GREAT AMERICAN SCANDALS

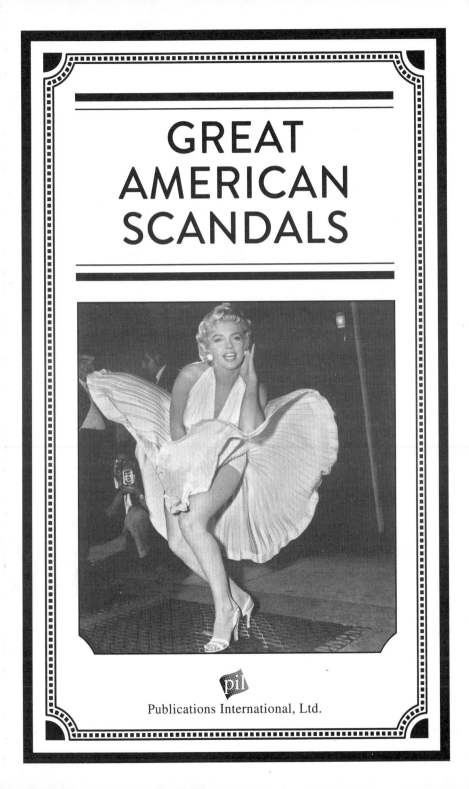

Publications International, Ltd.

Contributing writers: Jeff Bahr, Lisa Brooks, Katherine Don, Mary Fons-Misetic, Linda Godfrey, R.G.W. Griffin, Maya Henderson, Richard Knight Jr., Bill Martin, Michael Martin, Kimberly Morris, David Morrow, Lawrence Robinson, Paul Seaburn, Peter Suciu, Donald Vaughan, James Willis, and Kelly Wittmann

Images from the PIL Collection, Wikimedia, and Shutterstock.com

ISBN: 978-1-64030-631-8

Manufactured in China.

8 7 6 5 4 3 2 1

CONTENTS

Chapter 1: Lies, Bribes, and Other Unsavory Deeds............ 5

America's First Affair • Impeachment, Expulsion, and…Hero? • Stealing the President • The Teapot Dome Scandal • Con Artists, Fake Stocks, and Federal Agents: ABSCAM • The Keating Five • Heidi Fleiss and the World's Oldest Profession • Tyson Takes an Ear • An Olympic Bribe • The Man Who Bought Washington • James Traficant's Many Troubles • Michael Vick's Dog Fighting Shenanigans • An Olympic Athlete Tells a Lie

Chapter 2: Misconduct in High Office 29

The Pinchot-Ballinger Controversy • Truman's Revenue Scandal • Assassination Plots Against Castro • Notable Texas Political Scandals • The Iran-Contra Affair • The Ultimate He Said, She Said • Bush's String of Dismissals • Bridgegate

Chapter 3: Financial Swindles, Busts, and Turmoil 47

The Panic of 1792 • Black Friday: A Much Direr Meaning • The Whiskey Ring • A Railroad to Nowhere • Vegetable Oil: A Major Stock Market Threat? • A Fugitive Financier King • The Junk Bond King • Uncharitable Work • Enron: From Boom to Bust • Pure and Simple Greed • A Family of Fraudsters • A Telecom Cooks the Books • Hewlett-Packard's Spying Scandal • Too Big to Fail? • A Charlatan of Epic Proportions • Eight Ain't So Great

Chapter 4: Leaks, Hacks, and Spies 82

COINTELPRO • A Vietnam War Bombshell • Watergate • To Catch a Soviet Mole • Plamegate • A Computer Wiz Exposes the Truth • Sony's Embarrassing Hack • An Epic Data Breach

Chapter 5: Rants, Meltdowns, and Slips 100

Political Slips of Tongue • Sinead O'Connor's Primetime Protest • Janet's Wardrobe Malfunction • Rathergate • Mel Gibson's Crazy Rant • The Shock Jock Gets Booted • Britney Hits Her Breaking Point • TV's Highest Paid Loses His Cool • Brian Williams's Dramatizations

Chapter 6: They Did What?...................................121

A Master of Political Theater • Sister Aimee Dies for Love • The Much-Married Tommy Manville • A Rigged Game • A Rocker Weds, a Career Is (Almost) Dead • The Stanford Prison Experiment • The Kidnapping of a Publishing Magnate Heiress • The Talihook Scandal • Woody Allen's Idiosyncrasy • A Crying Shame • A Senator's Lewd Bathroom Behavior • A Private Matter Becomes a Public Spectacle • When Teachers Become Cheaters • Anything but a Shining Example • United's Public Relations Nightmare • PepsiCo's Epic Facepalm

Chapter 7: Cheaters, Dopers, and Fixers............................157

1919 World Series: It Ain't True, Is It? • Pete Rose: From Highest-Paid to Prison • Southern Methodist University's Death Penalty • A Plot for Naught • Mark McGwire and the Steroids Era • From Cheating Death to Cheating in Sport • Spygate • Bountygate • Deflategate

Chapter 8: Hollywood Headaches and Heartbreaks...........177

When Celebs Go Bad! • The Hollywood Sign Girl • A Law for the Future Uncle Fester • The Sex-sational Trial of Errol Flynn • Trouble for the Prince of Noir • Love on the Set: The Bergman-Rossellini Scandal • Scandalous Hollywood: Roman Polanski • A Comedian's Tragic End • Madonna's 1989 Hit: Brilliance or Blasphemy? • And the Oscar Goes to…? • The Curse of Billy Bob Thornton • Hollywood Drops the Ball • The Non-Scandal: Hollywood Does Good • 2017 Best Picture Oscar Flub • A Reckoning: Harvey Weinstein, #MeToo, and Time's Up

Chapter 9: Falls From Grace.....................................209

Aaron Burr: Hero or Villian? • Victoria Woodhull: An American Trailblazer • Frances Farmer: Tortured Soul • Wisconsin's Federal Scaremonger • Chappaquiddick • Bettie Page: From Girl Next Door to Impoverished Recluse • Resigning in Disgrace • Robert Bauman's Double Life • Gary Hart's Political Nosedive • Kobe Bryant: Adultery or Assault? • John Edwards's Serious Error • Rod Blagojevich: Another Corrupt Illinois Politician • A Socialite Topples a Four-Star General • Folly in the Big Apple

Chapter 10: Mysterious Deaths . . . or Murders.................243

The Rise and Fall of Fatty Arbuckle • William Desmond Taylor: A Macabre Puzzle • A 1924 Murder Mystery • The Mysterious Death of Thelma Todd • Ohio's Greatest Unsolved Murder Mystery • The Black Dahlia Murder Mystery • Lana Turner and the Death of a Gangster • Marilyn Monroe, an Untimely Death • Anything but Splendor: Natalie Wood • Unsolved: JonBenét Ramsey • The Deaths of Tupac and The Notorious B.I.G.

CHAPTER 1

LIES, BRIBES, AND OTHER UNSAVORY DEEDS

America's First Affair

Sometimes a man lusting after both the presidency and other women finds the two desires don't mix well. Such was the case in July 1791, when U.S. Treasury Secretary Alexander Hamilton began an affair with Maria Reynolds, a pretty 23-year-old woman who tearfully implored him for help as her husband had left her.

A few months later, Reynolds's husband, James, a professional con man, mysteriously returned and blackmailed Hamilton. Although he paid $1,750 to keep the affair quiet, Hamilton learned the sad truth that blackmailers are never satisfied. In 1797, the affair came to light, creating one of the first sex scandals in American politics. Although Hamilton apologized, many historians believe the damage to his reputation cost him the presidency he so coveted.

Impeachment, Expulsion, and . . . Hero?

The Constitution of the United States, which provided a framework of law and defined the executive, legislative, and judicial branches of government, remains one of the most important documents in our country. And many of those who signed were equally important in U.S. history: George Washington, Benjamin Franklin, and Alexander

Hamilton, to name a few. But one of the signers of the Constitution—William Blount—is remembered for another historic event: Blount became the first person to face impeachment by the House of Representatives.

A Tennessee Titan

Blount began his political career in the North Carolina legislature after serving in the American Revolutionary War. He spent two terms in the Continental Congress and was chosen as one of five delegates from North Carolina to attend the Constitutional Convention in Philadelphia. Some of the legislation Blount had introduced during the Congress later proved to be critical to the formation of what is now Tennessee, including a bill that established the city of Nashville. So, in 1790, President George Washington made Blount governor of the newly formed Tennessee Territory. Six years later, when Tennessee officially became a state, Blount was one of the state's first two senators.

Poor Decisions and a Bad Plan

But in the midst of all his political success, Blount was also an active land speculator. By the mid-1790s, Blount and his brothers had made a myriad of risky land investments, buying more than 2.5 million acres of western land. By 1795, the demand for this land had plummeted, and Blount and his family were deep in debt. Meanwhile, land speculators were worrying about the French—who had defeated Spain in the War of the Pyrenees—taking over Spanish-controlled Louisiana. This gave Blount an idea for a plan that would help him recoup his losses.

Blount enlisted the help of his friends John Chisholm and Nicholas Romayne in a scheme to convince Indians and frontiersmen to attack parts of Florida and Louisiana under Spanish control and give them to the British. In return, the British would allow free access to New Orleans and the Mississippi River to American merchants. In 1797, Blount wrote a letter outlining his entire conspiracy, which fell into the hands of Secretary of State Timothy Pickering—a politician who had always despised Blount. When Pickering saw the contents of the letter, he wasted no time in turning it over to President John Adams.

A National Disgrace but a Tennessee Hero

Adams, believing the letter was evidence of a crime, turned it over to the Senate. The Senate and House then formed special committees to investigate the matter, and Blount was ordered to testify. After consulting with two attorneys, Blount denied that he wrote the letter; however, two of his colleagues testified that the letter was, in fact, in his handwriting. On July 8, the House voted 41 to 30 to hold impeachment hearings, and the Senate voted 25 to 1 to expel Blount from his Senate seat. Instead of sticking around for the impeachment hearings, Blount fled to his home in Tennessee.

Chisholm and Romayne both confessed to their parts in the scheme, but Blount refused to answer any more questions and offered no repentance or apology. Ultimately, on January 11, 1799, with a 14 to 11 vote, the Senate defeated a resolution asserting that Blount was an impeachable officer. Thus, his impeachment was dismissed, despite exhibiting conduct "entirely inconsistent with his public trust."

Although Blount's reputation was tarnished throughout most of the country, his home state of Tennessee still welcomed him. When he returned to Knoxville after his Senate expulsion, he was greeted with a hero's military procession, and his allies in the state—including later President Andrew Jackson—remained loyal to him. He was elected to a state senate seat and became Speaker of the Senate in Knox County, where he served until his death in 1800.

Stealing the President

While he was alive, President Abraham Lincoln was loved and admired by many. Perhaps his popularity was the reason why, in 1876, a group of men decided that people would be willing to pay a lot of money to see the 16th president of the United States—even if he was dead.

Breaking Out Boyd

The plot was hatched in 1876, 11 years after President Lincoln's assassination by John Wilkes Booth. Illinois engraver Benjamin Boyd had been arrested on charges of creating engraving plates to make counterfeit bills. Boyd's boss, James "Big Jim" Kinealy, a man known around Chicago as the King of the Counterfeiters, was determined to get Boyd out of prison in order to continue his counterfeiting operation.

Kinealy's plan was to kidnap Lincoln's corpse from his mausoleum at the Oak Ridge Cemetery in Springfield, Illinois and hold it for ransom: $200,000 in cash and a full pardon for Boyd. Not wanting to do the dirty work himself, Kinealy turned to two men: John "Jack" Hughes and Terrence Mullen, a bartender at The Hub, a Madison Street bar frequented by Kinealy and his associates.

Kinealy told Hughes and Mullen that they were to steal Lincoln's body on Election Night, November 7, load it onto a cart, and take it roughly 200 miles north to the shores of Lake Michigan. They were to bury the body in the sand, to stow it until the ransom was paid. The plan seemed foolproof until Hughes and Mullen decided they needed a third person to help steal the body—a fellow named Lewis Swegles. It was a decision Hughes and Mullen would come to regret.

The Plan Backfires

The man directly responsible for bringing Boyd in was Patrick D. Tyrrell, a member of the Secret Service in Chicago. Long before their current role of protecting the president of the United States, one of the main jobs for members of the Secret Service was to track down and arrest counterfeiters. One of Tyrrell's informants was a small-time crook by the name of Lewis Swegles. Yes, the same guy who agreed to help Hughes and Mullen steal the president's body. Thanks to the stool pigeon, everything the duo was planning was being reported back to the Secret Service.

On the evening of November 7, 1876, Hughes, Mullen, and Swegles entered the Lincoln Mausoleum, unaware of the Secret Service lying in wait. The hoods broke open Lincoln's sarcophagus and removed the casket, and Swegles was sent to get the wagon. Swegles gave the signal to make the arrest, but once the Secret Service men reached the mausoleum, they found it to be empty. In all the confusion, Hughes and Mullen had slipped away, leaving Lincoln's body behind.

Unsure what to do next, Tyrrell ordered Swegles back to Chicago to see if he could pick up the kidnappers' trail. Swegles eventually found them in a local Chicago tavern, and on November 16 or 17 (sources vary), Hughes and Mullen were arrested without incident.

Lincoln Is Laid to Rest (Again)

With no laws on the books at the time pertaining to the stealing of a body, Hughes and Mullen were only charged with attempted larceny of Lincoln's coffin and a count each of conspiracy. After a brief trial, both men were found guilty. Their sentence for attempting to steal the body of President Abraham Lincoln: one year in the Illinois state penitentiary in Joliet.

As for Lincoln's coffin, it remains at its home in Oak Ridge Cemetery; it has been moved an estimated 17 times and opened 6 times. On September 26, 1901, the Lincoln family took steps to ensure Abe's body could never be stolen again: It was buried 10 feet under the floor of the mausoleum, inside a metal cage, and under thousands of pounds of concrete.

The Teapot Dome Scandal

The Teapot Dome Scandal was the largest of numerous scandals that plagued the presidency of Warren Harding.

Teapot Dome is an oil field reserved for emergency use by the U.S. Navy located on public land in Wyoming. Oil companies and politicians claimed the reserves were not necessary and that the oil companies could supply the Navy in the event of shortages.

In 1922, Interior Secretary Albert B. Fall accepted $404,000 in illegal gifts from oil company executives in return for leasing the rights to the oil at Teapot Dome to Mammoth Oil without asking for competitive bids. The leases were legal but the gifts were not. Fall's attempts to keep the gifts secret failed, and, on April 14, 1922, the *Wall Street Journal* exposed the bribes. Fall denied the charges, but an investigation revealed a $100,000 no-interest loan in return for leases that Fall had forgotten to cover up.

In 1927, the Supreme Court ruled that the oil leases had been illegally obtained, and the U.S. Navy regained control of Teapot Dome and other reserves. Fall was found guilty of bribery in 1929, fined $100,000, and sentenced to one year in prison. He was the first cabinet member imprisoned for his actions while in office. President Harding was not aware of the scandal at the time of his death in 1923, but it contributed to his administration being considered one of the most corrupt in history.

Con Artists, Fake Stocks, and Federal Agents: ABSCAM

What do a convicted con artist, fake Arab sheikhs, U.S. politicians, and the FBI have in common? They were all a part of a sting operation called ABSCAM in the late 1970s and 1980s.

An Elaborate Setup

In July 1978, the FBI set up an undercover operation in order to catch thieves dealing in stolen art. To help with the logistics, they brought a convicted con artist and swindler, Melvin Weinberg, and his girlfriend, Evelyn Knight, in on the plan. In exchange for their help, Weinberg and Knight—who were both facing prison sentences—were let out on probation. Weinberg helped the FBI create a fake company called Abdul Enterprises—the "AB" in ABSCAM. To make it look legitimate, Weinberg told the FBI to set up a million-dollar account under the name of Abdul Enterprises at the Chase Manhattan Bank.

Next, FBI employees posed as fictional Arab sheikhs named Kambir Abdul Rahman and Yassir Habib. The "sheikhs" were said to have millions of dollars to invest in the United States and were looking for profitable oil companies and rare art. Weinberg suggested art thieves who might be willing to do business with Abdul Enterprises, and within a few weeks, the FBI had recovered two paintings worth $1 million. The operation then switched focus to criminals who were dealing in fake stocks and bonds: thanks to the FBI's efforts, they halted the sale of approximately $600 million worth of fraudulent securities.

Political Targets

At this point, ABSCAM began taking aim at political corruption. A forger who was under investigation approached the fake sheikhs with the idea that they invest in New Jersey casinos, saying they could obtain licensing for the "right price." So for the first time in American history, the FBI began videotaping government officials as they were approached by the sheikhs' representatives and offered money in exchange for building permits, licenses, and "private immigration bills": proposed laws that would allow foreigners working for Abdul Enterprises into the country.

Thirty-one political officials were targeted during ABSCAM, and when it was all over, one senator and six congressmen were found guilty of bribery and conspiracy. Also convicted were three Philadelphia city councilmen, and Angelo Errichetti, the mayor of Camden, New Jersey. Errichetti was the first to be caught during the ABSCAM sting, when he accepted money in exchange for a casino license for Abdul Enterprises. Errichetti then introduced the "sheikhs" to Senator Harrison Williams and congressmen Michael Myers, Raymond Lederer, and Frank Thompson. All would later be convicted.

Entrapment?

In February 1980, ABSCAM was made public. Some had an ethical issue with the secretive videotaping employed by the FBI, as well as the fact that Weinberg was paid $150,000 and avoided prison thanks to his part. Many felt that the FBI was overzealous in its tactics and ABSCAM amounted to nothing short of entrapment. Still, all of the convictions due to ABSCAM were upheld in court. Following the controversy, however, Attorney General Benjamin Civiletti issued "The Attorney General's Guidelines for FBI Undercover Operations," which formalized procedures to be used during sting operations.

The Keating Five

After the banking industry was deregulated in the 1980s, savings and loan banks were allowed to invest deposits in commercial real estate in addition to residential. Many savings banks began making risky investments, and the Federal Home Loan Bank Board (FHLBB) tried to stop them, against the wishes of the Reagan administration, which was against government interference with business.

In 1989, when the Lincoln Savings and Loan Association of Irvine, California, collapsed, its chairman, Charles H. Keating, Jr., accused the FHLBB and its former head Edwin J. Gray of conspiring against him. Gray testified that five senators had asked him to back off on the Lincoln investigation. These senators—Alan Cranston of California, Dennis DeConcini of Arizona, John Glenn of Ohio, Donald Riegle of Michigan, and John McCain of Arizona—became known as the Keating Five, after it was revealed that they received a total of $1.3 million in campaign contributions from Keating. While an investigation determined that all five acted improperly, they all claimed this was a standard campaign funding practice.

In August 1991, the Senate Ethics Committee recommended censure for Cranston and criticized the other four for "questionable conduct." Cranston had already decided not to run for reelection in 1992. DeConcini and Riegle served out their terms but did not run for reelection in 1994. John Glenn was reelected in 1992 and served until he retired in 1999. John McCain continued his work in the Senate, and he unsuccessfully ran for president against Barack Obama in 2008.

Heidi Fleiss and the World's Oldest Profession

Imagine an entrepreneur who is so successful in her profession that she earns a million dollars in her first four months on the job, and she eventually starts turning away prospective employees because so many people want to work for her. Sounds like an ambitious company, right? No doubt a booming industry.

In the 1990s, that entrepreneur was Heidi Fleiss. And her profession was, well, the world's oldest.

Ring Management

Fleiss was born in Los Angeles in 1965, and by the time she was 13, was already showing a penchant for management. Perhaps a foreshadowing of her criminal future to come, a teenaged Fleiss ran a "babysitting ring" for her neighborhood, assigning different friends to different sitting jobs, but taking a cut of the money for herself.

In 1987, Fleiss was dating film director Ivan Nagy, who introduced her to a well-known Beverly Hills madam named Madam Alex. Alex dealt exclusively with wealthy clientele, and took young Fleiss under her wing. Alex's prostitutes were mostly middle-aged women wanting to leave the business, so Alex felt that Fleiss was the perfect fresh face to revamp the operation. Fleiss became a prostitute for a short time to learn about the profession, and by 1990, she set her sights on recruiting new women and starting her own prostitution ring.

A Quick Rise and Fall

By 1993, Fleiss was known as the "Hollywood Madam," and she was bringing in thousands of dollars a night from her working girls. She bragged that on a "slow" night she could still make $10,000, and a good night would bring in $100,000. But the profitable venture wouldn't last forever: in June 1993, Fleiss was arrested and charged by the state of California with five counts of pandering, and in 1994, federal tax evasion charges were filed against her.

The media was fascinated by the revelation of a "black book" which Fleiss supposedly maintained, with names and details of her clients. Fleiss refused to give up any names, but when she was arrested, she happened to have traveler's checks in her purse that belonged to actor Charlie Sheen. Sheen became the most prominent name to be connected to the Fleiss prostitution scandal, and he testified during her trial that he'd hired her call girls on at least 27 occasions.

A Troubled Life

Fleiss was convicted on the state charges, but they were later overturned. But in 1996, she was convicted of tax evasion and sentenced to seven years in prison. She served 20 months, and she was released to a halfway house in 1998, where she was ordered to perform 370 hours of community service. She was released from the halfway house in 1999, but she has lived a troubled life since then. After her release, she dated actor Tom Sizemore, who she later accused of domestic abuse—Sizemore was convicted and sentenced to 17 months in prison. Fleiss has also struggled with drug addiction, and she was arrested on drug charges in 2008. She attended a substance abuse program in 2009, and appeared on *Celebrity Rehab with Dr. Drew*, ironically, with her ex, Sizemore.

Fleiss has never completely extracted herself from the world of prostitution. She makes her home in Pahrump, Nevada—one of the few areas of the country where prostitution is legal. She dated and was briefly engaged to Dennis Hof, the owner of the brothel called the Moonlite Bunny Ranch, and she has made plans to open her own brothel. So far, her venture hasn't panned out, but who knows what the future may hold for the one-time Hollywood Madam.

Tyson Takes an Ear

It was the chomp heard 'round the world.

On June 28, 1997, boxers Mike Tyson and Evander Holyfield paired up for a fight billed as "The Sound and The Fury." Holyfield had dominated Tyson in their previous fight, winning after 11 rounds to be crowned with the World Boxing Association heavyweight title. While Tyson may have seen the match as a comeback opportunity, Holyfield bested him in the first two rounds. And it looked like Holyfield's momentum would carry him through the third round, until he— accidentally, according to the referee—head-butted Tyson. Tyson was left with a cut above his right eye, and that's when the unexpected happened: Tyson bit Holyfield's right ear.

Tyson wasn't immediately disqualified, but two points were deducted from his score. And then, at the end of the round, Tyson chomped down on Holyfield's left ear—and this time, the bite was so hard that part of Holyfield's ear was left on the floor of the ring. Tyson later claimed that Holyfield repeatedly head-butted him without penalty. "This is my career," he said. "What am I supposed to do? I've got children to raise. He kept butting me." This time, Tyson was immediately disqualified from the fight. His boxing license was suspended for 15 months and he was fined $3 million.

Marriage Woes

But surprisingly, biting off part of an opponent's ear may not be the worst of Mike Tyson's scandals. His yearlong first marriage to actress Robin Givens was well publicized for its tumultuous nature, with Givens accusing Tyson of abuse and mental instability. In a famous, and decidedly awkward, segment with Barbara Walters on the show *20/20* in September 1988, Tyson and Givens gave a joint interview where Givens said her husband suffered from manic depression and was "not a bad guy." But she also described him as "scary" and "intimidating," and said there were times when "he cannot control his temper." She admitted that she was "afraid" of the boxer, as he calmly sat beside her, showing little emotion. A month later, Givens filed for divorce, and the marriage was over by February 1989.

Prison and Redemption

Tyson's trouble with women came to a head in July 1991, when he was arrested for the rape of 18-year-old beauty contestant Desiree Washington. The scandal caused a media circus, with so many journalists converging on the Indianapolis courthouse where Tyson's trial took place that the lawyers for the case had to have police protection every time they walked inside. Tyson maintained his innocence, saying his contact with Washington was consensual, but the jury wasn't buying it: Tyson was convicted and sentenced to six years in prison and four years of probation. But the boxer continued— and still continues—to have supporters who believe his side of the story. He was released after three years, but he was required to register as a sex offender under federal law.

After his parole, Tyson returned to boxing and won many fights leading up to the infamous Holyfield bout. As for Holyfield, he needed eight stitches and 90 minutes of surgery to repair his ear. "I thought my ear had fallen off," he said after the match. But the two boxers have since made peace, with Tyson apologizing for the bite, and Holyfield offering forgiveness. The two even starred together in a hilarious 2013 Foot Locker commercial where, fittingly, Tyson gives Holyfield his ear back before embracing him in a bear hug.

An Olympic Bribe

The 2002 Winter Olympics were notable for being the first Olympic Games to be played after the September 11 attacks. President George W. Bush sat among the United States athletes and extended the declaration to open the games "on behalf of a proud, determined, and grateful nation." It was a moving and inspirational moment for the country and for the host town of Salt Lake City. But several years earlier, both the host city and the International Olympic Committee (IOC) were involved in the worst scandal in the Games' history, marring the reputation of the Games of Salt Lake City.

Outbid at Every Turn

Salt Lake City was not new to bidding on the rights to hold Olympic Games; in fact, they'd tried many times to host the event, bidding for the 1932, 1972, 1976, and 1992 games but losing the chance each time. In the late 1980s and early 1990s, Utah Economic Development Professional David Johnson and lawyer Tom Welch were charged with promoting Salt Lake City to the IOC in yet another attempt to convince the committee that they deserved to host the 1998 Games. They traveled extensively throughout the world to bring recognition to their city in hopes of scoring an Olympic bid; but despite their efforts, the 1998 Games ultimately went to Nagano, Japan.

Some felt that since the 1996 Summer Olympics had been awarded to Atlanta, it made sense for the IOC to choose a location outside the U.S. for the Winter Games. But others had a different theory: the Japanese bid committee was simply better at showing the IOC a good time. "We were giving out saltwater taffy and cowboy hats," one Salt Lake Organizing Committee member said, "and they were giving out computers." There were stories of IOC officials being lodged in the finest hotels, where they were wined and dined by geisha, the traditional Japanese hostess.

Show Me the Money

So what was Salt Lake City—known less for its hobnobbing hospitality and more for its conservative Mormonism and its namesake body of water—to do? Three words: spend, spend, spend. Interestingly, the IOC had asked the city of Nagano to destroy the records of their expenditures during their time in Japan; but estimates put the tab at around $14 million. The Salt Lake Organizing Committee spent more than $16 million to bring IOC members to their city, showing them the venues where the games would be held, and taking a cue from their Japanese counterparts and showering IOC members with gifts. And in June 1995, the expensive strategy worked: Salt Lake City was awarded the 2002 Winter Olympics.

But on November 24, 1998, a report was released that claimed the Salt Lake Organizing Committee was paying the tuition of the child of an IOC member. This went far beyond a mere "gift"—it seemed the committee was attempting to bribe the IOC. Swiss IOC member Marc Hodler even expressed his suspicion that such bribery had been going on for years, saying that a group of IOC members had been taking bribes since as early as 1990. The allegations resulted in investigations by the IOC, the United States Olympic Committee, the Salt Lake Organizing Committee, and the U.S. Department of Justice. It was discovered that IOC members had been given cash, travel, and expensive gifts, and their family members had even been offered jobs and healthcare.

Aftermath

Six IOC members were expelled from the committee—the first time such action was taken in 105 years—and four more were given warnings. Welch and Johnson, who had resigned their positions before the investigations began, were brought up on charges of bribery and fraud, but they were acquitted in December 2003. Salt Lake City was still allowed to host the games—a decision some questioned after the scandal broke. But IOC President Juan Antonio Samaranch made it clear that although some host cities may have behaved "unethically," it was the IOC itself that should be judged.

IOC Vice President Richard Pound admitted that the committee may have sent the wrong message over the years, with its history of allowing bid cities to lavishly wine and dine its members. However, he said, "When you're talking about substantial benefit going to family members of IOC board members, that's where we draw the line."

The Man Who Bought Washington

President Ulysses S. Grant, who would spend time in the lobby of the Willard Hotel in Washington, D.C. and speak to his constituents about their concerns, coined the term "lobbyist." Lobbying has become a crucial part of our country's democratic process, as lobbyists serve as the voices between the people and the government. In fact, if you've ever contacted a member of Congress to voice your opinion on an issue, you can consider yourself a lobbyist. But the practice is also fraught with scandal, as in the case of Jack Abramoff—or, as *Time* magazine dubbed him, "The Man Who Bought Washington."

From the Capital to Casinos

Abramoff relished his job as a lobbyist. He owned two restaurants near the Capitol building, leased expensive skyboxes at sports stadiums, and bought a fleet of casino boats, all to wine and dine his clients. But rival lobbyists noted that his tactics were often far outside the box of what was ethical, including padding invoices by billing for hours he didn't work, and paying journalists to write favorable op-eds about his clients.

In 1995, Abramoff began representing Native American tribes and their gambling interests. He managed to help defeat a Congressional bill that would have taxed Native American casinos, and he began representing more Indian interests, eventually working with 10 different tribes. Most of these tribes were naïve when it came to politics and lobbying tactics, and Abramoff saw a unique opportunity to take advantage of that fact.

Padding the Bills

One of these tribes was the Louisiana Coushattas, who owned a profitable casino, but were still $30 million in debt. Worried that state authorities were out to close down their source of income, the tribe turned to Abramoff and his partner, Michael Scanlon, to negotiate a 25-year gambling compact with the state. Abramoff and Scanlon convinced the tribe that they could help—for a price. True to their promise, Abramoff and Scanlon secured the future of the tribe's casino, but Abramoff told them they could have even more: "You can control Louisiana," he told tribal leaders. Intrigued, the tribe parted with $32 million over two years; but beyond their successful casino negotiation, the money produced nothing for them.

And the Coushattas weren't the only tribe to pay for nothing: Abramoff and Scanlon took $85 million in fees from various Indian tribes. But rather than use those millions to support the interests of Native Americans, the pair was secretly overbilling their clients by massive amounts and funneling the money back into their own pockets. The deception was discovered in 2005, and it was also discovered that the two had given gifts and campaign donations to legislators in return for votes and support. What's more, Abramoff and Scanlon left behind an email trail that detailed their plans for fraud and their nonchalant attitudes about scamming Native American tribes. In some emails, they referred to their clients as "monkeys," "troglodytes," and "morons."

The Bill Comes Due

Abramoff and Scanlon both pled guilty to various charges. In January 2006, Abramoff was sentenced to six years in prison for mail fraud, conspiracy to bribe public officials, and tax evasion. Scanlon was sentenced to 20 months in prison and 300 hours of community service. After his release from prison in December 2010, Abramoff wrote an autobiography titled *Capitol Punishment: The Hard Truth About Washington Corruption From America's Most Notorious Lobbyist.* The story of his lobbying scandal was also made into a feature film called *Casino Jack* starring Kevin Spacey as Abramoff.

James Traficant's Many Troubles

James Traficant was not your run-of-the-mill congressman. CNN once described the Ohio representative as a "maverick Democrat," and he was known for his eccentric dress (sometimes showing up to Congress in a denim suit) and his unkempt hairstyle (which was actually a toupee). He liked to give short, colorful speeches on the floor of the House, often ending them with "beam me up" in a nod to the old *Star Trek* franchise. He frequently voted with his Republican counterparts— especially on issues of abortion and immigration much to the chagrin of his fellow Democrats. In fact, when Traficant voted for Republican Dennis Hastert for Speaker of the House in 2001, Democrats were so frustrated with him that they stripped him of his committee assignments, making him the first member of the House of Representatives in more than a century without a committee assignment.

His Own Defense

Traficant's troubles only got worse from there. On May 4, 2001, he was indicted on charges of bribery, tax evasion, and racketeering when it was discovered that he was using campaign funds for personal use. This was not the first time Traficant had been indicted on such charges: In 1983, while working as a county sheriff, he was brought up on charges under the Racketeer Influence and Corrupt Organizations Act (RICO) when he was accused of accepting bribes. In true Traficant style, he represented himself in court—even though he was not a lawyer—and was ultimately acquitted of all charges. He became the only person to ever win a RICO case while representing himself.

So when his case went to trial in 2002, Traficant decided to once again to represent himself. Not only was the congressman accused of accepting gifts from constituents in return for political favors, but he was also accused of forcing employees in his office to work on his farm—staffers were asked to bale hay, clean horse stalls, and perform chores. But Traficant insisted that the whole thing was a set-up—it was, he said, revenge for his 1983 acquittal and orchestrated by federal prosecutors who like to hold grudges.

Scandal within a Scandal

This time, however, Traficant's defense strategy failed, and he was found guilty of all charges. He immediately lost his right to vote on legislation in the House, while the U.S. House Committee on Ethics reviewed his case. Their investigation resulted in a recommendation that Traficant be expelled from Congress, and on July 24, 2002, the House voted to expel him, 420 to 1. Interestingly, the one holdout was California representative Gary Condit, who was also in the midst of a scandal: Condit's affair with his intern, Chandra Levy, was exposed after the young woman disappeared and was later found murdered. Perhaps Condit's own significant troubles gave him empathy toward Traficant's plight.

Gone but Not Forgotten

Traficant spent seven years in prison and refused to receive any visitors while he was incarcerated. When he was released in 2009, 1,200 supporters welcomed him home with a banquet, where he defiantly told the crowd, "it's time to tell the FBI and the IRS that this is our country." He once again ran for Congress in 2010, running as an independent, but lost to his former aide, Tim Ryan. Sadly, on September 23, 2014, Traficant was gravely injured when a tractor he was driving flipped over and trapped him underneath. After four days on life support, Traficant died on September 27 at the age of 73. The unusual, controversial, and brazen congressman will not soon be forgotten.

Michael Vick's Dog Fighting Shenanigans

Quarterback Michael Vick spent 13 seasons with the NFL, spending most of his career with the Philadelphia Eagles and the Atlanta Falcons. He was the number one draft pick in the 2001 NFL draft, and it was easy to see why: Vick was known for his rushing abilities, and he broke records for the most rushing yards by a quarterback in a season with 1,039, and the most career rushing yards by a quarterback with 6,109. It's safe to say that at the beginning of his career, the football star was well on his way to a life of comfortable prosperity, provided he didn't do anything stupid.

And then he did something stupid.

Finding Trouble

Vick was born in Newport News, Virginia, on June 26, 1980. His family lived in a public housing project in a crime-ridden area of the city, where drug dealing and drive-by shootings were a way of life. But Vick and his second cousin, Aaron Brooks, spent a lot of time at their local

Boys and Girls Club learning the ins and outs of football. "Sports kept me off the streets," Vick would later tell *Sporting News* magazine.

Sports would not, however, keep him out of trouble forever. Vick maintained property in rural Surry County, Virginia, just across the James River from his hometown. On April 25, 2007, a search warrant was issued for the property resulting from a drug investigation of Vick's cousin, Davon Boddie. But instead of drugs, investigators found something even more disturbing. More than 70 dogs, some with signs of injuries, were discovered on the property, with evidence that they were used in an interstate dog fighting ring.

Unsettling Evidence

As state and federal authorities looked into the evidence, the details that emerged were upsetting—not only to animal rights activists, but to anyone who believes the axiom that dogs are man's best friend. Vick and his partners—Purnell Peace, Quanis Phillips, and Tony Taylor—created a dog fighting ring known as "Bad Newz Kennels," where spectators placed bets on the outcome and owners of winning dogs could collect tens of thousands of dollars. The dogs were also taken to locations in six other states to participate in fights. But the worst of the allegations concerned those dogs who were considered "underperformers"—if Vick and his partners weren't satisfied with a dog's fighting abilities, that dog would be killed by terribly inhumane methods including drowning, strangling, and shooting. Vick personally participated in killing at least eight dogs himself.

Prison, Bankruptcy, and a Comeback

In July, Vick and his partners were indicted on state and federal charges, and by August, all had pled guilty under plea bargain agreements. On December 10, Vick was sentenced for the federal charges to 23 months in prison, with Judge Henry E. Hudson questioning his remorse over "promoting, funding, and facilitating this cruel and inhumane sporting activity" and saying he didn't believe Vick had taken full responsibility for his actions. Vick was later sentenced on the state charges to three years in prison, which was suspended on condition of good behavior. He also deposited $1 million into an escrow account, which his attorneys used to help cover the costs of caring for the confiscated dogs and moving them into adoptive homes.

Before the dog fighting scandal, Vick's yearly income was estimated to be around $25 million. But due to his poor choices, he was forced to file for bankruptcy protection in July 2008. After he was released from prison, coach Tony Dungy took him under his wing and helped him with his return to the NFL. In 2010, while playing for the Philadelphia Eagles, he earned the Comeback Player of the Year award and was named the Eagle's starting quarterback. He has lobbied for H.R. 2492—the Animal Fighting Spectator Prohibition Act—which would establish penalties for spectators of illegal animal fights and make it a felony for adults to bring children to such fights. One can only hope that he has learned his lesson.

An Olympic Athlete Tells a Lie

In 2008, the world watched transfixed as the United States men's swim team—lead by superstars Michael Phelps and Ryan Lochte—won a total of 17 medals. It was Phelps's third Olympic appearance and Lochte's second, but it was the year that both swimmers would become household names.

Between the 2008 and 2012 Summer Olympics, Lochte earned more than $2 million from endorsement deals with various companies including Gillette, Gatorade, Ralph Lauren, and AT&T. And in 2013, the E! network debuted Lochte's reality series, *What Would Ryan Lochte Do?* Although the show—which chronicled Lochte's life as he prepared for the 2016 Summer Olympics—only lasted one season, the answer to that question became clear a few years later in Rio de Janeiro, when Lochte would "do" something pretty stupid.

A Scary Story

On August 14, 2016, while in Rio for the Summer Olympics, Lochte and teammates Jimmy Feigen, Gunnar Bentz, and Jack Conger claimed to have been robbed when men with guns forced them out of a taxi. The men had a police badge, and Lochte said that one of them pressed a gun to his forehead. Lochte's mother, Ileana Lochte, told media that the bandits stole the swimmers' wallets.

But over the next few days, various details of Lochte's story began to change: Instead of being forced out of the car, he said the team was robbed after using a bathroom at a gas station. And the gun hadn't been pressed against his head after all: it was several inches away. Brazilian police were confused about the murky details provided by the various team members, saying they had been highly intoxicated and confused.

Let's Go to the Videotape

By August 18, a better picture was emerging of what actually happened. The chief of civil police in Rio de Janeiro, Fernando Veloso, held a news conference and told reporters that security guards had stopped Lochte and the other swimmers after vandalizing a gas station. A video released shows the group pulling a sign off a wall, and then attempting to leave in a cab. Security guards then approach the cab to keep it from driving off, and the swimmers calmly exit the car. Lochte walks away after that, clearly under no threat whatsoever, and the other teammates sit on a curb, where police say they agreed to pay for the damages to the gas station. It is obvious that a robbery did not take place, and a gun was not present at the scene.

Apology Tour

Once the video came to light, Lochte attempted an apology, although he stopped short of saying he hadn't been robbed at gunpoint. According to him, the guards did, in fact, point guns at the swimmers and demand money before they could leave, and because of the "language barrier" the incident was stressful and "traumatic."

But a few days later, during an interview with Matt Lauer, he seemed a bit more remorseful, saying he "over-exaggerated" the story and apologized for the trouble he caused his teammates. He also did an interview for the Brazilian channel Globo, saying he was "110 percent sorry" for his actions.

CHAPTER 2

MISCONDUCT IN HIGH OFFICE

The Pinchot-Ballinger Controversy

President Theodore Roosevelt was known as a champion of conservation. It was the one thing he was most proud of during his presidency, and for good reason: Roosevelt established the United States Forest Service, five national parks, and 18 national monuments during his tenure. He established the Shoshone National Forest—the nation's first—along with 149 other national forests. He was adamant that these lands and wildlife be protected, and by the end of his term, he'd placed approximately 230 million acres of land under protection.

By Roosevelt's side in his conservation efforts was the first U.S. Forest Service Chief, Gifford Pinchot. Pinchot was an advocate of controlled use of natural resources, emphasizing the use of resources "for the service of man" while also maintaining those resources. He had critics on both ends of the conservation spectrum: those who believed solely in preservation thought that trees should never be harvested for timber, whereas those who opposed conservation altogether wanted more access to land for profit.

A New Administration

When Roosevelt's term came to an end in 1909, President William Howard Taft took over. He quickly replaced Roosevelt's Secretary of the Interior, James Rudolph Garfield, with his own, Richard A. Ballinger. It didn't take long for Ballinger to reverse some of Garfield's policies, returning three million acres of land to private use. Conservationists felt that Ballinger was out to reverse the benefits of Roosevelt-era land protection, and Pinchot agreed. He publicly accused Ballinger of siding with private trusts in his dealings with water power issues, and believed he may have been involved with some shady business regarding coal lands in Alaska. Meanwhile, the chief of the Portland, Oregon, field division of the General Land Office, Louis Glavis, expressed his own concerns about Ballinger's Alaska coal field dealings, and Pinchot assisted him in presenting evidence to the president.

Conservation Controversy and a Republican Rift

President Taft, however, disagreed with the findings. He assured the public that Ballinger had been part of no wrongdoing, and he tried to convince Pinchot that his administration was pro-conservation. Glavis, unsatisfied with the president's response, took his story to the press, and in November 1909 the magazine *Collier's* published an article entitled, "The Whitewashing of Ballinger: Are the Guggenheims in Charge of the Department of the Interior?" The article accused Ballinger of helping powerful interests illegally gain access to Alaskan coal fields, including the famous Guggenheim family.

Pinchot began to more vocally criticize Ballinger and Taft, and in January 1910, he sent a letter to Senator Jonathan P. Dolliver outlining what he believed was impropriety on the part of both men. He asked for hearings to be held to investigate Ballinger's actions, and he harshly denounced Taft. The president was incensed, and he immediately fired Pinchot from his position as chief forester. Although the U.S. House of Representatives did hold hearings on Ballinger, he was cleared of any wrongdoing.

The controversy caused a major rift between Roosevelt and Taft, with Roosevelt believing Taft had greatly betrayed the principles of conservation he held dear. The rift was so great that the Republican Party itself was split during the 1912 Presidential Election, with

Roosevelt running against Taft as a third party Progressive Republican—nicknamed the "Bull Moose Party." Although Woodrow Wilson won the presidency, Roosevelt remains the only third party presidential candidate to ever receive more than a third of the popular or electoral vote.

Truman's Revenue Scandal

President Harry S. Truman presided over some difficult times during our country's history: The atomic bomb era, the end of World War II, the "Red Scare," and the Korean War, just to name a few. In fact, Truman spent so much time dealing with significant issues that would later take up full chapters in history books that it's easy to forget that he was not immune to controversy. Like presidents before him and those who came after, Truman was also plagued by scandal.

Cold Corruption

In 1950, the Senate began investigating allegations of corruption among senior officials in the Truman administration. One of these officials was Truman's military aide, Harry Vaughn, who had been an associate of the president since World War I. The investigation discovered that Vaughn had been accepting bribes in return for political favors given to friends and businessmen. Perhaps the most interesting aspect of this discovery was the bribes themselves: Vaughn was given fur coats—and, strangely, deep freezers—from his associates. He gave one of these freezers to Bess Truman, but the appliances ended up being defective and the first lady's freezer broke within months. But defrosted freezer aside, Vaughn was found guilty of merely minor breeches of ethics. Truman stood beside his friend, pardoning the allegations, which some felt was an approval of Vaughn's actions.

Paying the Taxman

But the most serious scandal during Truman's tenure went far beyond freezers. Back in 1913, when the Sixteenth Amendment to the Constitution was ratified—giving Congress permission to impose tax on income—the Bureau of Internal Revenue (now the IRS) was created. By 1950, rumors began to swirl that some people with serious tax problems were able to bypass trouble by paying bureau officials to look the other way. The allegations became so serious that Delaware Senator John J. Williams demanded an investigation, and between 1951 and 1952, Congress and the Treasury Department paid closer attention to IRS tax collectors.

Their investigation revealed a pattern of serious corruption within the IRS, with high-level officials often accepting favors and payments in return for ignoring tax violations and evasion. More than a hundred employees—166 in all—were either fired or resigned due to the scrutiny. But Attorney General J. Howard McGrath thought that special prosecutor Newbold Morris was "too zealous" in his investigation, and subsequently fired him. This didn't sit well with Truman, who felt that rooting out the corruption was the best way to save his reputation with the public. So Truman dismissed McGrath and replaced him with James McGranery, whose vision more clearly aligned with Truman's.

Continued Controversy

Nevertheless, the Bureau scandal left a mark in the minds of the American people. Truman knew that the controversy, along with the ongoing and unpopular Korean War, were issues that would make a campaign for reelection an uphill battle. On March 29, 1952, he announced his decision to not run for reelection, throwing his support behind the Democratic nominee, Adlai Stevenson, and heavily criticizing his opponent, Dwight D. Eisenhower.

Eisenhower would go on to win the presidency, but this would not be the end of the Truman-era Bureau of Internal Revenue scandals. In 1956, two former Truman officials—Matthew J. Connelly and T. Lamar Caudle—were convicted of accepting bribes in exchange for helping a shoe distributer avoid prosecution for tax evasion. Both men were sentenced to six months in prison, but were later pardoned. Today, more than a hundred years after it was formed, the IRS continues to create controversy and scandal, and taxpayers continue to search for ways— legal and illegal—to avoid the dreaded agency.

Assassination Plots against Castro

American intelligence agencies were very active and successful during the Cold War. But how come no one could kill the leader of Cuba?

Perhaps no human being in history has survived more assassination attempts than Fidel Castro. A popular leader who overthrew the hated Cuban dictator Fulgencio Batista in 1959, Castro had first attempted to organize the people of Cuba directly into revolution, but he was thrown into prison in 1953. He had his first brush with assassination there: Batista ordered the guards to poison Castro, but none of them would do it. In 1955, after Batista made an election promise to free political prisoners, he ordered Castro's release. But the dictator was not about to let bygones be bygones. He sent an assassin named Eutimio Guerra to get close to Castro, but the revolutionary leader was suspicious of Guerra and gave him the slip. Castro seemed to lead a charmed life, and his revolutionary army moved from town to town fighting for Cuba until it was free of Batista.

After overthrowing the dictator and liberating Cuba, Castro was wildly popular with the majority of Cubans, although he was looked on with suspicion by almost everyone else. And because he received limited support from Cuba's traditional allies, including the United States, Castro had little or no choice but to ally Cuba with the Soviet Union. After all, he was just following the age-old maxim—"The enemy of my enemy is my friend." And what an enemy he made!

Before the Bay of Pigs

Most people think that the halfhearted backing of the Bay of Pigs invasion was the starting gun for hostility between Castro and John F. Kennedy, but it was Dwight Eisenhower who set the "Kill Fidel Contest" in motion in 1960 with what ultimately became Operation Mongoose—400 CIA agents working full-time to remove the Cuban dictator. At first, they decided to train paramilitary guerrillas to eliminate Castro in a traditional commando operation, but his immense popularity among the Cuban people made that impossible. The CIA did all the preliminary work on the Bay of Pigs. Then Eisenhower left office, and Kennedy came upon the scene.

The Bay of Pigs invasion turned out to be a fiasco, and a year and a half later the Cuban Missile Crisis almost triggered a full-scale nuclear war. America's only answer seemed to be to get rid of Fidel and try to turn Cuba back into a pliant banana republic (or in this case, sugarcane republic). But who would do it—and how?

Who's up to the Job?

The problem was that everyone wanted to get in on the act. The U.S. government hated having a Soviet base 90 miles from Florida. Batista Cubans, who'd lost their big-moneyed businesses, wanted their privileged lives back. Anticommunists such as FBI boss J. Edgar Hoover viewed a plot to assassinate Castro as a struggle against elemental evil. American businesses that relied on sugar felt the loss of their cheap supply. The Mafia, which had owned lucrative casinos and brothels in Havana, wanted revenge. As it turned out, the Mafia had the best shot—and they had help.

The CIA, being unable to handle the job themselves, hired Mafia members to terminate Castro with extreme prejudice. In exchange, the CIA pressured the FBI to offer the Mafia a certain amount of immunity in the United States. But the Mafia got used to the new leniency, which would end if Castro were killed, so they strung the Agency along with false promises to kill Castro if the CIA would continue to protect them from the FBI. Meanwhile, President Kennedy grew impatient. Changing the name of Operation Mongoose to Operation Freedom, he sent the American intelligence community in a full-time rush to whack Fidel. But after the Bay of Pigs, intelligence planners believed that conventional measures wouldn't work, so the attempts became stranger:

- During a United Nations meeting at which Castro was present, an agent working for the CIA managed to slip a poisoned cigar into Fidel's cigar case, but someone figured it out before Castro could light up.

- Another idea was to send Castro on an acid trip by dosing his cigars with LSD. He would appear psychotic, and his sanity would be questioned.

- Castro was an avid scuba diver, so the CIA sprayed the inside of a wet suit with tuberculosis germs and a fungal skin disease called Madura foot. Then they gave it to a lawyer heading to Havana to negotiate the release of Bay of Pigs prisoners. He was supposed to give the suit to Castro, but at the last minute the lawyer decided that the plot was too obvious and was an embarrassment to the United States, so he didn't take the suit with him.

- Perhaps the most infamous idea was to find out where Fidel's favorite diving spot was and prepare an exploding conch shell to kill him, but for many obvious reasons this plan was dropped as being unfeasible.

- Traditional assassination methods were also tried. Cuban exiles were sent to Havana with high-powered rifles and telescopic sights to take care of the problem with good old-fashioned lead, but none of them could get close enough to shoot Castro.

- One of Castro's guards was given a poison pen that worked like a hypodermic needle, but he was discovered before he could get close enough to inject the leader.

Not all the plots involved killing the Cuban leader. In another instance, a Castro aide was bribed to put special powder inside the dictator's boots—it contained a poison that would make his beard fall out. This never happened.

Starting in the 1970s, the CIA seemed to lose interest in these plans, and thereafter most attempts to kill the leader were carried out by Cuban exiles (with CIA funding, of course). Fabian Escalante, Castro's head of security, claimed that there have been 638 plots to kill Castro.

Before Fidel led a revolution, he came to the United States to try out for major league baseball. By all accounts, he was a terrific pitcher. If he had made the majors, recent history might have been very different. For one thing, a lot of amateur assassins would have had to find something better to do with their time.

Notable Texas Political Scandals

Next to football, politics may be the most popular sport in Texas. But with politics often comes scandal, and Texas has had more than its fill of that.

- Controversy dogged Lyndon Johnson in his first two runs for the U.S. Senate. In 1941, the member of Congress and future president ran for a vacant Senate seat in a special election against Texas governor W. Lee "Pappy" O'Daniel. Johnson initially appeared to be the winner but lost when some questionable returns were counted. He ran again in 1948, finishing second in a three-way Democratic primary to Coke Stevenson, but a runoff was forced when Stevenson failed to win a majority. Johnson won the runoff by 87 votes amidst accusations of fraud, including one that involved votes brought in by campaign manager (and future governor) John B. Connally that appeared to have been cast in alphabetical order. After a friendly judge struck down Stevenson's appeal, Johnson went on to win the general election.

- Billy Sol Estes was both a friend and an enemy of Lyndon Johnson. As a wealthy fertilizer salesman, Estes contributed to Johnson's campaigns for the Senate and the vice presidency. Unbeknownst to Johnson, much of Estes's wealth came from sources as odorous as his fertilizer. In the late 1950s, Estes lied about buying cotton from local farmers to obtain bank loans for nonexistent cotton and fertilizer he claimed was in storage. After his accountant and a government investigator died under suspicious circumstances, Estes and three associates were indicted on 57 counts of fraud. Two of these indicted associates also died suspiciously. Estes was found guilty of fraud and sentenced to eight years in prison, with an additional 15 years tacked on for other charges. His association with Johnson nearly caused President Kennedy to dump his vice president. The U.S. Supreme Court ultimately overturned Estes's conviction in 1965, however, on the grounds that having TV cameras and reporters in the courtroom (uncommon at that time) deprived him of a fair trial. After Johnson's death, Estes accused his one-time friend of involvement in a conspiracy behind the Kennedy assassination.

• The Texas Sharpstown Scandal is named for the Sharpstown master-planned community near Houston and its backer, banker and insurance company manager Frank Sharp. Sharp made loans of $600,000 from his bank to state officials, who then bought stock in his insurance company. They next passed legislation to inflate the value of the insurance company, which allowed the officials to sell their stock profitably. The huge profits aroused the suspicions of the SEC in 1971, and charges were filed against Sharp and others. The governor, lieutenant governor, and House speaker, among other state officials, were accused of bribery. Sharp received three years' probation and a $5,000 fine. One victim of the fraud, Strake Jesuit College Preparatory, lost $6 million.

• Democrat Jim Wright represented Texas in Congress for 34 years, serving as Speaker of the House from 1987 to 1989. In 1988, Republican Newt Gingrich led an investigation by the House Ethics Committee into charges that Wright used bulk purchases of his book to get around congressional limits on speaking fees and that his wife had been given a job to get around a limit on political gifts. Wright was forced to resign from Congress in 1989, and Gingrich eventually became Speaker of the House with his own subsequent ethics violations.

• George Parr was a political force in Duval County from the 1920s to the 1960s. Replacing his brother in 1926 as county judge, Parr used legal and illegal tactics to convince the county's majority Mexican-American population to support the Democratic Party. Parr was convicted of income tax evasion in 1934 and served nine months with little effect on his influence as the "Duke of Duval County." He found questionable votes to help Lyndon Johnson win the 1948 Democratic senatorial primary and was linked to but never accused of at least three murders of political opponents. While appealing a conviction and five-year sentence for federal income tax evasion in 1975, Parr died by suicide.

The Iran-Contra Affair

On July 8, 1985, President Ronald Reagan told the American Bar Association that Iran was part of a "confederation of terrorist states." He failed to mention that members of his administration were secretly planning to sell weapons to Iran to facilitate the release of U.S. hostages held in Lebanon by pro-Iranian terrorist groups. Profits from the arms sales were secretly sent to Nicaragua to aid rebel forces, known as the contras, in their attempt to overthrow the country's democratically elected government. The incident became known as the Iran-Contra Affair and was the biggest scandal of Reagan's administration.

The weapons sale to Iran was authorized by Robert McFarlane, head of the National Security Council (NSC), in violation of U.S. government policies regarding terrorists and military aid to Iran. NSC staff member Oliver North arranged for a portion of the $48 million paid by Iran to be sent to the contras, which violated a 1984 law banning this type of aid. North and his secretary Fawn Hall also shredded critical documents. President Reagan repeatedly denied rumors that the United States had exchanged arms for hostages, but later stated that he'd been misinformed. He created a Special Review Board to investigate. In

February 1987, the board found the president not guilty. Others involved were found guilty but either had their sentences overturned on appeal or were later pardoned by George H. W. Bush.

The Ultimate He Said, She Said

On October 30, 1989, President George H.W. Bush nominated lawyer and judge Clarence Thomas to fill Robert Bork's seat on the United States Court of Appeals for the District of Columbia Circuit. His confirmation hearing was uneventful, and the U.S. Senate confirmed Thomas on March 6, 1990.

Just over a year later, on July 1, 1991, President Bush once again nominated Thomas to fill an empty seat. Thurgood Marshall, the first African-American to serve on the United States Supreme Court, was retiring due to poor health, and Bush felt that Thomas would be an honorable replacement for the groundbreaking justice. This time, however, Thomas's confirmation hearing would lack the routine predictability of his previous hearing. And the resulting bout of "he said, she said" would make the name of Clarence Thomas forever synonymous with another: Anita Hill.

High Ambition

Thomas and Hill first met when Hill worked as an attorney for Thomas at the U.S. Department of Education in 1981. In 1982, Thomas became chairman of the U.S. Equal Employment Opportunity Commission (EEOC), and Hill followed him along as his assistant. Hill then moved on with her career, becoming a professor, first at Oral Roberts University and later at the University of Oklahoma College of Law. Thomas, meanwhile, was said to be "openly ambitious for higher office," and a seat on the Supreme Court would give him the highest office in the country. But first came the formality of confirmation.

At first, Thomas's confirmation hearing was fairly uneventful, although there was some concern about filling Marshall's seat with a justice who was more conservative. Many civil rights groups opposed Thomas for his criticism of affirmative action, and feminists were concerned that he might not support *Roe v. Wade*. Still, all was going well until just before the conclusion of the hearings, when an FBI interview with Anita Hill was leaked, and she was called to testify.

He Said, She Said

Hill alleged that while she was working for Thomas at the Department of Education and the EEOC, Thomas repeatedly pressured her to go on dates, which she declined. Once she'd rebuffed him many times, Thomas moved on to speaking about sexual subjects during work situations. Hill's testimony was often graphic, but matter-of-fact, as she calmly described the harassment she said she endured. Several other witnesses were never called, although two of Thomas's former assistants submitted written statements in support of Hill, despite the fact that neither would say they'd been harassed. Hill stuck to her accusations even when her credibility was questioned, saying, "I am not given to fantasy. This is not something I would have come forward with if I was not absolutely sure of what I was saying."

But just as stubborn was Thomas, who adamantly denied the accusations, saying the hearing had become "a circus" and "a national disgrace." He said he felt "shocked, surprised, hurt, and enormously saddened" that Hill would accuse him of harassment, especially since he'd considered her a friend. He claimed to have never asked Hill out on any dates, although he admitted that he would occasionally drive her home after work and the two would "argue about politics." And former colleague Nancy Altman, who shared an office with Thomas at the Department of Education, testified that she never heard him say anything inappropriate.

Stalemate

By the time the hearing was over, only one thing was certain: one person was telling the truth, and one person was lying. But each gave such compelling, believable testimony that it was impossible to know which was which. The Judiciary Committee was split 7-7, and Thomas's nomination was sent to the Senate. He was confirmed by a narrow 52-48 vote—the closest vote for approval of a Supreme Court nominee in more than a century.

Today, Thomas is considered the most conservative member of the Supreme Court, and he is known not only for his quiet and stoic demeanor but also for his thoughtful intellect. Hill is now a professor of social policy, law, and women's studies at Brandeis University. She is still lauded for bringing awareness of harassment in the workplace, and she has a legacy that lives on in the current #MeToo movement.

Bush's String of Dismissals

In 1993, after President Bill Clinton took office, Attorney General Janet Reno fired 93 of 94 United States attorneys in federal districts. Similarly, after President Donald Trump began his term in 2017, Attorney General Jeff Sessions dismissed 46 attorneys; many more had already resigned in anticipation of such a move. Some saw these firings as "scandalous," but the truth is, it's quite normal. U.S. attorneys are political appointees, chosen by the president to carry out policy, and it's up to each administration to decide which attorneys to retain and which to dismiss. It stands to reason that each president prefers attorneys who align with their political vision.

Out with the Old and in with the Interim

But in December 2006, almost two years into President George W. Bush's second term, seven U.S. attorneys were dismissed for reasons that were unclear, in an unprecedented and scandalous move. As is the case with every administration, the seven attorneys in question were appointed by President Bush at the beginning of his term, so questions arose about the true motives behind the firings.

To add to the controversy was a new provision in the USA PATRIOT Act that removed a 120-day term limit on interim U.S. attorneys. When a vacancy opens up, the U.S. Attorney General—in this case, Alberto Gonzales—can immediately appoint an interim attorney, unlike the president's U.S. attorney appointees, who must be confirmed by the Senate. By removing the 120-day term limit on U.S. Attorney General appointees, it opened the door to "interim" attorneys with indefinite terms, who could bypass Senate confirmation. So were the dismissals a way to remove attorneys who had been confirmed by the Senate to replace them with the administration's own choices?

What Was the Reason?

The rationale behind the firings was murky, at best, with the administration saying the attorneys had been dismissed due to "job performance" issues, even though most of them had recently received positive feedback on evaluations from the Department of Justice. Critics speculated that the dismissals were politically motivated, and that the attorneys were fired for failing to prosecute Democrats or, conversely, for prosecuting Republicans. And the resulting investigations into the firings proved to be just as confounding. Despite hours of testimony by Attorney General Gonzales and Department of Justice staff members, changing and contradictory statements made the administration's role in the controversy unclear.

Much Ado about Nothing?

By mid-September 2007, nine Department of Justice staff members— including Attorney General Gonzales—had resigned. A year later, the Justice Department's Inspector General released a report that concluded the dismissals had been politically motivated. The new Attorney General, Michael Mukasey, appointed special prosecutor Nora Dannehy to investigate the scandal and to give her opinion on whether any of the key players should be brought up on charges. But in July 2010, prosecutors closed the investigation without filing any charges, determining that there was not enough evidence to prove a criminal act had occurred.

Not everyone felt that Bush's dismissal of the attorneys should have created such an uproar. As *National Review* contributing editor Andrew C. McCarthy stated, it was "much ado about nothing." After all, if it is acceptable for a president to entirely revamp the Department of Justice at the beginning of a term, why is some transition not acceptable in the middle of a term? Perhaps the controversy was made worse by the Bush administration's bumbling management of the case. But there was one silver lining: on June 14, 2007, Congress repealed the provision in the USA PATRIOT Act that removed the 120-day term limit for interim attorneys, and President Bush immediately signed it into law.

Bridgegate

Anyone who lives in a big city knows the stresses and challenges of a daily commute. It's not unusual for speedy traffic to transform to a painstaking crawl during rush hour, turning what should be a quick trip into a slow-motion nightmare. Usually, this frustrating vehicular situation is merely a byproduct of so many cars on the road—it's not a deliberate action, it's just what happens when everyone is trying to get somewhere at the same time. But in September 2013, the traffic torment on the George Washington Bridge between New Jersey and New York *was* a deliberate action, and it may have cost a governor his shot at the presidency.

Gridlocked

The George Washington Bridge is a double-decker toll bridge that connects Fort Lee, New Jersey, and the island of Manhattan, and it is owned by the Port Authority of New York and New Jersey. It is the busiest motor vehicle bridge in the world, with 29 toll lanes spread across three toll plazas. The bridge is heavily traveled by commuters who work in New York City but live in the much cheaper neighborhoods of New Jersey, as well as by tourists eager to take in some sights. Even on a "slow" day the bridge is crowded with city traffic.

But on September 9, 2013—the first day of the school year—commuters from Fort Lee were taken aback to discover unexpected lane closures. Normally, three lanes are reserved in the toll plaza exclusively for Fort Lee traffic; but on this day, two of those lanes were closed off. There had been no warning—not even to police departments—that these closures were going to take place, and traffic in Fort Lee ground to a halt, impeding both school buses and emergency response vehicles. The inexplicable closures lasted all week, until finally, on September 13, the executive director of the Port Authority, Patrick Foye, demanded that the lanes be reopened. But why had the lanes been closed to begin with?

A Fake Study with Real Consequences

When reporters began asking questions, they were originally told that the lane closures were part of a traffic study. But the *Wall Street Journal* questioned this excuse, quoting sources saying that there was no traffic study. It was revealed that not even Foye had been notified of the closures, and when he reopened the lanes, he questioned whether the closures had broken state or federal laws. The New Jersey legislature then held a hearing on the matter, questioning Governor Chris Christie, who denied any knowledge of the incident. So, who ordered the closures?

Emails turned over to the legislature revealed the source as Christie's deputy chief of staff, Bridget Kelly. Kelly emailed Port Authority executive David Wildstein on August 13 saying it was "time for some traffic problems in Fort Lee." Wildstein then went to George Washington Bridge manager Robert Durando and told him to close the lanes on September 9, citing the fake "study." He instructed Durando not to tell anyone about the closures, saying it would impact the study's results.

How Much Did Christie Know?

When Christie heard the whole story, he fired Kelly, saying, "I am stunned by the abject stupidity shown here." His administration's review of the lane closures found that Kelly and Wildstein—as well as Port Authority deputy executive director Bill Baroni—were responsible for the traffic turmoil on the bridge, and the whole thing was orchestrated to punish Fort Lee Mayor Mark Sokolich for his refusal to endorse Christie's reelection.

While no evidence was found to suggest that Christie knew of the plot beforehand, many believe he must have been complicit in the plan his staff carried out. As a result, his political standing was damaged, and the once-popular contender for the 2016 Republican Presidential Nomination dropped out of the race quickly after the New Hampshire primary. Meanwhile, lane closures or not, traffic in New Jersey continues to cause nightmares.

CHAPTER 3

FINANCIAL SWINDLES, BUSTS, AND TURMOIL

The Panic of 1792

In this day and age, where televisions, Internet, and smartphones are as ubiquitous as the humans who use them, we are used to hearing stories of scandal and corruption. But the world was filled with con men and people seeking to make a profit at the expense of others long before we could read about their transgressions at the click of a mouse. In fact, the story of William Duer and Alexander Macomb—considered to be the very first people to participate in insider trading—goes all the way back to 1792.

The Senator

Duer was an unlikely choice to be pegged as a criminal: He was a senator in the first New York State Legislature and a member of the Continental Congress, and he later became a modestly successful businessman, supplying lumber to the American army. In 1779, he married Lady Catherine Alexander, a descendant of several prominent New York families; George Washington was a guest at the wedding. By 1789, Alexander Hamilton appointed Duer the first Assistant Secretary to the U.S. Treasury, and he was enjoying a comfortable, prosperous life in the still-new United States.

The Landowner

Macomb, as well, was hardly someone to be suspected of corrupt behavior. A respected merchant, fur trader, and shipping magnate, Macomb owned large tracts of land in several U.S. states, including four million acres in New York. In 1788, he built a large mansion in New York City that, in 1790, was leased by the federal government to serve as the second presidential mansion for Washington. He was active in civic affairs, served in the state assembly, and was a father to 10 children.

The Scheme

But Duer and Macomb were also both serial speculators, often biting off more than they could chew when it came to investments. In the winter of 1791, Duer and Macomb—acting on the inside knowledge Duer had gained at his post at the Treasury—began speculating on the newly formed Bank of the United States. They anticipated that stock prices would rise dramatically, and their hope was that they could corner the U.S. debt securities market. So the two businessmen began taking out loans all across the city—from banks, shopkeepers, and business owners—to finance their scheme. But by the beginning of 1792, it became apparent that stock prices weren't rising as quickly as the duo had hoped, and Duer and Macomb began to default on their loans. Investors began pulling their money out of the Bank of the United States, the price of securities fell more than 20 percent, and panic ensued.

The Fix

Hamilton managed to halt the panic by encouraging banks to continue making loans at a higher rate of interest and authorizing hundreds of thousands of dollars in open-market purchases of securities. By the fall of 1792, market demand was back to normal and the economy continued to grow. But Duer and Macomb would never benefit from the thriving economy. Both men were sent to debtor's prison, where Duer spent the rest of his life, dying in 1799 at the age of 56. Macomb was eventually released from prison, but the once wealthy merchant never regained his sizeable fortune.

Black Friday: A Much Direr Meaning

The words "Black Friday" probably conjure up images of after-Thanksgiving sales, when crowds of bargain hunters are eager to get a head start on their holiday purchases. But more than a century ago, on September 24, 1869, the words had a much direr meaning.

The Price of Gold

Before the Civil War, gold had been the standard currency in the United States. But during the war, the government authorized the printing of $450 million in paper "greenbacks" to help fund the Union's wartime efforts. President Ulysses S. Grant intended to return the country to the gold standard by redeeming the greenbacks with gold, and his policy was to sell the precious metal at weekly intervals. This served to control the price of gold: when the government sold it, the price went down; when they didn't sell, the price went up.

This effect did not go unnoticed by a couple of scheming speculators named James Fisk and Jay Gould. Fisk and Gould, who were directors of the Erie Railroad, reasoned that if the government were to hold on to its gold longer, the price would increase exponentially. Since there was only about $20 million in gold in circulation at any time, a savvy investor could buy large amounts of gold and "corner" the market and sell for huge profits.

Cornering the Market

But in order for such a plan to work, Fisk and Gould would have to convince the president to hold on to the gold in the Treasury. So they befriended a small-time speculator named Abel Corbin, who was married to President Grant's sister, and let him in on the scheme to corner the gold market. Now that they had an inside man, they were able to get closer to the president and began to plant suggestions that the government shouldn't sell so much gold. Corbin would invite Fisk and Gould to social functions, where they'd engage in friendly banter with the president and argue against the government sale of gold, saying that high gold prices would benefit farmers who sold their harvests overseas. The president's brother-in-law would heartily agree, and over time the ideas began to have an effect.

By the first week of September, President Grant had changed his mind about the weekly gold sales, and he ordered the Treasury to halt the sales for the next month. Fisk and Gould sprang into action, buying up as much gold as they could, and just as they'd planned, the price climbed. What was a $100 piece of gold in August sold for more than $140 by September. And then Corbin made a mistake: he wrote the president to ask him if he was holding firm on his new gold policy, and the question aroused suspicion. Grant began to suspect that his brother-in-law was involved in a gold scheme, and he was furious to discover he'd been manipulated.

Crashing Down

So on September 24, President Grant ordered that $4 million in gold be released from the Treasury, and the price immediately dropped. Both Fisk and Gould's corner and the U.S. stock market broke: the market fell 20 percentage points, and some of Wall Street's smaller firms were bankrupt. Speculators were ruined, foreign trade stopped, and farmers, who had been the basis for Fisk and Gould's gold arguments, lost 50 percent of the value of their harvests.

Amazingly, Fisk and Gould—the scheming investors who'd planned the entire debacle—escaped any conviction or even financial hardship due to their actions. Even after an official investigation by Congress, the two were able to avoid jail time or fines, and Fisk even avoided paying back his massive losses, saying a third party had made trades without his knowledge. The manipulators remained wealthy men for the rest of their lives.

The Whiskey Ring

In September 1869, James Fisk and Jay Gould started the Black Friday panic when they attempted to corner the gold market. The scandal tarnished Grant's reputation, and he started to lose support from some of his fellow Republicans in Missouri. So Grant sent General John McDonald—the supervisor of the U.S. Treasury Department's internal revenue for the St. Louis area—to Missouri to round up some support for the struggling president. But instead of turning attention to something other than the controversy surrounding Grant's administration, McDonald introduced the country to a brand-new scandal.

Don't Drink and Bribe

In an effort to raise money for Grant, McDonald—along with what would grow to hundreds of other accomplices—partnered up with whiskey distillers in a scheme to benefit both parties. The distillers would pay federal agents huge bribes, and in return, the agents helped the distillers evade taxes. Tax on whiskey was 70 cents per gallon; but if a distiller bribed a federal agent, his whiskey was only taxed at 35 cents a gallon, and he could make impressive profits.

The Whiskey Ring, as it came to be known, spread from St. Louis to Chicago to New Orleans to Washington D.C. The plotters in the conspiracy included politicians, reporters, revenue service agents, shopkeepers, and, of course, whiskey distillers. Even Grant's private secretary and good friend, General Orville E. Babcock, participated in the ring. But with so many people in on the conspiracy, it was only a matter of time before the whole thing came crashing down.

The First Special Prosecutor

In 1875, word of the Whiskey Ring reached the U.S. Secretary of the Treasury, Benjamin Bristow. Bristow had already seen the effects of the Black Friday panic and the Credit Mobilier scandal, and he'd had enough of the corruption. Working secretly and without Grant's knowledge, Bristow used information he'd heard from members of the ring to conduct raids across the country on May 10, 1875. More than 200 men were indicted—with 110 eventual convictions, including McDonald—and $3 million in taxes was recovered.

After the ring was exposed, Grant appointed John B. Henderson as a special prosecutor—the country's first—to avoid any appearance of a conflict of interest. One of Henderson's indictments was Babcock, but Grant's longtime friend insisted to the president that he was innocent. When Henderson not only refused to accept Babcock's appeal of innocence but also suggested that Grant might have known about the ring, Grant fired him and replaced him with James Broadhead.

The Damage Is Done

Grant himself testified during Babcock's trial, and the president's secretary became the only major player in the Whiskey Ring to win an acquittal. However, the public's trust was gone, and Babcock was forced to resign his position. Bristow resigned as well, as members of Grant's cabinet—disgruntled that their friends and associates had been scrutinized—refused to speak to him. And Grant, although not involved in the Whiskey Ring himself, found his reputation marred by so many scandals during his presidency. He left office in 1877 for less controversial pursuits: traveling around the world with his family.

A Railroad to Nowhere

When we think of scandals, the Union Pacific Railroad probably isn't the first thing to come to mind. But this 32,000-mile freight hauling system was part of one of the earliest American political corruption controversies.

A Railroad to Nowhere?

In the 1860s, the federal government agreed to provide the Union Pacific Railroad with $100 million in capital to help build a transcontinental rail line from the Missouri River to the Pacific coast. The project was daunting: it would require 1,750 miles of rail construction through some of the harshest environments in the country. And once finished, the route would be unpopular with travelers, as the western United States was mostly undeveloped east of the California border. In fact, many who opposed the new railway called it a "railroad to nowhere" and saw it as an unprofitable venture.

A Company within a Company

Because of the predicted difficulties and the fact that few passengers would likely pay to use the new railway, private financers refused to invest in the project. So, Union Pacific corporate leaders, including entrepreneur George Francis Train and Union Pacific vice president Thomas C. Durant, came up with an idea. They formed a business called Credit Mobilier of America in 1864 and portrayed it as a construction company. The group convinced not only the general public but also the government that this fake company had agreed to be the principle contractor for the railroad project. Union Pacific representatives then made agreements with Credit Mobilier to construct the new railway at rates that were significantly higher than the actual cost.

Union Pacific billed the U.S. government with the invoices from Credit Mobilier, which reflected the inflated prices. Since the two companies were presumably independent of one another, no one questioned the costs. While the operating costs of the construction added up to $50,720,959, the U.S. government paid a total of $94,650,287, a profit of $43,929,328 for Credit Mobilier. This "profit" made the fake company a huge success, and their stock began to soar.

Congressional Complicity

But there's even more to the story. In 1867, Credit Mobilier replaced Thomas C. Durant with Massachusetts Congressman Oakes Ames. Ames began to offer members of Congress Credit Mobilier stock at par value, which was much cheaper than its market value. The congressmen could then sell their shares at market value to investors eager to own stock in the "successful" company. In return, the members of Congress granted Credit Mobilier generous government subsidies and land grants.

Participants in the corruption barely tried to hide it, with both Union Pacific and Credit Mobilier stockholders getting rich off the scheme. So it's not surprising that public suspicion began to grow, and in 1872, the New York City newspaper the *Sun* broke the story of the scandal. The paper reported that Credit Mobilier had received far more money for the railroad than it had actually cost to build, and soon many investors were bankrupt.

Congress investigated 13 lawmakers who were accused in the scam. These included the incoming Vice President Henry Wilson—who was able to prove that he had paid for stock in his wife's name and with her money—and James A. Garfield, who denied any involvement and was later elected president. Also accused was Vice President Schuyler Colfax, who subsequently left politics and never ran for office again. In a strange twist of fate in this train tale, Colfax died in 1885—after he suffered a heart attack while running to catch a train.

Vegetable Oil: A Major Stock Market Threat?

On November 22, 1963, President John F. Kennedy was assassinated in Dallas, Texas. Most of us, whether we actually remember the event or have just read about it in history books, are acquainted with the tragic story. But far fewer know that this national crisis overshadowed a major threat to the stock market—a threat that revolved around, of all things, vegetable oil.

Making a Career of Swindling

The story began with Tino De Angelis, a Bronx-born commodities trader who learned how to be a con man at an early age. By the time he was a teenager, De Angelis was working in a meat and fish market where he managed 200 employees, and he soon took over the Adolph Gobel Company in North Bergen, New Jersey. While running the company, he decided to take advantage of the National School Lunch Act and sold the government two million pounds of subpar, uninspected meat. He overcharged by tens of thousands of dollars, and his attempted con was quickly uncovered. The Adolph Gobel Company went bankrupt, and De Angelis moved on to his next venture: vegetable oil.

In 1955, he started the Allied Crude Vegetable Oil Refinery to take advantage of another government program, Food for Peace. The Food for Peace program sold goods to Europe at low prices to help boost its post-war economy. De Angelis shipped massive amounts of low-quality shortening and vegetable oil to Europe with great success. By 1962, he was doing so well that he decided to try to corner the market on soybean oil, so he bought up large quantities of oil and took out huge loans with Wall Street banks. He used his money to buy soybean oil futures to drive up the price of his oil holdings.

Oil and Water

De Angelis became a customer of American Express's new field warehousing division, which made loans to companies using their inventory as collateral. Amex would write a warehouse receipt for the vegetable oil De Angelis had in stock, and he could then exchange the receipts for cash at a bank. The schemer soon realized the easy money he could make this way, and he began falsifying receipts for nonexistent oil. Amex, of course, needed to occasionally inspect the tanks at the refinery to make sure De Angelis had the oil he claimed to have. But unbeknownst to the inspectors, many of the tanks were filled with water, with only a small bit of oil floating on top. De Angelis also cleverly connected some of his tanks with pipes, so he could transfer oil from one tank to an empty tank, making it appear that all tanks were full.

De Angelis didn't stop with Amex; over time, he got loans from 51 different companies, including Proctor & Gamble and Bank of America. Strangely, no one seemed to notice that the amount of vegetable oil De Angelis claimed to have was more than the Department of Agriculture reported for the entire United States. Obviously, this swindle couldn't last forever; eventually, inspectors were tipped off by mistakes and bribes within Allied Crude. They inspected the tanks more thoroughly and found the water, and De Angelis was revealed as a fraud.

An Unexpected Event

The soybean oil futures market crashed, and the value of the loans was immediately wiped out. Allied Crude filed for bankruptcy on November 19, 1963, and all 51 companies that De Angelis went to for loans were stuck with the mess he created. Millions of dollars were never accounted for. Two of the brokerage houses De Angelis had used, Williston and Beane and Ira Haupt and Co., were suspended from trading by the New York Stock Exchange, and by November 22, traders were close to panic.

And then came the news that President Kennedy had been shot. Suddenly, the panic that had begun with the vegetable oil debacle reached a fever pitch, and at 2:07 p.m., trading was stopped by NYSE officials to calm down investors. The market remained closed for the next three days, as the country mourned the loss of the president. When it reopened on Tuesday, November 26, the break from trading was enough to restore a sense of normalcy to the market.

As for De Angelis, he was sentenced to seven years in prison. Later, he would involve himself in a Ponzi scheme involving the livestock industry, and in 1992 he was sentenced to prison after attempting to buy more than a million dollars' worth of meat from a New York company using a forged check. Apparently even prison was not enough to teach this career swindler a lesson.

A Fugitive Financier King

On November 23, 2007, American financier Robert Vesco died of lung cancer in Havana, Cuba. Reportedly he was buried in Colon Cemetery, but some insist that he is still alive, having fled to Sierra Leone after faking his own death. It is fitting that the man once dubbed "the undisputed king of the fugitive financiers" would stir up as much controversy at the end of his life as he did throughout the rest of it.

Devious Dropout

Vesco was born and raised in Detroit, Michigan, where he quit both high school and later engineering school in favor of delving into the world of finance. In 1968, at the young age of 33, Vesco had managed to acquire International Controls Corporation (ICC), a holding company that owned an airline and several manufacturing plants, and the two-time school dropout was worth $50 million.

Vesco's first financial misstep was in 1970. That's when he swooped in to buy troubled mutual fund investment company Investors Overseas Service, Ltd. (IOS) from its jailed founder, Bernard Cornfeld. Vesco then used IOS investments to cover his own investments in ICC, moving IOS investor funds into dummy corporations. When his actions were discovered, Vesco took his corporate jet and fled to Costa Rica before any charges could be filed against him.

Life on the Lam

Right before he left the country, Vesco made illegal contributions totaling $250,000 to Richard Nixon's reelection campaign in a last-ditch effort to avoid trouble from the SEC. Vesco was hoping to convince Nixon's Attorney General, John N. Mitchell, to intercede on his behalf to the SEC, but his ploy failed.

Now a fugitive in Costa Rica, Vesco invested $2.1 million into a company that was founded by the Costa Rican president, Jose Figueres, and in return, Figueres passed a law that guaranteed Vesco could not be extradited to the United States. The "Vesco Law," as it was commonly called, was repealed in 1978 when Rodrigo Carazo was elected the new Costa Rican president. Vesco then bounced around between the Bahamas, Antigua, and Nicaragua, all of which ignored extradition requests from the United States. He continued to conduct shady business deals and grew his wealth, even appearing several times on the *Forbes* list of the wealthiest people in the world.

Cuban Quandary

In 1982, Vesco moved to Cuba; the country agreed to admit him provided he stayed out of financial deals. This didn't prevent him from finding trouble, however. In the 1990s, Vesco partnered with Richard Nixon's nephew, Donald Nixon, who asked the Cuban government to help him conduct trials on an herbal immunity booster. Cuba agreed to provide manufacturing facilities and doctors for the studies. But not long after trials began, Vesco was arrested and accused of being a foreign agent, and Nixon was held for a month on suspicion of involvement in the "international drug trade." Nixon was eventually allowed to leave Cuba, but Vesco was charged with defrauding foreign investors and illicit economic activity.

Vesco was jailed in a Cuban prison for 13 years, and released in 2005. Two years later, he supposedly died of lung cancer, but Cuban authorities never actually reported his death publicly, and he was buried in an unmarked grave. Some want to believe that he's still on the run, elusive as ever, but the reality is probably much simpler: Robert Vesco couldn't run from his own final fate.

The Junk Bond King

In the financial world, bonds with a high credit rating are known as investment-grade bonds. But those with a high default risk are known as speculative or noninvestment grade, or are known by their popular nickname: junk bonds. And in the 1980s, no one was better at manipulating junk bonds than Michael Milken—the "Junk Bond King."

Meteoric Rise

Milken graduated from the University of California, Berkeley in 1968, where he became interested in investing. To educate himself on the process, he read studies written by W. Braddock Hickman, who, at the time, was the president of the Federal Reserve Bank of Cleveland. Hickman surmised that a portfolio of noninvestment grade bonds could offer greater risk-adjusted returns than a portfolio full of investment-grade bonds.

Milken then moved on to the Wharton School of the University of Pennsylvania, where he earned an MBA. He began working for investment banks, eventually ending up at the firm Drexel Burnham Lambert, where he created a high-yield bond trading department. By 1976, less than a decade after beginning his career, Milken was making around $5 million a year. By the 1980s, Milken was a superstar in the financial world, with some calling him the most powerful American financier since J.P. Morgan.

Trouble Ahead

But all was not as perfect as it seemed: As early as 1979, Milken and his colleagues were under constant scrutiny by the SEC for what it deemed was possible unethical and illegal behavior. It seemed, however, that Milken played everything by the book, even though he felt that some securities laws were a hindrance to free trade.

But by 1986, cracks were beginning to show in Drexel Burnham Lambert's façade. First, a managing director in the mergers and acquisitions department, Dennis Levine, was charged with insider trading. Then, after Levine pled guilty to four felonies, he implicated one of his partners, stock trader Ivan Boesky. And as part of a plea deal, Boesky also agreed to name a name: Michael Milken. This prompted the SEC to launch a new investigation into Drexel's operations. The chaos within the firm also caught the attention of Rudy Giuliani—who at that time was the United States Attorney for the Southern District of New York—and he began his own investigation.

For two years, both investigations focused on Milken's department, with Drexel insisting that Boesky was simply a criminal telling lies in return for a reduced sentence. The evidence was mounting, however, and by 1988, the SEC sued Drexel for insider trading, stock manipulation, defrauding its clients, and stock parking. Giuliani was also convinced of wrongdoing and threatened to indict Drexel under RICO. In order to avoid the RICO indictment, Drexel began to negotiate with Giuliani; but when Giuliani demanded that Milken leave the firm if he was ever indicted, Drexel's board refused the terms.

Paying His Dues and Giving Back

It only took two days before they changed their minds. Drexel's own lawyers discovered a suspicious limited partnership that Milken had set up. Through this partnership, Milken had been selling stock warrants to his own children and to managers of money funds, which was a breach of Drexel's regulations and may have constituted self-dealing and bribery. Drexel immediately pleaded guilty to six counts of stock parking and stock manipulation, and several money managers were consequently convicted on bribery charges.

As for Milken, he was indicted on 98 counts of racketeering and fraud. He pleaded guilty to six counts of securities and tax violations, and he was sentenced to 10 years in prison. He was also ordered to pay a total of $1.1 billion in fines and repayments to investors. After 22 months, Milken was released from prison, he and has since focused his energies on philanthropy through his Milken Family Foundation. Milken also founded the Prostate Cancer Foundation and a nonprofit called FasterCures, which focuses on accelerating medical research.

Uncharitable Work

The United Way of America, which partners with many charitable organizations to pool fundraising and support efforts, has been around since 1887. Back then, church leaders in Denver, Colorado, formed the Charity Organization Society to help collect funds for 22 different agencies. This evolved into Community Chest organizations, which were established throughout the United States and the world.

A New Name and a Rise to the Top

One such Community Chest was located in South Bend, Indiana, where Army Lt. William Aramony began his post-Korean War career. Aramony had a knack for raising funds and endorsing charities, and he was quickly promoted to an executive. By 1970, he was hired as CEO of the governing body of the Community Chest, the United Community Funds and Council of America. He wasted no time reorganizing the company, and he renamed it the United Way of America, which he headquartered in Alexandria, Virginia.

Aramony brought in great amounts of publicity through a partnership with the National Football League, and he created a core strategy that helped raise even more money, resulting in donations that went from $787 million in 1970 to $3.1 billion by 1990. He was called a "visionary" and a "genius" and seemed to be exactly the kind of person the United Way needed to fulfill its mission.

Whispers of Trouble

But just as the organization was enjoying such promising success, rumors started to swirl about its illustrious leader. Aramony and his wife, Bebe, had been estranged since 1988, and the office gossip began centering around the CEO's alleged teenaged girlfriend. This in itself would have been enough to tarnish the reputation of the 63-year-old, but there was even more to the story. In late 1990, United Way's chairman, Edward A. Brennan, was sent an anonymous note that accused Aramony of using charity money to fund his affair with the young woman.

Aramony denied this accusation, of course, but after he divorced Bebe in 1991, some of his expenses with the organization came to light. He often flew first class, was driven by chauffeurs, and bought expensive gifts for friends. Independent investigators were hired and they discovered a history of poor recordkeeping and sloppy accounting, but they did not find any direct evidence that Aramony had done anything wrong. They did, however, note that the records did not distinguish between business expenses and personal expenses.

Uncharitable Work

Aramony announced his retirement on February 27, 1992. Despite the lack of evidence found by the independent investigators, the story was enough to catch the attention of the FBI, the IRS, and the U.S. Postal Service, and they began their own investigations into the matter. They discovered that Aramony had been using United Way money to fund trips to gamble in Las Vegas, lobster dinners at fancy restaurants, and furnishings for an apartment in Manhattan and another in Miami. But Aramony's worst transgression was using United Way money to lavish expensive trips and gifts on his mistresses, the youngest of whom was only 17 when she began dating the CEO.

Aramony was indicted on federal charges and his case went to trial in 1995. Four of his former mistresses testified against him, as well as his former assistant, who stated that she replaced the names of Aramony's mistresses with clients' names in his expense accounts and used United Way funds to purchase personal items for him. The disgraced CEO was sentenced to seven years in prison and fined $300,000.

According to his son, Robert, Aramony stayed true to his lifelong career of helping others, even behind bars. Aramony developed a mentoring program while in prison that helped prepare inmates for job interviews after release. His advice to fellow prisoners? "Hold your head high, speak honestly about your past mistakes, and explain with confidence why you are ready for a new opportunity."

Enron: From Boom to Bust

For a company that seemed to have everything going its way, the end sure came quickly.

In the 1990s, the U.S. Congress passed legislation deregulating the sale of electricity, as it had done for natural gas some years earlier. The result made it possible for energy trading companies, including Enron, to thrive. In effect, the law allowed a highly profitable market to develop between energy producers and those local governments that buy electricity—a system kept in place because of aggressive lobbying by Enron and other such firms. By the turn of the twenty-first century, Enron stock was trading for $80 to $90 a share.

Trouble in the Waters

All was not smooth sailing, however, for the energy giant. Its new broadband communications trading division was running into difficulties, its power project in India was behind schedule and over budget, and its role in the California power crisis of 2000—2001 was being scrutinized. Then, on August 14, 2001, CEO Jeffrey Skilling announced he was resigning after only six months in his position. He also sold off 450,000 shares of Enron stock for $33 million.

Ken Lay, the chairman at Enron, affirmed that there was "absolutely no accounting issue, no trading issue, no reserve issue, no previously unknown problem" that prompted Skilling's departure. He further asserted that there would be "no change or outlook in the performance of the company going forward." Though he did admit that falling stock prices were a factor behind Skilling's departure, Lay elected to assume the CEO position.

A Suspicious Appearance

Enron's financial statements were so confusing because of the company's tax strategies and position hedging, as well as its use of "related-party transactions," that Enron's leadership assumed no one would be able to analyze its finances. A particularly troubling aspect was that several of the "related-party" entities were, or had been, controlled by Enron CFO Andrew Fastow (who may or may not have realized that he was being groomed as a scapegoat).

Sound confusing? Good, then the plan worked. And if all this could confuse government regulatory agencies, think of how investors must have felt. Stock prices slowly started sliding from their highs at the beginning of 2001, but as the year went on, the tumble picked up speed. On October 22, for instance, the share price of Enron dropped $5.40 in one day to $20.65. After Enron officials started talking about such things as "share settled costless collar arrangements" and "derivative instruments which eliminated the contingent nature of restricted forward contracts," the SEC had a quote of its own: "There is the appearance that you are hiding something."

Things Fall Apart

The landslide had begun. On October 24, Lay removed Fastow as CFO. Stock was trading at $16.41. On October 27, Enron began buying back all of its shares (valued around $3.3 billion). It financed this purchase by emptying its lines of credit at several banks.

On October 30, in response to concerns that Enron might try a further $1-2 billion refinancing due to having insufficient cash on hand, Enron's credit rating was dropped to near junk-bond status. Enron did secure an additional billion dollars, but it had to sell its valuable natural gas pipeline to do so.

Enron desperately needed either new investment or an outright buyout. On the night of November 7, Houston-based energy trader Dynegy voted to acquire Enron at a fire-sale price of $8 billion in stock. It wasn't enough.

The sale lagged, and Standard & Poor's index determined that if it didn't go through, Enron's bonds would be rated as junk. The word was out that Lay and other officials had sold off hundreds of millions of dollars of their own stock before the crisis and that Lay stood to receive $60 million dollars if the Dynegy sale went through. But the last straw was that Enron employees saw their retirement accounts—largely based on Enron stock—wiped out.

By November 7, after the company announced that all the money it had borrowed (about $5 billion) had been exhausted in 50 days, Enron stock was down to $7.00 a share. The SEC filed civil fraud complaints against Arthur Andersen, Enron's auditor. And on November 28, the sky fell in: Dynegy backed out of the deal to acquire Enron, and Enron's stock hit junk-bond status. On December 2, 2001, Enron sought Chapter 11 protection as it filed for the biggest bankruptcy in U.S. history. Around 4,000 employees lost their jobs.

Who Killed Enron?

There was blame aplenty:

- Ken Lay and Jeffrey Skilling were indicted for securities and wire fraud. Lay was convicted on six of six counts; Skilling was convicted on on 19 of 28 counts. Skilling was sentenced to 24 years and four months in prison. Lay avoided prison time by dying of a heart attack before he was sentenced.

- Arthur Andersen accountants signed off on this fraud. Why? They were getting a million dollars a week for their accounting services. The firm was convicted of obstruction of justice for shredding documents related to the Enron audit and surrendered its licenses and right to practice. From a high of more than 100,000 employees, Arthur Andersen is now down to around 200. Most of them are handling lawsuits.

- Investors bought stock in a company they didn't understand for the greedy promise of quick money.

- Stock ratings companies said it was a great investment, even though they had no idea what shape Enron was in.

- Investment bankers who knew that Enron was shaky bought in for a shot at quick and easy profits.

- And we can't forget the Enron employees who knew that something was fishy yet stayed silent because they were getting paid. There were a few whistleblowers, but the ones who knew and said nothing earned their places at the unemployment office.

Pure and Simple Greed

Tyco International was a company that specialized in preventing loss. With headquarters in Princeton, New Jersey, the business dealt mostly in fire and safety systems and security systems. So it was quite the scandal when, in 2002, CEO Dennis Kozlowski and CFO Mark H. Swartz were accused of exactly what Tyco products worked so hard to prevent: the theft of millions of dollars.

Shady Dealings

The trouble began when Manhattan District Attorney Robert Morgenthau began investigating Kozlowski for tax evasion. During the course of his investigation, he discovered some shady accounting practices within Tyco, including the forgiveness of a $19 million, no-interest loan to Kozlowski, and another $10 million loan that was forgiven, with all interest billed to the company. As Morgenthau dug further, he found that Kozlowski and Swartz had taken as much as $600 million from the firm. It was also discovered that Kozlowski and Swartz sold about $100 million in stock in the prior fiscal year but then claimed to have never sold stock.

As the investigation continued, Kozlowski resigned, saying only that he was under investigation for tax evasion, and on September 12, 2002, Kozlowski and Swartz were indicted on charges of enterprise corruption. Morgenthau alleged that the two had stolen more than $170 million from Tyco and acquired another $430 million by way of fraud in the sale of company shares.

A Scandalous Trial

In October 2003, the trial of the former executives began. The jury was shown video of lavish parties and luxury furnishings bought with Tyco money, and a report released by Tyco described the extravagant lifestyle its former CEO was living with his stolen company money. The list of items purchased by Kozlowski was staggering: In addition to a $16.8 million apartment on Fifth Avenue in New York City plus $11 million in furnishings, the report described items like a $15,000 dog umbrella stand, a $6,000 shower curtain, a $2,900 set of coat hangers, and a $445 pincushion!

Interestingly, the trial itself ended with a scandal, as one of the jurors, Ruth Jordan, was supposedly seen making an "OK" sign as she walked by the defense lawyers. The gesture received much publicity and lead people to believe that the trial was rigged in favor of the defendants. On April 4, 2004, a mistrial was declared, and a new trial began in January 2005.

Finally, on June 17, 2005, Kozlowski and Swartz were convicted of all but one of the more than 30 counts against them. Each received a sentence of no less than eight years and four months and no more than 25 years in prison. Kozlowski and Swartz were both granted parole in 2014. A remorseful Kozlowski told the parole board that he stole out of "greed, pure and simple." He apologized for his part in the scandal, saying, "I can't say how sorry I am and how deeply I regret my actions."

A Family of Fraudsters

The Greek word *adelphoi* means "brothers." So when brothers John and Gus Rigas started a cable system company in the tiny town of Coudersport, Pennsylvania, in 1952, they named it Adelphia. Twenty years later, John would consolidate several cable companies into one operator, Adelphia Communications. The company, with the help of many acquisitions in the 1980s and 1990s, grew into the fifth-largest cable company in the United States. And the "brothers" moniker continued to be relevant throughout the corporation's growth, as many members of the Rigas family, including John's sons Timothy and Michael, enjoyed executive status within Adelphia. But the "family" aspect of this company was also part of its undoing.

The Fall of a Cable Giant
By the year 2000, Adelphia had an impressive 5.5 million subscribers after several mergers and acquisitions. Although the acquisitions had left it with debt, analysts still felt the company was well-positioned to be profitable. But on March 27, 2002, Adelphia officials disclosed an

astounding $2.3 billion in debt that the Rigas family had taken out as loan agreements for their private trust, Highland Holdings. And while the family was responsible for repaying the debt, if they were unable to do so, Adelphia would be liable.

When the debt was revealed during Adelphia's quarterly conference call, Wall Street analyst Oren Cohen asked the question that many were no doubt wondering: How did the Rigas family plan to pay back billions of dollars without asking Adelphia for assistance? Instead of responding, the Rigas family avoided the question and answered with silence. Almost immediately, Adelphia stock began to fall, and the investigation into the previously unrecorded debt began.

A Family Affair

Within two months, John, Timothy, and Michael Rigas resigned from the company. The SEC discovered that the family had used the loan money to buy Adelphia stock and purchase cable companies, build a private golf course for the family, maintain private timberland, and pay staff members. Every time they misused company funds, the Rigas family would manipulate the accounting to hide the transactions and give Adelphia a falsely inflated financial appearance. John and Timothy were both charged with bank fraud, wire fraud, and securities fraud, and the elder Rigas—who was 80 years old at the time of his trial—was sentenced to 15 years in prison, and his son was sentenced to 20.

A Hero?

In December 2015, John's lawyers appealed for a "compassionate release" for their client, stating that he was ill with terminal bladder cancer and had less than six months to live. A judge ordered the elder Rigas's release on February 19, 2016, and he returned to Coudersport, where local media reported that he was welcomed back as "a hero." One resident described Rigas as "the kindest person I have ever known." As of 2018, Rigas—who was described by the Associated

Press as "frail" more than a decade ago—continues to fight his cancer, and he continues to insist that he and his son Timothy are innocent.

A Telecom Cooks the Books

Before telecommunications giant Verizon became a household name, it was originally made up of two corporations: MCI Communications and WorldCom. For a while, the merged company was known simply as WorldCom, and it became the United States' second-largest long-distance telephone company after AT&T. By the end of the twentieth century, CEO Bernard Ebbers was a very wealthy man; but soon scandal and bankruptcy would change the trajectory of the corporation, and the name WorldCom would fade as a new wave of communications leaders would take its place.

The Rise and Fall of a Telecom

Just before the turn of the century, the telecommunications industry enjoyed immense growth. The rise of high-speed internet caused a huge competition for new networks and new customers, and a plethora of small startup companies jumped into the mix, hoping to capitalize on the relatively new appeal of the World Wide Web. But suddenly, a downturn in the stock market brought everything to a halt. Investors were no longer willing to take a chance on independent startups and instead stuck with established names with a history of profit.

But even large companies weren't immune to the falling stock market—even AT&T and Sprint, two of the three largest behemoths in the telecommunications industry, had to regroup and restructure in an effort to maintain revenue. But the third of those large behemoths, WorldCom, took a decidedly dangerous route to maintain the appearance of profitability.

Cooking the Books

Ebbers, along with CFO Scott Sullivan, controller David Myers, and director of general accounting Buford Yates, immensely inflated WorldCom's assets by filing expenses as investments and manipulating reserves. In 2002, after the fraud had been ongoing for at least two years, a team of internal auditors worked in secret to uncover exactly what had happened, originally discovering $3.8 billion improperly recorded. WorldCom's board of directors immediately dismissed Sullivan, and Myers resigned. Meanwhile, the SEC began their own investigation into the company, ultimately discovering a total of $11 billion in inflated assets. At the time, it was the largest accounting fraud in U.S. history.

Bankruptcy and Justice for the Little People

On July 21, 2002, WorldCom filed for Chapter 11 bankruptcy. The company was ordered to pay $750 million in cash and stock to the SEC, to help pay back wronged investors, and the SEC and WorldCom reached a $2.25 billion civil penalty agreement. But perhaps the harshest penalty was reserved for former CEO Ebbers: on March 15, 2005, Ebbers was found guilty of fraud, conspiracy, and filing false documents with regulators. He was sentenced to 25 years in prison, and he is serving his time at Oakdale Federal Correctional Institution in Louisiana.

The story was not without a ray of hope, however. Shortly before it filed for bankruptcy, WorldCom let go 5,100 employees—although that number would eventually reach 30,000—who formed a group called "exWorldCom 5100." The group created a website and enlisted the help of the AFL-CIO in an effort to recover the severance pay and benefits they felt they were owed. While WorldCom itself was unable to pay anything due to bankruptcy, the website provided a place for ex-employees, friends, and even politicians to make donations into a fund to help those without severance benefits. The fund provided enough to help many employees make ends meet while they searched for new jobs, proving that corporate greed can be overcome by the generosity of the "little people."

Hewlett-Packard's Spying Scandal

As with many popular tech companies, Hewlett-Packard's origins were modest. Founded in a one-car garage in Palo Alto, California, in 1939 by William Redington Hewlett and David Packard, the company eventually grew to be a powerhouse. Between 2007 and 2013, it was the world's leading PC manufacturer, and in 2009, Hewlett-Packard was number nine on the Fortune 500 list. That's not bad for a company with a history of a spying scandal that could have torched its reputation and harmed sales.

A Worrisome Leak

The trouble began in January 2006, when Hewlett-Packard's chairwoman, Patricia Dunn, noticed that information discussed at board meetings was somehow making its way to the media. Tech website CNET had published an article that described Hewlett-Packard's long-term strategy plan, which was not meant to be public knowledge. Convinced there was a leak within the company, Dunn hired a team of independent security experts to find the source. Those experts, in turn, hired private investigators to look into the matter, and that's when things got dicey.

The private investigators employed a technique known as "pretexting," in which they impersonated board members and journalists. The investigators would call the phone company and pretend to be the person they were targeting, armed with personal information to bolster their claim. In this way, they were able to obtain phone records for Hewlett-Packard board members and nine journalists, including reporters for CNET, the *New York Times*, and the *Wall Street Journal*. As a result of the shady investigation, board member George Keyworth was discovered to be the source of the leak, although he claimed that the information he provided the media was in the best interests of the company. Regardless, he resigned on September 12, 2006.

Investigating the Investigators

But that didn't end the controversy, as Keyworth's leaks took a backseat to the methods used to uncover them. The day before Keyworth's resignation, CNET published a letter sent to Dunn from the United States House Committee on Energy and Commerce which stated that it had been investigating online "data brokers" who sell information obtained by "lies, fraud, and deception," and they were dismayed by Hewlett-Packard's use of pretexting. The committee demanded that Hewlett-Packard provide them with the name of the firm they used to conduct their investigation as well as the names of anyone within the company who was involved in the investigation and the names of the targeted individuals.

On September 22, Dunn resigned as chairwoman, saying that her presence on the board was a "distraction." And on September 28, Dunn and CEO Mark Hurd testified before the House Committee on Energy and Commerce, where Dunn insisted that she believed all of the phone records were obtained legally. Several high-ranking Hewlett-Packard employees, including Ann Baskins, who resigned as Hewlett-Packard's general counsel the day she was to appear as a witness, invoked the Fifth Amendment and refused to answer questions.

Silver Lining

Dunn was eventually brought up on criminal charges in California, but all of the charges were later dismissed. One private investigator, Bryan Wagner, faced federal charges after illegally obtaining a journalist's Social Security number, and he was sentenced to three months in prison. Amazingly, before the Hewlett-Packard scandal, pretexting was more of a legal "gray area" and not clearly illegal. But thanks to the Hewlett-Packard controversy, Congress passed the Telephone Records and Privacy Protection Act of 2006, which now makes pretexting—which was previously merely "wrong"—outright illegal.

Too Big to Fail?

In 1984, Continental Illinois Bank and Trust Company became the largest bank to ever fail in U.S. history. At the time, Continental Illinois was the seventh-largest bank in the country, with approximately $40 billion in assets. During a Congressional hearing that discussed the Federal Deposit Insurance Corporation's intervention in the bank's troubles—the FDIC gave Continental Illinois $4.5 billion in an effort to rescue them—U.S. Congressman Stewart McKinney said the bank was "too big to fail."

Decades later, in 2010, Federal Reserve Chair Ben Bernanke gave a detailed definition for the catchphrase: "A too-big-to-fail firm is one whose size, complexity, interconnectedness, and critical functions are such that, should the firm go unexpectedly into liquidation, the rest of the financial system and the economy would face severe adverse consequences." He went on to say that when the government bails out large firms, it is not out of "favoritism" but rather an effort to protect the overall economy.

A Bailout

But not everyone is convinced that these "too big to fail" corporations are deserving of government bailouts. Such was the case in 2008. That's when the government provided a $180 billion loan to insurance and finance corporation AIG, which had sold huge amounts of insurance without safeguarding their investments. In the fourth quarter of 2008, AIG recorded the largest loss in corporate history: $61.7 billion. But it wasn't just the government bailout that had people enraged; after accepting the bailout, AIG paid its executives $165 million in bonuses. While the bonuses were retention bonuses, paid in an effort to convince employees to stay on at AIG and help untangle the company's financial mess, Americans were understandably outraged that a firm bailed out by the government could find the money to pay executives such large sums.

A Bankruptcy

Not every firm was bailed out during the 2008 financial crisis. Lehman Brothers, which had been the fourth-largest bank in the United States and had been in operation since 1850, filed for bankruptcy after the collapse of the housing bubble. The corporation had originated many subprime mortgages—loans made to people who may have trouble paying them back—and suffered a loss in stock price and a greatly reduced number of clients. Although executives at the firm appealed for a bailout or for a stronger institution to help, Lehman Brothers ended up collapsing. It was the largest bankruptcy in U.S. history and led to a week of panic on Wall Street.

A Takeover

And then there were Bear Stearns and Washington Mutual, two more banks caught up in the subprime mortgage debacle. There was one more option besides bailout or bankruptcy, and that was a takeover by a larger bank. JPMorgan Chase, the largest bank in the United States, swooped in to buy both firms in the midst of their certain collapse. But even this takeover was not without controversy: both Bear Stearns and Washington Mutual felt their sale price to JPMorgan was far too low, and several lawsuits resulted from the whole affair.

Congressman McKinney probably had no idea that one day his "too big to fail" phrase would be at the center of so much drama and controversy.

A Charlatan of Epic Proportions

"Greed is good," said Gordon Gekko in Oliver Stone's 1987 hit movie *Wall Street*. Greed resides at the center of the financial industry. For the powerful real-life stockbroker Bernie Madoff, greed knew no boundaries.

Madoff, a well-respected broker who became chairman of the Nasdaq in 1990 and served in the position in 1991 and 1993, orchestrated the largest Ponzi scheme in history: an estimated $65 billion fraud. He conned thousands of investors and would later pled guilty to 11 felony charges—including money laundering, perjury, and fraud—and earn a prison sentence of 150 years.

Madoff was, according to the *New York Times*, a "charlatan of epic proportions, a greedy manipulator so hungry to accumulate wealth that he did not care whom he hurt to get what he wanted."

Small Beginnings

Madoff founded Bernard L. Madoff Securities in 1960. He started his firm with a paltry $5,000 he saved from lifeguarding. His wife's father allowed Madoff to work out of his Manhattan accounting firm. A market maker, Madoff dealt in over-the-counter penny stocks. He was also, Madoff would later recall in an interview, a "little Jewish guy from Brooklyn" who felt like he was on the outside looking in.

Madoff steadily grew his business—and reputation—as he embraced new trading technology and crafted friendships with industry regulators. While traders described him as obsessive, paranoid, secretive, and manipulative, Madoff earned the trust of employees, investors, and Wall Street. At the same time, Madoff was overseeing a massive con involving fraudulent transactions on an epic scale.

He later claimed that a handful of powerful clients known as the "Big Four" forced him into a Ponzi scheme in the early 1990s.

A Confession

In the late 1990s, Frank Casey, an investment firm executive, asked a colleague to look into Madoff's trades. The colleague, Harry Markopolos, quickly became suspicious and suspected a Ponzi scheme. Casey told PBS *Frontline* that Markopolos compared Madoff's returns to a baseball player "hitting .925 straight for 10 years in a row." Markopolos sent an eight-page memo to the SEC, but the agency did not follow up with an investigation. He wrote additional memos to the SEC, and in January 2006, the SEC launched an investigation.

Finally, at the height of the 2008 financial crisis, Madoff's jig was up.

On December 10, 2008, Madoff allegedly confessed to his sons that his business was a massive Ponzi scheme. The next day, authorities arrested Madoff on one count of securities fraud, and he was released on $10 million bail. In June 2009, a federal judge sentenced Madoff to 150 years in prison. He did not appeal the sentence.

Taking Responsibility?

The Department of Justice announced in December 2017 that it had begun to return money to Madoff's victims, including thousands of respected individuals and institutions. The initial distribution included

$772.5 million, a fraction of the more than $4 billion in assets recovered for the victims. An additional $504 million was announced in April 2018.

In a 2011 interview with Barbara Walters, Madoff said he has no fear because "I'm no longer in control of my own life." He told Walters that he took full responsibility for his crimes, but he said, "Nobody put a gun to my head. I never planned to do anything wrong. Things just got out of hand."

Even prison hasn't keep Madoff's profit-motivating instincts at bay, however. At one point, the aging criminal reportedly purchased hot chocolate packets from the commissary and sold them for a profit in the prison yard.

Eight Ain't So Great

It's not uncommon for a salesperson to convince a customer that they should buy another complementary item: perhaps a scarf to go with an outfit, or a protective cover for a computer, or the special "sports package" for a new car. This practice is known as "cross-selling," and it isn't only practiced at retail stores or on new car lots. In fact, in 2016, cross-selling became a focus in one of the banking industry's largest fraud scandals—a scandal that continues to create controversy.

A High-Pressure Sales Culture

In 2013, the *Los Angeles Times* published an article investigating the sales culture at Wells Fargo & Company, the financial services company headquartered in San Francisco. They discovered that employees were often burdened with unattainable quotas, leading to a very high-pressure work environment. The article didn't garner much initial attention; but fast forward to 2016, when the Consumer Financial

Protection Bureau announced that Wells Fargo would be fined $185 million for illegal activity.

Suddenly, Wells Fargo's pressure tactics were coming to light: in order to maintain its reputation as the most successful cross-seller in the financial world, the bank's employees were encouraged to cross-sell financial products—such as checking accounts, savings accounts, and credit cards—in order to meet their stringent quotas. This, by itself, could be seen as nothing more than an annoying sales tactic; however, if quotas were not met, employees were then pressured to resort to unethical—and often illegal—measures.

Eight Is Great

Employees opened credit cards for pre-approved customers without their consent, created fraudulent checking and savings accounts, and even enrolled the names of homeless people into fee-accruing financial products. To create these fake accounts, employees would use a process called "pinning" where the client's personal identification number would be set to 0000; the process allows bankers to access the clients' accounts and enroll them in products the customers never authorized.

When the scandal broke, Wells Fargo immediately placed ads in newspapers taking responsibility for the controversy, but they denied that it was a result of any high-pressure sales culture. Employees believed otherwise, however, citing CEO John Stumpf's favorite mantra: "eight is great." Stumpf coerced bankers into selling at least eight different products to each customer, a feat that was often impossible to accomplish without resorting to fraudulent strategies.

In September of 2016, the Senate Banking Committee held a hearing on the issue led by Senator Elizabeth Warren. Warren called for Stumpf's resignation. Less than a month later, Stumpf resigned, saying that it would help Wells Fargo to "move forward." The bank also abolished all of its sales goals, so quotas will no longer influence employees' sales tactics.

An Ongoing Controversy

The original Consumer Financial Protection Bureau investigation discovered 1,534,280 unauthorized deposit accounts and 565,433 credit card accounts, but by August 2017, nearly 1.4 million more fake accounts had been discovered. Wells Fargo's troubles don't end there: they've also been accused of forcing customers to buy insurance, ripping off small mom-and-pop businesses with credit card fees, and coercing elderly members of the Navajo Nation to open savings accounts. And in April 2018, federal investigators ordered the bank to pay a $1 billion fine. With new information still coming to light, it seems that Wells Fargo may have years of damage control ahead of them.

CHAPTER 4

LEAKS, HACKS, AND SPIES

COINTELPRO

The night of March 8, 1971, was one for the history books. Muhammed Ali and Joe Frazier paired off in the "Fight of the Century" at Madison Square Garden in New York City, going for 15 rounds until Frazier was declared the winner. Stars from Burt Lancaster to Woody Allen to Frank Sinatra were in attendance, and the event was broadcast in 50 countries in 12 different languages. Surely, for anyone who watched, it was a night to remember.

But as millions of people around the world observed the drama unfolding in the boxing ring, a quieter, but much more significant, drama was unfolding 100 miles to the southwest, just outside of Philadelphia. Under the cover of darkness, a group of burglars broke into the FBI offices in Media, Pennsylvania, and stole a bundle of files. They didn't realize it at first, but what they had in their hands would blow the cover off one of the FBI's most controversial and notorious operations.

Threatened by Dissent?

In the 1950s and 1960s, members of anti-war, civil rights, and New Left movements developed growing suspicions that they were being watched—specifically, by J. Edgar Hoover's FBI. But with no proof, there was little they could do about their concerns. By the 1970s, when U.S. involvement in Southeast Asia was becoming more and more unpopular, William Davidon, a professor at Haverford College—an institution founded on peaceful Quaker values—decided to do something about his suspicion that the FBI was "suppressing dissent" by infiltrating peace groups.

Davidon recruited a group of anti-war activists and formed the Citizens' Commission to Investigate the FBI. On the night of the Ali-Frazier fight, the group broke into the unsecured offices in Media and stole dossiers. Some of the memos were titled "COINTELPRO," which made no sense to the group as they began reading; eventually, congressional hearings would reveal the meaning to be "Counter-Intelligence Program." The FBI established this program in 1956, in order to infiltrate the Communist Party USA; however, it didn't stop there.

Disturbing Tactics

The COINTELPRO project targeted the Socialist Workers Party, the Ku Klux Klan, the Nation of Islam, the Black Panther Party, and numerous anti-war and New Left political movements. Specific members of these groups were under surveillance, including civil rights leaders Martin Luther King Jr. and Malcolm X, Black Panther Party supporter and actress Jean Seberg, and even Ernest Hemingway, who was pinpointed because of his ties to Cuba. The FBI not only infiltrated these groups and kept an eye on their members but also used numerous questionable and downright illegal tactics in their surveillance. From preventing and disrupting Vietnam War protests, to launching smear campaigns against targets, to ordering raids on homes of black militant leaders—it seemed there were few avenues the FBI wasn't willing to take.

In fact, COINTELPRO resulted in assassinations more than once. The most famous case was the assassination of Fred Hampton, the chairman of the Chicago Black Panther Party. One of the FBI's infiltrators, William O'Neal, provided floorplans of Hampton's apartment and slipped him barbiturates before the FBI raided his home. Hampton, drugged and asleep, could not even react when the apartment he was sharing with eight other Black Panther members was raided. Hampton and one other member were shot and killed; the other seven members were arrested on charges of aggravated assault and attempted murder.

The End?

When the Citizens' Commission group realized what they'd stolen, they sent copies to news outlets across the country. Many publications were hesitant to publish any of the information, but several independent papers, as well as the *Washington Post*, did decide to publish. Over the next few weeks, more and more information about COINTELPRO was released by the media, and within a month, Hoover announced that the program was over. Many lawsuits were filed against the FBI, and in 1976, the Select Committee to Study Governmental Operations with Respect to Intelligence Activities of the United States Senate—often called the "Church Committee" in reference to its chairman, Idaho Senator Frank Church—launched an investigation into COINTELPRO in which they concluded that the FBI "violated specific statutory prohibitions and infringed the constitutional rights of American citizens."

Although COINTELPRO was "officially" terminated in April 1971, the FBI has continually faced scrutiny over the decades for its tactics. Some counterterrorism methods have been criticized for employing "COINTELPRO-like" methods, and the FBI continues to face accusations of improper surveillance, by groups like People for the Ethical Treatment of Animals, Greenpeace USA, and the Black Lives Matter movement. It seems that as long as there are special interest groups, the FBI will take a "special interest" in their operations.

A Vietnam War Bombshell

On June 13, 2011, the U.S. government declassified 7,000 pages of a study entitled "Report of the Office of the Secretary of Defense

Vietnam Task Force." The wordily titled study's release was not a random choice; it was the 40th anniversary of its controversial leak to the press in 1971. At that time, the report was better known by its much catchier nickname: the Pentagon Papers.

An Unpopular War

By 1971, the United States had been entrenched in the Vietnam War for 16 long years. The conflict waged between pro-communist North Vietnam, backed by the Soviet Union and China, and anti-communist South Vietnam, which was backed by the United States, South Korea, and Australia. As the war dragged on, American support for U.S. government actions in the region shrunk. People lost faith in the government's assurances that the war was winnable, and the anti-war mood grew into protests, demonstrations, and even riots.

Secrets Revealed

In the midst of this turmoil, a reporter for the *New York Times* by the name of Neil Sheehan was tipped off to the existence of a highly classified report. The report detailed U.S. political and military involvement in Vietnam from 1945 to 1967. Sensing a big story, Sheehan contacted Daniel Ellsberg, an ex-U.S. Marine Corp officer and former strategic analyst for the Department of Defense. At the beginning of the war, Ellsberg had been a supporter of U.S. involvement in the region and helped to compile the report at the end of the study in 1967. A few years later, however, Ellsberg, like so many other Americans, had come to believe the war was a lost cause. And what's more, he believed that the American people had a right to know what was contained in the lengthy, secretive report.

So, in June of 1971, with doubts about the government's actions weighing on his mind, Ellsberg—who, by this time, was working as a senior research associate at MIT's Center for International Studies— decided to turn over portions of the report to Sheehan. And on June

13, the *New York Times* published the first of a series of front page articles about the report, which revealed that several presidential administrations had misled the public on U.S. involvement in Vietnam. The report even revealed that the John F. Kennedy administration had an active part of the overthrow and assassination of South Vietnamese President Ngo Dinh Diem in 1963. The publication of these bombshells set off a media frenzy, and the report was quickly dubbed the Pentagon Papers.

Freedom of the Press

Needless to say, the Nixon administration was not happy to see government secrets splashed across the front page of the *New York Times*. After only three articles had been published, the U.S. Department of Justice got a temporary restraining order against the *Times*, citing a threat to national security. This did not sit well with the newspaper, which fought back in the case of *New York Times Co. v. United States*. While the *Times* was tied up in court, the *Washington Post* picked up the slack and began publishing their own articles featuring the Pentagon Papers. Once again, the government attempted to silence the publication; however, this time they were not successful. As the *Post* continued to publish articles and the case made its way to the Supreme Court, 10 other newspapers across the country got their hands on the report and started publishing their own articles. The Pentagon Papers had taken on a life of their own.

Ultimately, on June 30, 1971, the Supreme Court ruled 6-3 in favor of the media, and all news organizations across the country were free to publish whatever parts of the report they chose. The Nixon administration indicted Ellsberg on criminal charges of conspiracy, espionage, and stealing government property, but those charges were later dropped when it was discovered that a secret team had broken into Ellsberg's psychiatrist's office to find information about him.

The issues of government secrecy and freedom of the press stirred up by the scandal still reverberate today, even inspiring the 2017 film *The Post*, which starred Meryl Streep and Tom Hanks.

Watergate

Watergate is the name of the scandal that caused Richard Nixon to become the only U.S. president to resign from office.

On May 27, 1972, concerned that Nixon's bid for reelection was in jeopardy, former CIA agent E. Howard Hunt, Jr., former New York assistant district attorney G. Gordon Liddy, former CIA operative James W. McCord, Jr., and six other men broke into the Democratic headquarters in the Watergate Hotel in Washington, D.C. They wiretapped phones, stole some documents, and photographed others. When they broke in again on June 17 to fix a bug that wasn't working, a suspicious security guard called the Washington police, who arrested McCord and four other burglars. A cover-up began to destroy incriminating evidence, obstruct investigations, and halt any spread of scandal that might lead to the president.

On August 29, Nixon announced that the break-in had been investigated and that no one in the White House was involved. Despite his efforts to hide his involvement, Nixon was done in by his own tape recordings, one of which revealed that he had authorized hush money paid to Hunt.

To avoid impeachment, Nixon resigned on August 9, 1974. His successor, President Gerald Ford, granted him a blanket pardon on September 8, 1974, eliminating any possibility that Nixon would be indicted and tried. *Washington Post* reporters Bob Woodward and Carl Bernstein helped expose the scandal using information leaked by someone identified as Deep Throat, a source whose identity was kept hidden until 2005, when it was revealed that Deep Throat was former Nixon administration member William Mark Felt.

To Catch a Soviet Mole

By all appearances, Robert Hanssen was a typical American. Born and raised in Chicago, Hanssen graduated from William Howard Taft High School in 1962; he graduated from Knox College with a degree in chemistry in 1966. He dabbled with the idea of becoming a dentist, and he met his wife, Bonnie, in dental school. After they married in 1968, Hanssen dropped out of dental school and decided to pursue business instead, earning an MBA in 1971. After working as an internal affairs investigator for the Chicago Police Department, he got a job as a special agent with the FBI in 1976. He and his growing family— Hanssen and his wife eventually had six children—moved from Gary, Indiana, to New York City so he could work in the field office there. A staunch Catholic, he was known as a quiet family man and a hard worker. Robert Hanssen's life, it would seem, was so stable it was almost boring.

When people get bored, they often take up hobbies—something to pass the time and bring a bit of excitement to life. Those seeking adventure might explore skydiving or mountain climbing; but Hanssen took a different route: he became an FBI mole, passing information to Soviet and Russian intelligence services.

Secrets and Lies

Hanssen's double life began in 1979, just a few years after joining the FBI. After being transferred to counterintelligence and tasked with compiling a list of Soviet agents, he volunteered his services to the Soviet military intelligence agency, GRU. He began leaking information to them, including the identity of CIA informant Dmitri Polyakov, who was later executed by the Soviets. A year later, in 1980, Hanssen's wife caught him with some suspicious documents, and he admitted to her that he'd been spying for the Soviets. He claimed that he'd given them nothing of importance, but Bonnie insisted he confess to a priest and immediately cease his espionage activities.

In 1981, Hanssen was transferred to Washington, D.C., where he worked in the FBI's budget office and had access to information about wiretapping and electronic surveillance, and three years later he was transferred to the Soviet analytical unit. True to his word, he had no contact with the Soviets during these years; but in 1985, Hanssen sent a letter to the KGB, once again offering his services as a spy. This was the beginning of an on-and-off espionage career that would last more than fifteen years. Hanssen gave the Soviets—and, after the dissolution of the Soviet Union in 1991, the Russians—thousands of pages of classified materials over the years. These included identities of Soviets spying for the U.S., information about the U.S. nuclear program and details about American spying methods.

Red Flags

Throughout the years he was spying, occasional concerns would be raised about Hanssen. In 1990, his own brother-in-law, also a member of the FBI, recommended that Hanssen be investigated for possible espionage after spotting a pile of cash in his home; however, no action was ever taken. Several years later, another FBI mole who had been spying for the Russians, Earl Edwin Pitts, told the Bureau he suspected that Hanssen was also a spy. But once again, no action was taken.

But Hanssen couldn't keep dodging bullets forever. The FBI expressed confusion about how certain information was leaking to the Russians even after they'd caught several moles within the organization. So in 1994, they organized a mole-hunting team to locate "Graysuit"—the codename for the suspected spy. After years of false leads and dead ends, the FBI finally found an ex-KGB agent who was willing to share information—for a price. They paid $7 million for a file that included an audiotape of Hanssen speaking with KGB agent Aleksander Fefelov, and their investigation was finally on a roll. With Hanssen now under surveillance, the FBI "promoted" him in order to keep an eye on him. On February 18, 2001, Hanssen drove to Foxstone Park in Vienna, Virginia, and taped a bag full of classified information to the underside of a footbridge. FBI agents immediately rushed in to arrest him, and Hanssen, apparently unsurprised, commented, "What took you so long?"

The End of the Spy Game

Interestingly, Hanssen was never motivated by any political or ideological beliefs, but rather by good, old-fashioned financial gain. He was paid around $1.4 million in cash and diamonds by Moscow throughout the course of his espionage career. Hanssen also wrote in a letter to the Russians that he was inspired to be a spy when he was only 14 years old, after reading the memoirs of Kim Philby, a British double agent.

Whatever his motivations, the outcome for Hanssen was dire: he was sentenced to 15 consecutive life sentences with no possibility of parole, and is living out his days at a Colorado federal supermax prison. To his credit, he apologized for his behavior when he was sentenced, stating, "I am shamed by it." He was especially remorseful for the pain he caused his family, saying, "I have opened the door for calumny against my totally innocent wife and our children. I hurt them deeply. I have hurt so many deeply."

Plamegate

In March 2003, the United States—along with assistance from the United Kingdom, Australia, and Poland—invaded Iraq, and began a weeks-long incursion dubbed Operation Iraqi Freedom. U.S. President George W. Bush and U.K. Prime Minister Tony Blair asserted that the goal of the operation was "to disarm Iraq of weapons of mass destruction, to end Saddam Hussein's support for terrorism, and to free the Iraqi people."

In July of the same year, journalist Robert Novak published a column in which he revealed the identification of covert Central Intelligence Agency officer Valerie Plame, resulting in her dismissal from the CIA and leaving several sensitive operations hanging in the balance. On the surface, the two occurrences would seem to be unrelated; but a closer look reveals a much more complicated and intricate web.

Diplomatic Connections

Valerie Plame, who began her CIA career in 1990, married former U.S. diplomat Joseph C. Wilson in 1998. One of only a handful of people who knew his wife's status within the CIA, Wilson had been posted in several African countries throughout the course of his diplomatic career, including Togo, South Africa, and Niger. He was also the last American diplomat to meet with Iraqi dictator Saddam Hussein after Iraq's 1990 invasion of Kuwait.

So in 2002, when rumors stirred of Iraq's interest in Niger's uranium, Plame sent a memo to her superiors at the CIA, stating that her husband still had contacts within the country—including with the Prime Minister and Director of Mines—and might be able to assist in uncovering any Iraq-Niger connections. Soon after, Wilson traveled to Niger and spoke to Mai Manga, the former minister of mines, who insisted he knew of no sales of uranium to Iraq. Wilson also spoke to former Niger Prime Minister Ibrahim Assane Mayaki, who only mentioned that a businessman interested in "expanding commercial relations" between Niger and Iraq had approached him. According to Mayaki, no mention of uranium was ever made.

Fateful Words

Almost a year later, during the 2003 State of the Union address, President Bush uttered what would come to be known as the "16 words": "The British government has learned that Saddam Hussein recently sought significant quantities of uranium from Africa." The information came from the September Dossier, an investigation performed by the British government into Iraq's weapons capabilities, and the findings were part of what lead to the eventual invasion of Iraq in March of that year.

Months after the invasion, in July 2003, Wilson published an op-ed in the *New York Times* in which he described his trip to Niger and questioned the basis for the war, stating, "I have little choice but to conclude that some of the intelligence related to Iraq's nuclear weapons program was twisted to exaggerate the Iraqi threat." And this is where the "Plame affair" truly began: Novak published his column a week later, where he not only stated that Plame was the one who recommended Wilson for the trip to Niger, but he also named her as a covert CIA officer. The question was, how did Novak procure this classified information?

The Plame Blame Game

Many were convinced that the Bush administration deliberately blew Plame's cover as retaliation for Wilson's article about the Iraq War. The United States Department of Justice requested an FBI investigation into the matter, but no one was ever indicted or convicted concerning the leak. White House Deputy Chief of Staff Lewis "Scooter" Libby was, however, indicted on several charges, including obstruction of justice and perjury.

Ultimately, it was discovered that State Department Official Richard Armitage was the source of the classified information, but he insisted that he hadn't meant to reveal any sensitive intelligence; it was merely an inadvertent remark he made during an interview with Novak. Whatever the sources or reasons for the leak, Plame herself has taken everything in stride, becoming a successful writer and spy novelist whose book *Fair Game: My Life as a Spy, My Betrayal by the White House* was made into a 2010 film starring Naomi Watts.

A Computer Wiz Exposes the Truth

If you ever feel like someone is watching you, you may be correct. And that "someone" may be the government. According to former CIA contractor Edward Snowden, you should have the right to know about such surveillance; but not everyone thinks that the public should be privy to every scheme and plan the government puts into place.

A Computer Wizard

Edward Snowden attended high school near Baltimore, Maryland, but dropped out in his sophomore year. He then spent his time developing a love of computers and technology and eventually earned a GED. After a brief stint in the army, Snowden obtained a job as a security guard at the University of Maryland's Center for Advanced Study of Language. The center is sponsored by the National Security Agency, and the job required Snowden to gain high-level security clearance. Soon after, at the age of 23, young Snowden was hired as a technical/IT expert for the CIA. Snowden, who, despite dropping out of high school is believed to have a high IQ, has said that it was easy for him to land the job because he is a "computer wizard."

By 2007, Snowden was working as a cyber security expert with diplomatic cover in Geneva, Switzerland. It was during this time that he came to question the function of the U.S. government and wondered whether his own job was doing more harm than good. According to an article published in the *New York Times*, Snowden's supervisor at the CIA had suspicions that the young "computer wizard" was trying to break into classified computer files. These suspicions, however, went unnoted for years.

Collecting the Truth

Snowden left the CIA in 2009 and began working as a contractor for the NSA and CIA for Dell Computers. For four years, he worked as an expert in cyber counterintelligence at various U.S. locations. In March 2012, he was assigned to Hawaii, where he worked for the next fifteen months. The last three months were with the IT consulting firm Booz Allen Hamilton, a job which Snowden admits he deliberately sought in order to gather more data about the NSA's surveillance activities.

Beginning in December 2012, Snowden reached out to several journalists, including Glenn Greenwald of the *Guardian*, documentary filmmaker Laura Poitras, and Barton Gellman of the *Washington Post*. In early 2013, Snowden began providing them with classified documents, sometimes using encrypted emails with the codename "Verax"—from the Latin for "truth."

The Beginning of Snowden's End?

Knowing that the release of the information he'd leaked was imminent, in May 2013 Snowden flew to Hong Kong. By early June, the *Guardian* had published the first of the revelations they'd been provided, which detailed how the NSA, on a daily basis, collected millions of Americans' email and telephone data from Verizon. Subsequent reports by the *Guardian*, the *Washington Post*, the *New York Times*, and Germany's *Der Spiegel* detailed more about government surveillance programs, including wiretaps, collection of emails and instant messages, and cell phone tracking. And Snowden's revelations went beyond U.S. soil: the leaked documents exposed U.S. spy operations in dozens of countries, including Brazil, France, China, Germany, and Mexico. The U.S. also worked closely with Australia, the U.K., and Canada in their global surveillance programs.

On June 9, 2013, the *Guardian* revealed Snowden's identity at his own request. The jig, as they say, was up. United States federal prosecutors charged Snowden with theft of government property and two counts of violating the Espionage Act. The whistleblower took refuge in Moscow, Russia, which has granted him temporary asylum.

While many consider Snowden a hero for exposing the secrets of the U.S. government, others—including United States Navy Admiral and NSA Director Michael S. Rogers—believe his actions have harmed the global fight against terrorism. One thing is certain: Snowden knew the risk he was taking in leaking so much sensitive information. As he once wrote to Gellman, "I understand that I will be made to suffer for my actions, and that the return of this information to the public marks my end."

Sony's Embarrassing Hack

The 2014 comedy film *The Interview* tells the story of two tabloid journalists who produce an entertainment talk show with an unlikely fan: North Korean dictator Kim Jong-un. The journalists—played by James Franco and Seth Rogen—manage to land an interview with Kim with the hope that they will be taken more seriously in their profession. But when the CIA gets wind of their interview, they recruit the unwitting pair for a much more dangerous undertaking: the assassination of Kim Jong-un.

A silly, unlikely premise to be sure, and it's certainly nothing that anyone would ever take seriously, right? Well, according to the FBI, the film with the ridiculous plotline may have caused a much a larger uproar than anyone expected.

A Message from the GOP

The trouble started on November 24, 2014, when employees at Sony Pictures—the studio that backed *The Interview*—attempted to log in to their computers but were greeted with an ominous message from a group calling itself the "Guardians of Peace," or GOP. The message threatened to release personal data, including employees' "secrets" if the GOP's unspecified "request" was not met. The information stolen by the group included emails, personal information about employees and their families, salaries, and copies of unreleased Sony films. Sony Pictures executives Michael Lynton and Amy Pascal sent a memo to employees after the leak, saying, "we unfortunately have to ask you to assume that information about you in the possession of the company might be in their possession."

Soon afterward, the hackers began leaking yet-unreleased films and confidential data online, and messages alleged to be from the hackers began demanding that *The Interview*—which they called a "movie of terrorism" — be pulled from theaters. Ironically, the hackers also threatened terrorist attacks against any theaters that screened the film on its December 25 release date.

The Work of the Hermit Kingdom?

On November 28, the technology news website Re/code was the first to suggest a North Korean link to the hack. It is difficult to find the perpetrators of cyberattacks, because all of the evidence left behind is digital. But U.S. officials also began to suspect the North Korean government, saying they were "99 percent" sure that the secretive regime was behind it. Even before the hack, North Korea had expressed its indignation with the film to the United Nations, saying that "to allow the production and distribution of such a film" would "be regarded as the most undisguised sponsoring of terrorism as well as an act of war." Clearly, North Korea was not a fan.

Sony Pictures scrambled to get the leak of information under control, but before they could, many emails, which revealed the behind-the-scenes operations at Sony, were released. These included messages between Pascal and film producer Scott Rudin in which Rudin refers to actress Angelina Jolie as "a minimally talented spoiled brat," and an email exchange where they discuss an upcoming meeting with President Barack Obama using language and terms that were deemed racist. The latter resulted in Pascal's eventual resignation from Sony. The hackers also released scripts of several then-unreleased Sony films, including *Annie*, *Still Alice*, and the James Bond feature *Spectre*.

On December 19, the FBI officially named North Korea as the source of the hack. Ultimately, Sony decided to cancel the formal premiere of *The Interview*, instead releasing it as a digital download. But 300 theaters across the county still opted to screen the film on its opening day. The film was widely panned by critics, but thanks to all the controversy it stirred up, *The Interview* has still managed to pull in $40 million in online and on-demand sales.

An Epic Data Breach

We've all seen the commercials for websites that provide people with credit scores: a person is thinking of buying a car or renting a house, but first, they check to be sure their credit score passes muster. Or someone shares their big dreams for the future with a friend, and the friend replies with, "Have you checked your credit score?" The scores are important, of course, because any time a consumer applies for a loan, the lender will check credit history to decide whether or not to approve the loan.

In the U.S., there are three major companies that compile credit reports: Experian, TransUnion, and Equifax. Obviously, the information collected by these companies is sensitive and personal, and it includes social security numbers, credit card numbers, and driver's license numbers. In a way, the fact that these companies collect this information is good, because it helps consumers prove their identity when they decide to buy cars or houses. But no one would want all of this information to fall into the hands of a hacker; unfortunately, that's exactly what happened in 2017.

A Breach in Security

Sometime between May and July 2017, hackers breached the computer systems of Equifax and stole information concerning approximately 145 million Americans. Thousands—and possibly millions—of British and Canadian residents were also affected. The breach was discovered on July 29, and on September 7, Equifax alerted the public to the cybercrime. The data breach alone was enough to tarnish Equifax's reputation, and immediately after the public announcement, its stock fell more than 13 percent. But facts that came to light afterwards raised questions about how the company handled the entire ordeal.

Stunning Delays

For one thing, the delay in alerting the public was widely criticized. If Equifax knew of the hack in July, why did they wait until September to inform consumers? The company insisted that the delay in disclosing the hack was due to the amount of time it took to determine the extent of the breach and how much data was compromised. But between August 1 and August 2—after Equifax knew about the hack but before they informed the public—three executives sold off about $1.8 million in personal shares of Equifax stock. The company released a statement on September 7 insisting that the executives "had no knowledge that an intrusion had occurred at the time they sold their shares." Still, the timing was extremely suspect.

Another issue that garnered criticism was the fact that Equifax was notified of a weakness within its systems in March 2017, and the firm was even provided with a patch to fix the vulnerability. However, Equifax didn't apply the patch until July 30—the day after the breach was discovered. In fact, a smaller hack had occurred in March, which may have been carried out by the same perpetrators who later breached the system in May. Equifax failed to heed the warning signs of impending crisis, and consumers later paid the price.

You Can't Fix Stupid

Finally, Equifax provided the public with a website where people could go to check and see if their information had been compromised; but in a strange and ironic twist, the company mistakenly linked consumers to an unofficial fake website. A software engineer named Nick Sweeting, who apparently wanted to demonstrate how easily consumer information can be obtained, created the site. He set up a fake "phishing" site—a site that gathers sensitive info like passwords and credit card numbers—with an address similar to Equifax's official website. Fortunately, Sweeting's intentions weren't malicious—he merely wanted to prove a point. And he certainly did: during an October hearing of the House Digital Commerce and Consumer Protection subcommittee, in which former Equifax CEO Richard Smith admitted "mistakes were made," Representative Greg Walden said what many were thinking: "I don't think we can pass a law that can fix stupid."

CHAPTER 5

RANTS, MELTDOWNS, AND SLIPS

Political Slips of Tongue

Presidents and other politicians have a lot to say and not much time to say it; in their haste, the message often gets lost on its way from the brain to the mouth and comes out in funny, embarrassing, and memorable quotes. Here are some favorites.

1. Ronald Reagan: As president, Reagan sometimes veered from his carefully written speeches with disastrous results. In 1988, when trying to quote John Adams, who said, "Facts are stubborn things," Reagan slipped and said, "Facts are stupid things." Not known as an environmentalist, Reagan said in 1966, "A tree is a tree. How many more do you have to look at?" His most famous blooper came during a microphone test before a 1984 radio address when he remarked, "My fellow Americans, I am pleased to tell you I just signed legislation which outlaws Russia forever. The bombing begins in five minutes."

2. Al Gore: Al Gore served as vice president under Bill Clinton from 1993 to 2001. During the 1992 campaign, he asked voters skeptical of change to remember that every Communist government in Eastern Europe had fallen within 100 days, followed by, "Now it's our turn here in the United States of America." Gore has often been incorrectly quoted as saying that he invented the Internet, but his actual comment in 1999 was the following: "During

my service in the United States Congress, I took the initiative in creating the Internet."

3. Richard Nixon: Richard M. Nixon was the 37th president of the United States, serving from 1969 to 1974. He is the only U.S. president to have resigned from office. Famous for telling reporters, "I am not a crook," Nixon once gave this advice to a political associate: "You don't know how to lie. If you can't lie, you'll never go anywhere." Nixon couldn't cover up Watergate, and he couldn't cover up bloopers like that, either.

4. Richard J. Daley: Mayor Richard J. Daley served as the undisputed leader of Chicago during the turbulent 1960s. The Democratic National Convention was held in Chicago in August 1968, but with the nation divided by the Vietnam War and the assassinations of Martin Luther King, Jr., and Robert F. Kennedy fueling animosity, the city became a battleground for antiwar protests, which Americans witnessed on national televisi on. When confrontations between protesters and police turned violent, Daley's blooper comment reflected the opinion of many people: "The police are not here to create disorder, they're here to preserve disorder."

5. Texas House Speaker Gib Lewis: A true slow-talkin' Texan, many of Texas House Speaker Gib Lewis's famous bloopers may have influenced his colleague, future president George W. Bush. While closing a congressional session, Lewis's real feelings about his peers slipped out when he said, "I want to thank each and every one of you for having extinguished yourselves this session." He tried to explain his problems once by saying, "There's a lot of uncertainty that's not clear in my mind." He could have been describing his jumbled reign as Texas speaker when he commented, "This is unparalyzed in the state's history."

6. Dan Quayle: Before President George W. Bush took over the title, Dan Quayle was the reigning king of malaprops. Serving one term as vice president from 1989 to 1993, Quayle's slips of the tongue made him an easy but well-deserved target for late-night talk shows. His most famous blunder came in 1992 when, at an elementary school spelling bee in New Jersey, he corrected student William Figueroa's correct spelling of potato as p-o-t-a-t-o-e. Quayle didn't really help the campaign for reelection when, at a stop in California, he said, "This president is going to lead us out of this recovery."

7. Spiro Agnew: Spiro Theodore Agnew served as vice president from 1969 to 1973 under President Nixon, before resigning following evidence of tax evasion. This slip expressed his true feelings on this matter, "I apologize for lying to you. I promise I won't deceive you except in matters of this sort." Agnew also didn't endear himself to poor people in 1968 when he commented, "To some extent, if you've seen one city slum, you've seen them all."

8. George W. Bush: Reflecting about growing up in Midland, Texas, President George W. Bush said in a 1994 interview, "It was just inebriating what Midland was all about then." Back in those days, Dubya was known to be a heavy drinker, so misspeaking the word invigorating was a real Freudian slip.

9. George H. W. Bush: With Dan Quayle as his vice president, the bloopers of President George H. W. Bush sometimes got overshadowed, but he still managed some zingers. While campaigning in 1988, he described serving as Ronald Reagan's vice president this way: "For seven and a half years I've worked alongside President Reagan. We've had triumphs. Made some mistakes. We've had some sex . . . uh . . . setbacks." When it

comes to presidents 41 and 43, you could say that the slip doesn't fall far from the tongue.

Sinead O'Connor's Primetime Protest

On October 3, 1992, the musical guest on variety show *Saturday Night Live* was Sinead O'Connor. O'Connor's album *I Do Not Want What I Haven't Got* had helped the Dublin-born singer gain considerable fame in the United States, mainly due to her hit version of Prince's song, "Nothing Compares 2 U." During that night's *SNL* broadcast, O'Connor performed an a cappella version of Bob Marley's song "War." The anti-apartheid song, which was inspired by a 1963 speech given by Ethiopian Emperor Haile Selassie, was a heavy choice for the comedy program, but not altogether surprising, given O'Connor's nonconformist style.

Halfway through the song, the singer changed some of the lyrics about fighting racial injustice to words about fighting child abuse. She reached the last line in the song—"We are confident in the victory of good over evil"—and as she sang the word "evil" she produced a picture of Pope John Paul II. As the stunned audience looked on, O'Connor tore the picture into pieces, threw them at the camera, and proclaimed, "Fight the real enemy!"

Why Did She Do It?

At the time, Ireland was in the midst of a sexual abuse scandal within the Irish church—an atrocity that would soon come to light in the United States, as well—and O'Connor was frustrated by the lack of action taken to protect children. O'Connor herself says that she endured physical abuse at the hands of her parents, and she has advocated on behalf of abused children. But to American audiences, her actions seemed very much a random, nonsensical outburst, aimed at an image many consider sacred. At best, her protest was confusing; at worse, it was downright offensive.

Confusion and Complaints

While the audience in the studio may have been silent, the audience watching on television at home was quick to voice anger over the stunt. NBC received 4,400 calls about the incident, and all but seven of them were complaints. But the network was just as blindsided as the rest of the country: NBC had no prior knowledge of O'Connor's plan, as during rehearsals she had held up a picture of orphaned children at the end of the song. After the live broadcast, *SNL* creator Lorne Michaels said he was "stunned" and that "the air went out of the studio."

The next week, guest host Joe Pesci delivered his opening monologue and held up the same picture and said if he'd been there to see O'Connor live, he, "would have gave her such a smack." The audience reacted with huge applause. A week later, the National Ethnic Coalition of Organizers gathered hundreds of O'Connor's cassettes and CDs and ran over them with a 30-ton steamroller in front of Rockefeller Center. Even pop star Madonna—who is known for her own controversial antics—said that O'Connor should have found another way to express her anger. "I think there is a better way to present her ideas rather than ripping up an image that means a lot to other people," she said.

No Regrets?

While her anger over the treatment of children was understandable, even the defiant O'Connor eventually realized that her expression of emotion may not have been in the best taste. In a 1997 interview with the Italian newspaper *Vita*, the singer asked the Church for forgiveness. But she continues to say that she's never regretted her actions on *SNL*, although she admits that Americans may have found it confusing. "It's very understandable that the American people didn't know what I was going on about," she has stated. She has also said that tearing up the picture of the pope wasn't meant to be specifically about "the man," but rather about "the office and the symbol of the organization that he represents." If O'Connor wanted to create controversy, she definitely succeeded.

Janet's Wardrobe Malfunction

Scandals are often bestowed with nicknames in homage to the infamous Watergate scandal. The catchy, colorful monikers allude to the nature of the controversy: For instance, "Bridgegate" incensed New Jersey drivers after they were blocked from reaching the George Washington Bridge, and "Deflategate" angered football fans who already had plenty of reasons to hate the New England Patriots. So when a scandal has been dubbed "Nipplegate," eyebrows are raised and curiosity is piqued.

For a Moment, Everyone Forgot about the Game

The incident occurred during Super Bowl XXXVIII, which aired live on the CBS network on February 1, 2004. While only diehard fans will be able to recall who played and who won the game (the New England Patriots beat the Carolina Panthers 32-29), everyone who was watching that day remembers the halftime show. The show featured Jessica Simpson, P. Diddy, Nelly, and Kid Rock, but the highlight of the entertainment was the appearance of Janet Jackson, who sang her popular hits "All for You" and "Rhythm Nation."

But the crowd in the stadium was even more excited when Justin Timberlake made a surprise appearance. The duo launched into a duet of Timberlake's song "Rock Your Body," complete with plenty of suggestive dance moves and innuendo. And then came the song's final—and strangely prophetic—line: "I'm gonna have you naked by the end of this song." As he sang the line, Timberlake ripped off a part of Jackson's costume, briefly revealing her breast, which was covered only by a nipple shield. The broadcast immediately cut to an aerial view of the stadium, but for almost a second, 143 million viewers saw more of Janet Jackson than they'd ever seen before.

Was It an Accident or Not?

Speculation ran rampant over whether the stunt was planned or accidental. Many thought it was a deliberate publicity stunt, and if so, it had the desired effect: "Janet Jackson" became the most searched term in internet history, and the moment was the most replayed television moment in TiVo's history. In fact, 35,000 new subscribers signed up for TiVo after the incident, perhaps dismayed that their own televisions lacked the ability to record and replay scenes.

But Jackson's representatives insisted that the incident had not gone according to plan; Timberlake was supposed to rip away her costume to reveal a red lace bra which then "collapsed." Planned or not, the FCC fined CBS $550,000 and increased overall fines for indecency violations. Broadcasters also began adding a five-second delay to live shows to avoid any similar events in the future.

Jackson released an apology for inadvertently flashing viewers, but she said she couldn't understand why she was receiving so much attention when "there are much worse things in the world." Timberlake apologized as well, calling the event a "wardrobe malfunction," which would later become such a popular phrase that it was eventually added to Merriam-Webster's Collegiate Dictionary.

Man vs. Woman

Often lost in the salacious undertones of the scandal is the subsequent treatment of Jackson and Timberlake, who had very different experiences. Jackson was required to release a videotaped apology and was banned from attending that year's Grammy Awards, whereas Timberlake was not required to apologize and attended the Grammys as planned. Years later, Timberlake would admit that he "probably got 10 percent of the blame" for what happened, and he lamented that "America is harsher on women." FCC Chairman Michael Powell stated it was "really unfair" that so much blame was placed on Jackson, especially when Timberlake was the one who removed her clothing.

Incidentally, just after the halftime show, a British streaker ran out onto the field, stripped, and performed a dance in nothing but a thong. But because of Nipplegate, it was too little, too late. The most shocking moment of the night was already history.

Rathergate

For several decades, Americans relied on the "Big Three" news anchors at ABC, NBC, and CBS—Peter Jennings, Tom Brokaw, and Dan Rather—to deliver timely, accurate broadcasts of the important issues in the world. So few would have guessed that one of Rather's reports would cause such an uproar that it would lead to his retirement and later be named on a *TV Guide* list of "TV's Ten Biggest Blunders."

An Exclusive Story?

The kerfuffle began just two months before the 2004 Presidential Election between George W. Bush and John Kerry. CBS News producer Mary Mapes was given copies of documents that allegedly spoke critically of President Bush's Air National Guard service from 1972 to 1973. Lieutenant Colonel Bill Burkett, who claimed that they came from the files of Bush's commander, the late Lieutenant Colonel Jerry B. Killian, provided the documents.

The contents of the Killian documents painted President Bush in an unfavorable light: supposedly, he had disobeyed orders while serving in the Guard, and had been grounded from flying, but Killian had been pressured by those higher up to improve Bush's dismal record. On September 8, 2004, Rather went on the air in a *60 Minutes* broadcast, and presented the documents, stating that they "were taken from Lieutenant Colonel Killian's personal files." Rather also claimed that the documents' authenticity had been verified, saying, "We consulted a handwriting analyst and document expert who believes the material is authentic."

Questions of Authenticity

Almost immediately after the broadcast, internet forums and blogs began to question Rather's insistence that the documents were real, with many pointing out that the spacing and font used in the Killian documents were identical to computer-generated documents created in 2004, whereas a typeset document from the 1970s would look much different. What's more, it was discovered that Burkett, who provided the documents, made many conflicting and unsubstantiated claims about Bush over the years, calling his credibility into question. He even claimed to have inexplicably burned the original Killian documents after faxing copies to CBS.

Further investigation into the matter revealed that CBS asked four experts to review the documents, but none of them were able to definitively authenticate the material. Two of the experts recommended to Mapes that she contact a typewriter expert named Peter Tytell; but when Tytell contacted CBS, he was told they "did not need him anymore."

The Fallout

Once the scandal broke, CBS attempted to come up with more evidence that the documents were authentic, but within a week their defense started to crumble. They produced experts that insisted the documents could have been created in the 1970s, but they still had no hard evidence. As suspicion about the Killian documents grew, CBS began to backtrack, questioning Burkett's reliability and claiming that he admitted that "he deliberately misled the CBS News producer." And CBS News president Andrew Heyward stated that using the documents "was a mistake, which we deeply regret." Mapes was subsequently terminated from her position at CBS.

As for Rather, he left the network on March 9, 2005, his 24th anniversary as anchor. He continued to defend his report on the Killian documents, saying that while they have never been authenticated, they've never been proven to be forgeries, either.

Mel Gibson's Crazy Rant

Every child of the 1970s or 1980s was a Mel Gibson fan. The star of films like *Mad Max*, the *Lethal Weapon* series, and *Braveheart* was not only handsome and charismatic on screen, but by all appearances, his private life was admirable, as well. Married to the same woman, Robyn, for more than 25 years—a rarity in Hollywood—and father to seven children, Gibson was seen as a family man, whose conservative Catholic upbringing provided him with a stable foundation to navigate the ethically challenged showbiz industry and a rocky world.

Trouble Ahead

But there were hints of trouble in Gibson's life, even before he became famous. The actor's father, Hutton Gibson, is a member of an ultra-conservative branch of Catholicism known as Sedevacantism, which rejects many of the modern teachings of the church. Hutton is also a well-known conspiracy theorist who has often doubted the reality of the Holocaust and believed that the September 11 attacks were carried out by "remote control." The elder Gibson has stated that the Holocaust was "mostly fabricated" and he believes the Jews in Europe were not imprisoned and murdered but simply emigrated to other countries. His son was no doubt exposed to these disturbing, anti-Semitic views, and they may have influenced him more than anyone realized.

Gibson's personal struggles began at a young age, and he was drinking by the time he was 13. He struggled with alcohol for decades, despite gaining a reputation for his professional behavior on Hollywood sets, and he has also stated that he has bipolar disorder. This combination of alcoholism, changing moods, and his father's extreme views converged one night in 2006, in a confrontation that would damage Gibson's career. And it would be another decade before the Oscar-winning actor and director started to recover from the fallout.

A Bizarre Tirade

That night, July 28, 2006, Gibson was pulled over for speeding in Malibu, California. The officer who pulled him over described Gibson as being "cooperative" until it became apparent that the actor was intoxicated. When the officer then told Gibson he was being arrested for drunk driving, Gibson tried to run to his car, but he was quickly subdued and placed in the back of the officer's police car. Drunk and defeated, Gibson then began ranting about his fame and his worry that the incident would soon be public. Understandable, perhaps; but his demeanor changed from worry to anger, and Gibson provided the officer with a profanity-laced tirade en route to the sheriff's department.

In addition to telling the officer, James Mee, that he would "regret you ever did this to me," Gibson inexplicably yelled, "The Jews are responsible for all the wars in the world." He then asked the officer, "Are you a Jew?" Mee, was, in fact, Jewish, and Gibson's erratic behavior unnerved him so much that he called ahead to the sheriff's department and requested a sergeant meet him in the parking lot so he wouldn't need to deal with the belligerent man alone. Ultimately, Gibson pleaded no contest to a drunk driving charge and was given three years' probation and ordered to attend self-help meetings.

Apologies and Forgiveness

Gibson's worry that the story would go public was well founded, of course, and soon his bizarre meltdown was the talk of gossip columns across the country. He quickly released several apologies, including one specifically addressed to the Jewish community, where he asked to meet with Jewish leaders "to discern the appropriate path for healing." He insisted that "hatred of any kind goes against my faith," and he later entered a treatment program to battle his alcoholism.

For the next decade, most of Hollywood turned its back on Gibson, and he only participated in a handful of film projects. There were some, however—including actor Robert Downey Jr., who himself fought his way back from drug abuse and legal troubles—who called for forgiveness. And in 2016, Gibson finally saw a turnaround in the industry's attitude toward him: he directed the Oscar-winning film *Hacksaw Ridge* and was honored with a Best Director nomination. For now, at least, Gibson is back in the spotlight.

The Shock Jock Gets Booted

Women's sporting events don't always get the respect they deserve. Even in the years since Title IX of the Education Amendments Act of 1972 prohibited discrimination in education programs, schools and universities often struggle to find popularity for their women's programs. Instead, fans flock to university football games and revel in the "March Madness" of men's basketball. It would stand to reason that when a women's team performs well and accomplishes something great, they deserve some positive recognition, too.

Worthy Opponents

So in 2007, when the Rutgers University women's basketball team made it to their first ever NCAA Championship game, people were talking. Especially since the team had had a dismal start—they lost four of their first six games—but still managed to claw their way back to the top. The underdogs made it to the final four, where they beat Louisiana State University 59-35, holding their opponents to the lowest score ever recorded in a Final Four game. In the championship game, they faced the University of Tennessee, but the Volunteers proved to be too much for the Scarlet Knights, and they were defeated 59-46. Still, Rutgers' impressive showing throughout the season earned them much respect from the sporting world, with journalists calling them a "Cinderella" team and praising their "suffocating defense" that had helped them win so many games.

The Shock Jock

And then there was Don Imus. The "shock jock" radio host of *Imus in the Morning* has always been known for his irreverent, often offensive jibes, never holding back with the insults. Some of his more famous remarks include calling radio host Rush Limbaugh "a fat, pill-popping loser," referring to Peabody Award-winning journalist Gwen Ifill as a "cleaning lady," and calling *60 Minutes* journalist Lesley Stahl a "gutless, lying weasel."

While Imus may have been readily forgiven for these rude quips, his comments on April 4, 2007—the day after the NCAA Championship Game—were not soon forgotten. That day, Imus and his executive producer, Bernard McGuirk, were discussing the previous night's game; but the talk soon turned to the players themselves. Imus called them "rough girls," and McGuirk then said they were "hardcore hos." Imus ran with the description and took it one step further, switching it up to "nappy-headed hos."

The backlash was immediate, with outrage expressed by everyone from fellow "shock jock" Howard Stern to activist Al Sharpton, who condemned the "abominable, racist, and sexist" remarks. Imus tried to downplay the incident, saying it was simply "some idiot comment meant to be amusing," but no one seemed very amused. The captain of the Rutgers women's basketball team, Essence Carson, spoke about Imus's comments at a news conference on April 10, saying the team was "highly angered at his remarks but deeply saddened with the racial characterization they entailed." Carson and her fellow players felt that the "degrading comments" Imus made overshadowed a moment when they should have been celebrating. Carson went on to say that Imus had "stolen a moment of pure grace" from the team.

Too Little, Too Late

Imus issued an apology for the "thoughtless and stupid" remark, saying, "it was completely inappropriate, and we can understand why people were offended." He was suspended for two weeks, and several sponsors pulled their ads from his show. But many, including Al Sharpton, *Time* magazine journalist Joe Klein, and *Chicago Tribune* columnist Clarence Page, called for Imus to be fired; and on April 12, 2007, CBS Radio cancelled *Imus in the Morning*.

Just hours after his firing, Imus met with the Rutgers women's basketball team and their coach, C. Vivian Stringer, to discuss the controversy. Afterwards, Stringer stated that the team had accepted Imus's apology, reiterating the fact that the team had never called for Imus to be fired. Stringer was impressed that Imus still came to the meeting hours after being fired, saying, "let's give him credit for that."

Imus returned to radio less than a year later, hopefully having learned some lessons from the gracious members of the Rutgers women's basketball team.

Britney Hits Her Breaking Point

On February 16, 2007, pop superstar Britney Spears walked into Esther's Haircutting Studio in Tarzana, California, and asked owner Esther Tognozzi to give her a buzz cut. Tognozzi, perhaps a bit taken aback by the request, refused; but that didn't deter Spears. She picked up some electric clippers and took matters into her own hands, shaving off her long locks as dozens of paparazzi snapped photos outside. The subsequent pictures of her bald head—along with headlines like the *New York Daily News*'s "Britney Shears"—spread through the gossip pages like wildfire. And everyone was asking: What happened to the singer we all knew and loved?

Early Success
Britney Jean Spears was born on December 2, 1981, and spent most of her childhood in Kentwood, Louisiana, where she loved singing and dancing and performed in many children's talent shows. In 1992, she was cast in *The Mickey Mouse Club* alongside some very good company: the soon-to-be-famous Christina Aguilera, Justin Timberlake, Ryan Gosling, and Keri Russell. The show was cancelled in 1996, but Spears had already made an impact on the entertainment industry and stayed in touch with record producers and executives. Her first album, *...Baby One More Time*, was released in January 1999 and was an immediate hit, and her career took off like a rocket.

Troubled Relationships
For the next few years, Spears enjoyed her status as one of the most popular performers in the world. Her first four albums each debuted

at number one, and she won a Grammy for Best Dance Recording for her song "Toxic." Her personal life, however, was a strange mix of ups and downs. In January 2004 she impulsively married childhood friend Jason Allen Alexander, but had the marriage annulled just 55 hours later. Then in July of that year, she became engaged to backup dancer Kevin Federline, who she'd met only three months earlier. At the time of the engagement, Federline's ex-girlfriend, Shar Jackson, was still pregnant with their child, and the love triangle was the focus of much media attention.

Spears and Federline were officially married on October 6, and the couple wasted no time starting a family. Less than a year later, on September 14, 2005, Sean Preston was born. Within a few months, Spears was pregnant with baby number two, and on September 12, 2006, Jayden James was born. But the marriage was soon over— Spears filed for divorce in November, citing irreconcilable differences. The end of her marriage sent Spears into a downward spiral from which it would take years to recover.

The Breaking Point

The shaved head incident came after several months of delving into the Hollywood club and drug scene, when Spears was often photographed with notorious party girls Paris Hilton and Lindsay Lohan. Friends and family were worried about the pop star's well-being and encouraged her to try rehab. She checked into a facility in Antigua, but just 24 hours later checked herself out and returned to California, where she attempted to see her kids. When she was told that she'd need to get help before she could see them, something inside her seemed to snap. She wandered into the hair salon, and soon her bald head was a major news headline.

But that was just the beginning of the pop star's meltdown: after a couple more short stints in rehab and unsuccessful attempts to see her kids, her behavior grew increasingly bizarre. In another famous incident, she attacked a photographer's car with an umbrella when she got frustrated with the paparazzi. And that's not all: she wore multicolored wigs and was seen making drug store runs in the middle of the night; she was charged with hit-and-run and driving without a license when she crashed into a car in a parking lot; and at one point she even inexplicably affected a fake British accent. By January 2008, Spears was denied even visitation rights to her children, after being rushed to the hospital while under the influence of "an unknown substance."

Comeback

But the hospitalization proved to be the turning point for the troubled singer, who was committed to a psychiatric ward for five days and placed under conservatorship of her father and attorney. Faced with the wakeup call she needed, Spears slowly began to rebound, winning MTV Video Music Awards for her single "Piece of Me," recording a new album, *Circus*, and regaining visitation rights to her children. She was even able to bring Sean and Jayden along with her on her comeback tour in 2009.

Most recently, Spears wrapped up an immensely popular Las Vegas residency show, with the final performance bringing in nearly $1.2 million a record for a single show in Las Vegas. Lucky for Spears, her career—and her hair—grew back to its former glory.

TV's Highest Paid Loses His Cool

In 2010, it seemed like Charlie Sheen was on top of the world. The actor—who was born Carlos Estevez to his famous father, Martin Sheen, and mother, Janet Templeton—was already known for a string of hit films, including *Platoon*, *Wall Street*, *Young Guns*, and *Major*

League. But his real success came with his wildly popular television comedy, *Two and a Half Men*, in which he starred with Jon Cryer and Angus T. Jones. Sheen's character—named, aptly, Charlie—was an affluent jingle writer with a beach house in Malibu who regularly entertained a revolving cast of women. Sheen's oft-publicized relationships, including a revelation that he was a client of infamous madam Heidi Fleiss, led some fans to believe that the show was often more truth than fiction. Either way, the show was a great success, and was nominated for a total of 46 Emmy Awards. By 2010, Sheen was the highest paid actor on television, earning a staggering $1.8 million per episode.

Road to a Meltdown

But Sheen's life had also been riddled with serious troubles for years. In 1998, at only 32 years old, Sheen suffered a stroke, and it was later discovered that the malady was brought on by cocaine use. His drug abuse problems continued over the next decade, with several unsuccessful stints in rehab. In January 2011, *Two and a Half Men* went on hiatus while Sheen attempted to complete another rehab program. But on February 14, Sheen appeared on the radio talk show *The Dan Patrick Show* and blamed the show's producers for the halt in production, saying he was ready and able to work but no one else was.

Then, a week later, the star went on *The Alex Jones Show* and ranted about the show's creator, Chuck Lorre, calling him a "charlatan" and throwing in a few anti-Semitic remarks. CBS responded by halting production of the show for the rest of the season, and Sheen shot back with some nonsensical comments, saying, "I have defeated this earthworm with my words—imagine what I would have done with my fire-breathing fists." But the most famous words uttered in the midst of his bizarre meltdown came during appearances on *Today* and *Good Morning America*. Sheen introduced his two live-in girlfriends he called "the goddesses," repeatedly talked about "winning," and claimed he didn't need rehab because it was "for normal people, people that aren't special, people that don't have tiger blood, you know, Adonis DNA."

A Personal Admission

With Sheen apparently coming unhinged, CBS terminated his contract on March 7 and replaced him with Ashton Kutcher. Sheen filed a $100 million wrongful termination lawsuit, claiming to have brought in "more than a billion dollars" for the show and saying the only reason he was fired was because of Lorre's "bruised ego." But Sheen's increasingly erratic behavior spoke for itself.

Once the controversy died down, Sheen began working on a new show, *Anger Management*, which ran for 100 episodes. On November 17, 2015, the actor returned to the *Today* show to make an announcement: "I am here to admit," he said, "that I am, in fact, HIV positive." Later, he went on *The Dr. Oz Show* to explain that his strange meltdown had been a side effect of using too much testosterone cream. "That was a very specific period of time that did feel very out-of-body and very just detached from all things real," he said. "I felt superhuman during some of that." Hopefully Sheen has finally figured out how to pull his life together and can truly start "winning."

Brian Williams's Dramatizations

It was a harrowing story.

NBC correspondent Brian Williams, appearing on the NBC news program *Dateline* on March 26, 2003, recounted to Tom Brokaw a story of riding in a military helicopter that was dodging enemy fire while flying over Iraq during the U.S. invasion of the country. In the segment, which was titled, "Target Iraq: Helicopter NBC's Brian Williams Was Riding

In Comes Under Fire," Williams described how the helicopter flying in front of his own was hit with a rocket-propelled grenade, or RPG, and had to make an emergency landing.

Years later, Williams would tell his story again, with even more frightening details. On a March 2013 episode of *Late Show With David Letterman*, the correspondent said that "two of the four helicopters" in his group were hit with fire from RPGs and AK-47s, including the one he was riding in. And in a January 2015 segment on the *NBC Nightly News*, Williams said that "the helicopter we were traveling in was forced down after being hit by an RPG." Williams certainly wouldn't be the first journalist to face a dangerous situation during a time of war. But there was one problem: his story simply wasn't true.

A Murky Memory

Shortly after Williams appeared on *Nightly News*, soldiers who had been riding in the helicopters on the day in question began raising suspicions on social media about Williams's retelling of the situation, with many of them doubting that the correspondent's helicopter had been hit by an RPG. On February 4, 2015, as uncertainties about his honesty mounted, Williams offered an apology—both on Facebook and on *Nightly News*—where he said he "made a mistake in recalling the events of 12 years ago." Williams claimed that his "constant viewing" of a video from his time in Iraq which showed an area impacted by weapons fire caused him to mix up timelines and accidentally "dramatize" what actually happened.

Williams then gave a more detailed interview to the military newspaper *Stars and Stripes*, in which he said he "assumed" his helicopter had been hit with small-arms fire and the fear he felt during the chaotic experience made his memories "a fog." He told the newspaper: "All we knew is we had been fired upon." However, several pilots who had been flying the helicopters that day contradicted even the "small-arms fire" claim, saying that the helicopter formation had not been fired upon at all that day.

A Pattern of Embellishment

On February 7, Williams announced he would be taking a leave of absence from the *Nightly News*, as he himself had become "too much a part of the news." Soon after, some of Williams's other stories were called into question, as inconsistencies and contradictions in his claims came to light. Some of these included statements he made after Hurricane Katrina, where he alternately described hearing about a suicide inside the New Orleans Superdome but later claimed to have witnessed it himself. He also told another story on *The Daily Show* in 2006 where he claimed to have been riding in an Israeli Air Force Black Hawk helicopter that was nearly hit by rockets fired from Lebanon. It would seem as if flying in targeted helicopters was quite a common occurrence for Williams.

On February 10, NBC News president Deborah Turness announced that Williams would be suspended for six months without pay. In a statement, Turness said that Williams "has a responsibility to be truthful and to uphold the high standards of the news division at all times." But with even some of Williams's older, innocuous anecdotes being questioned—such as his claim of being robbed at gunpoint while selling Christmas trees as a teenager, or his story about rescuing puppies when he served as a volunteer firefighter—the damage to Williams's credibility may haunt him for the rest of his career.

CHAPTER 6

THEY DID WHAT?

A Master of Political Theater

William Langer was born in 1886, three years before North Dakota was officially added to the Union. But he would become one of the state's most notorious political characters, maintaining popularity even after fighting off scandal. Historians have called him "a master of political theater," and his tale demonstrates why.

A Path to the Governor's House

Langer began his political career in 1914 as a Republican with the Nonpartisan League (NPL). But it wasn't long before he was making enemies within the NPL, clashing with founder and leader Arthur C. Townley and attempting to close down a bank that provided the NPL with most of its cash. In 1920, Langer announced he would be running for governor, but he was defeated by the party's incumbent, Lynn Frazier.

Realizing that the NPL ran the show in North Dakota, Langer began mending fences with the party, and after years of campaigning, he was finally elected governor in 1932. He promised to lower taxes and reduce the state budget, and he was popular with the farmers in the area, issuing a moratorium that prohibited mortgage foreclosures on locally operated farms in the state.

One Misstep

Morale in North Dakota was high, and Langer seemed to be doing a great job in his role as governor. And then in 1933, he began requiring that all state employees donate 5 percent of their salaries to the NPL and for a subscription to the *Leader*, a weekly newspaper owned by officials within his administration. This in itself was not prohibited by law, and was actually quite a common practice at the time. Most employees were even happy to donate some of their salary, as they were grateful for the jobs that Langer's administration had created.

It wasn't until donations were taken from highway department employees—who were paid by the federal government—that a red flag was raised. One of Langer's political enemies, Senator Gerald P. Nye, demanded an investigation into the donations, and U.S. Attorney P.W. Lanier concluded that the donations were a conspiracy to defraud the federal government.

Trial After Trial

A conspiracy trial began in May of 1934, and on June 29, Langer was found guilty and sentenced to 18 months in prison. He was removed from office on July 17 and replaced by Lieutenant Governor Ole Olson. But that wasn't the end of it: on May 7, 1935, the conviction was overturned, and a new trial was ordered when it was discovered that the original jury had been hand-picked by the prosecution. Langer was retried—not just once, but twice, when the first retrial ended in a hung jury.

Finally, in December 1935, Langer was acquitted, having maintained his innocence throughout the whole ordeal. Langer insisted that bitter political rivals who wished to see him ruined, including Lanier and the judge who presided over the first two trials, had targeted him. But Langer, not willing to allow an enemy to destroy his career, shrugged off the scandal and was once again elected governor of North Dakota in 1936.

Sister Aimee Dies for Love

Did a well-known early twentieth century evangelist stage her own death?

Sister Aimee Semple McPherson (1890—1944) was a woman far ahead of her time. In a male-driven society, McPherson founded a religious movement known as the Foursquare Church. Using her natural flamboyance and utilizing modern technologies such as radio, McPherson reached thousands with her Pentecostal message of hope, deliverance, and salvation. But turbulent waters awaited McPherson. Before the evangelist could grow her church to its fullest potential, she'd first have to survive her own "death."

The Seed Is Planted

It was said that McPherson was something of a firebrand right from the get-go. Born Aimee Elizabeth Kennedy in Salford, Ontario, the future evangelist was daughter to James Kennedy, a farmer, and Mildred "Minnie" Kennedy, a Salvation Army worker. As a teenager, the inquisitive Aimee often came to loggerheads with pastors over such weighty issues as faith and science—even as she openly questioned the teaching of evolution in public schools.

In 1908, Aimee married Robert James Semple, a Pentecostal missionary from Ireland. The marriage was short-lived. Semple died from Malaria in 1910, but their union produced a daughter, Roberta Star Semple, born that same year.

Working as a Salvation Army employee alongside her mother, Aimee married accountant Harold Stewart McPherson in 1912. One year later they had a son, Rolf Potter Kennedy McPherson. But this marriage would also dissolve. Citing desertion as the cause for their rift, Harold McPherson divorced his wife in 1921.

By this point McPherson was well on her way as an evangelist. In 1924 she began to broadcast her sermons over the radio. This new electronic "reach," coupled with McPherson's flair for drama, drew hordes into her fold. From an evangelistic standpoint, it was the best of times. But as Dickens demonstrated in the immortal opening line of *A Tale of Two Cities*, such heady times rarely come without strings attached. McPherson would soon experience this directly—ostensibly from the afterworld.

Gone with the Tide?

On May 18, 1926, the shocking news broke like a wave crashing against a beach: Nationally famous evangelist Aimee Semple McPherson had gone missing while swimming in the Pacific Ocean near Venice Beach, California. She was presumed drowned. Adding to the tragedy, two of her congregants perished while searching for her in the ocean. Despite continued efforts, no trace of McPherson—or her body—could be found.

From Death Comes Life

Oddly, police received hundreds of tips and leads that suggested that McPherson hadn't drowned at all. One letter, signed "The Avengers," said that Aimee had been kidnapped and demanded $500,000 for her safe return. One month later, a very alive McPherson emerged near Douglas, Arizona. She claimed she had been kidnapped and held in a shack in Mexico. No such shack, however, could be found.

Even stranger, radio operator and church employee Kenneth G. Ormiston vanished at precisely the same time as McPherson. Gossip spread like wildfire that the married Ormiston and McPherson had in fact shacked up for a month of tawdry, un-Christianlike romance. Charges of perjury and manufacturing evidence were brought against McPherson and Ormiston but were inexplicably dropped months later.

Scandal Sells

Despite the scandal, McPherson's church continued to grow by leaps and bounds. McPherson married a third time in 1931, but she was divorced once again by 1934. In 1944, Aimee Semple McPherson died from an overdose of sedatives. Her death was ruled accidental, but many believed that McPherson had in fact died by suicide. Whatever the cause of her death, the woman of faith who faltered at love left behind a strong legacy. By the end of the twentieth century, the church she founded boasted more than two million members worldwide.

The Much-Married Tommy Manville

Thomas Franklyn Manville Jr.—flamboyant Manhattan socialite and heir to the Johns-Manville asbestos fortune—earned minor celebrity and a place in Guinness World Records for being the American man married the most times in the 20th century.

Manville appeared to revel in his reputation and frequently made self-deprecating comments that made for memorable sound bites.

"I propose to anybody . . . Sort of an introduction."

During his lifetime (1894—1967), Manville racked up 13 marriages to 11 different women. Why the hankering to get hitched? Well, part of his marriage compulsion may have been motivated by financial gain. You see, when Tommy's wealthy father died, his father's will set up a trust for Tommy—but he was only entitled to withdraw from the interest. However, the will reportedly stipulated that Tommy would receive a million dollars from the principal when he married. The loophole? It didn't specify that only the first marriage was eligible for the payout!

"I've only had lunch with her once or twice, [but] . . . I think this could be one of the richest experiences of my life."

The above statement was made while Manville was still married to his eighth wife. He was referring to a brunette nightclub singer named Ruth Webb. Ruth managed to avoid becoming wife number nine, but perhaps Manville regretted that he went another route.

"I'm done with blondes."

Manville's love of women and reciting marital vows was only matched by his passion for fast cars. In fact, as a parting favor, Manville typically gifted each wife with an automobile on their way out. Other than that, Manville barely had to tap into his $20 million bank account while freeing himself from his first eight marriages.

But wife number nine, blond bombshell Anita Frances Roddy-Eden, caused quite a headache. When they wed in 1952, the dancer was 30 years Manville's junior. And she didn't age much in the 12 days they were married. She hauled the eccentric playboy to court and took the stand with accusations of "extreme mental cruelty." Among her claims: Manville drank excessively, and when she questioned his morning gin consumption, he threatened to kill her with a gun. Plus, he allegedly hung photos of his previous wives around the house and constantly talked about his exes. She even said that while they were still married, he tried proposing to her twin sister, Juanita Patino, the ex-wife of a Bolivian tin tycoon. A bit of a sassy character herself, Roddy-Eden Manville remarked that if they were unable to come to terms with a satisfactory settlement, "I am still his wife, and I am going to be the widow Manville!"

"She cried, and the judge wiped her tears with my checkbook."

Ultimately, Roddy-Eden Manville walked away with $260,000—a sizable sum at the time and significantly more than any of her predecessors received. She went on to pen and publish a biography entitled *The Many Wives and Lives of Tommy Manville*.

"When I meet a beautiful girl, the first thing I say is 'Will you marry me?' The second thing I say is 'How do you do?'"

Over the years, Manville's notoriety made its mark on popular culture. Anita's book inspired a campy musical by Jackie Curtis called *Lucky Wonderful: 13 Musicals About Tommy Manville*. Manville is also referenced in Irving Berlin's song "What Chance Have I With Love." Furthermore, it is widely believed that Manville was the basis for Gary Cooper's serial marrying character in the 1938 movie *Bluebeard's Eighth Wife*.

A Rigged Game

Before there were shows like *Who Wants to Be a Millionaire?*, *The Price is Right*, or even *Jeopardy*—which has aired since 1964— families tuned in to watch Jack Barry host the quiz show *Twenty One*. The show, which debuted in 1956, consisted of two players who would be confined to separate booths, where they could not see or hear each other. They would take turns answering questions posed by Barry, unaware of how their competition was faring. Each question was worth between one and 11 points, based on the difficulty of the question. If a contestant answered correctly, they would earn points; but if they answered incorrectly, the same number of points would be subtracted from their score. The first player to earn 21 points would win the game.

It sounds like a fun game with a nice element of competition, right? But the truth was that *Twenty One* was hardly a game at all; in fact the show turned out to be more of a casting call for actors than the quiz show it purported to be.

The Underdog

In the beginning, *Twenty One* was an honest game: the first episode featured two contestants who were not manipulated in any way; but unfortunately, they also weren't very bright. Producer Dan Enright felt that they made a mockery of the quiz format and called the episode "a dismal failure." And the show's sponsor, Geritol, threatened to pull out if the game didn't get its act together. So what was a boring quiz show to do? In the case of *Twenty One*, it began providing contestants with scripted answers and decided who would win and who would lose.

One of the "winners" was Herbert Stempel, a literal genius with a 170 IQ who could have easily competed fairly on a trivia show. But when he signed on for *Twenty One*, he became a part of the deception employed by the show: Stempel was grilled on the correct answers and how to answer them, and he was even asked to dress in a modest, frumpy fashion, so as to give him the appearance of an underdog.

Taking a Dive

After several weeks on the show, Stempel's appeal began to wear off; ratings dropped, and producers realized they needed a new "winner" to energize the audience. So, they chose college professor Charles Van Doren, who was billed as a "clean-cut, All-American boy." Van Doren and Stempel played to a tie for four weeks, which kept viewers on the edge of their seats: when a game ended in a tie, the scores were erased and a new game began, and the stakes were raised by $500 per point.

Finally, the producers decided it was time for Stempel to lose, and they asked him to incorrectly answer a question: What motion picture won the Academy Award for 1955? Stempel has since said that it was difficult for him to give an incorrect answer, since the correct answer—*Marty*—was one of his favorite films. Stempel recalls that he almost made a split-second decision to answer correctly—he had already been feeling a bit disgruntled, since he was told that he would not be receiving as much money as he won. But producer Dan Enright promised him a television job when it was all over, so, reluctantly but dutifully, Stempel threw the game, and Van Doren won.

Game Over

But the promised job never materialized, and Stempel, who had to watch Van Doren gaining popularity off a game they both knew was rigged, decided enough was enough. He contacted journalist Jack O'Brien at the New York City *Journal-American*, and blew the whistle on the quiz show. At first, his accusations were seen as jealousy over Van Doren's success; but when another game show, *Dotto*, was abruptly cancelled after it was found to be providing players with answers, investigators started to take things seriously.

In the fall of 1958, New York assistant district attorney Joseph Stone began to look into the allegations, and he found several other former *Twenty One* contestants who vouched for the scripted nature of the show. The controversy caused ratings to plummet, and on October 17, 1958, the show aired its last broadcast.

Disgraced, Barry and Enright were barely heard of for years after the scandal. Barry eventually began hosting game shows again and starred on *The Generation Gap* in 1969, and the two produced several shows together in the 1960s and 1970s. As for Stempel and Van Doren, the former contestants have led fairly quiet lives since the scandal, but the two gained a bit of fame once more when the controversy was adapted into the 1994 film *Quiz Show*, starring John Turturro as Stempel and Ralph Fiennes as Van Doren.

A Rocker Weds, a Career Is (Almost) Dead

In 1957, Jerry Lee Lewis had it all after clawing his way to the top of the rock 'n' roll world with his electrifying piano playing and howling, sexy vocals. That is, until he married his 13-year-old cousin.

The High Climb to Fame and Fortune

It hadn't been easy for Jerry Lee Lewis. He was born in 1935 into grinding poverty in Ferriday, Louisiana. Though his family was devoutly Christian (his cousin, Jimmy Swaggart, would one day gain fame and notoriety as a preacher), the young Lewis was drawn to the rhythm and blues he heard on the radio and at Haney's Big House, an African American juke joint "on the other side of the tracks." When Lewis's parents mortgaged their farm to buy him a piano, they hoped he would make music for the Lord. Instead, Jerry began to tour the southeast playing rockabilly, an early form of rock 'n' roll.

Lewis was signed by Sun Records in Memphis, Tennessee, in late 1956 and immediately began backing such important artists as Carl Perkins and Johnny Cash on piano. But Lewis wanted to be a star in his own right, even though some told him it would be impossible unless he abandoned the piano for the guitar. He soon proved the naysayers wrong with two huge piano-driven hits called "Whole Lotta Shakin' Goin' On" and "Great Balls of Fire." Although many early rock 'n' roll artists traded on sexual innuendo, very few matched Lewis in their brazenness. His sex-drenched lyrics and orgasmic yelps caused some radio stations to boycott him, but this forbidden fruit aspect only made "the kids" want his music more.

Lewis's Lolita

Lewis knew he could get away with a lot in his personal life, and he took full advantage of that. He married his second wife, Jane Mitcham, 23 days before his divorce from his first wife, Dorothy Barton, was final. Then he divorced Jane, too. No one seemed to care or expect any better of him, so Lewis continued with his wild ways, womanizing and carousing his way across the United States on booze-soaked tours. Fans liked their rock 'n' roll devil to be as bad as could be, so perhaps by the age of 22, Lewis figured there was nothing he could do to push them too far. Oh, but there was: Lewis married a 13-year-old girl who still believed in Santa Claus. And she was his cousin.

Myra Gale Brown was actually Lewis's first cousin, once removed—the daughter of Lewis's first cousin, J. W. Brown, who was the bass guitar player in Lewis's band. But the combination of this blood relationship and her tender age caused an international scandal when it was reported while Lewis was on his first tour of Britain in 1958. Only one journalist, Ray Berry, had shown up at London Airport to greet Lewis and Myra, and Berry sure got one heck of a scoop when Lewis started flapping his gums about his most recent plunge into matrimony. The British tabloids had a field day with the story, and the tour was canceled after only three performances.

Rock 'n' Roll Repercussions

Back home in the United States, Lewis was blacklisted from both radio and television, and his career was nearly destroyed. His reputation as one of the hottest, most exciting stage acts in history saved him from complete ruin, however. Though his nightly concert fee dropped drastically from the $10,000 it once was, $250 a night wasn't exactly peanuts in the 1950s. Lewis was at least able to afford a comfortable, if not luxurious, lifestyle for him, his child bride, and the two children they eventually had.

Jerry Lee Lewis and Myra Gale Brown were married for 13 years, divorcing in 1970. Lewis, who was inducted into the Rock 'n' Roll Hall of Fame in 1986, toured the United Kingdom, the scene of the scandal, as recently as 2008. Brown later became a real estate agent in Atlanta, Georgia.

The Stanford Prison Experiment

On August 14, 1971, 12 young men were rounded up from their homes in Palo Alto, California, by police officers. They were handcuffed and searched as confused neighbors looked on, then hauled off to prison, where they were booked, fingerprinted, and left blindfolded in a holding cell. Over the next few days, they would be subjected to psychological and physical abuse by callous and power-hungry prison guards, driving some of them to breakdowns.

And amazingly, they all volunteered for the experience.

Flip of a Coin

It's no wonder the young men's neighbors who had witnessed their "arrests" were confused: the "prisoners" were all middle-class college students with no histories of crime or drug abuse. They were heading to prison not due to behavior, but rather for experimental reasons. Stanford University psychology professor Philip Zimbardo—with a grant from the U.S. Office of Naval Research—created the experiment to study the dynamic between prisoners and guards. He placed an ad in a local newspaper asking for volunteers, and out of 70 respondents, chose 24 to participate in the study. They were then divided into two groups based on a coin flip; half of the men were designated "prisoners," and the others were "guards." Zimbardo became the "superintendent" and an undergraduate research assistant was the "warden."

Zimbardo consulted with an ex-prisoner to turn the basement of the Stanford Psychology Department building into a realistic mock-up of a prison. Windows were boarded up, regular doors were taken off rooms and replaced with doors with steel bars, and a closet was converted into the "solitary confinement" cell. The young men who were assigned guard status were given mostly free reign to keep order, within reason—they could not physically hurt the prisoners, or deny them food or water. They were given wooden batons, dressed in the same khaki shirts and pants, and given mirrored sunglasses so the prisoners couldn't see their eyes.

The prisoners, meanwhile, were stripped, given a smock to wear, and outfitted with a heavy chain on their ankle "to remind prisoners of the oppressiveness of their environment." They were then forced to cover their heads with nylon stockings to simulate having their hair shaved off. Each prisoner was assigned a number, and that was considered his identification for the rest of the experiment.

It Starts Getting Real

Although the first day of the experiment was rather uneventful—the guards and prisoners were both feeling out their new roles and hadn't quiet embraced their parts yet—by the second day, things started to take a disturbing turn. After some of the prisoners barricaded themselves into a cell, the guards debated how to restore order. They broke into the cell, stripped the prisoners naked, took their beds away, and placed the leader of the rebellion into solitary confinement. They then used psychological tactics, like allowing "good" prisoners to use a "privilege cell," where they got their clothes and beds back, and were given special food to eat. In this way, the guards managed to divide the prisoners and destroy the solidarity they once felt.

But the guards didn't stop there. Feeling the rush of power, they began forcing prisoners to do push-ups when they misbehaved, denied them trips to the toilet, and took away their mattresses so they'd have to sleep on concrete. Prisoners were rounded up several times a day for "counts"—sometimes in the middle of the night—when they would have to repeat their numbers, reinforcing the idea that their individuality had been taken away.

Breakdowns and a Shutdown

Only 36 hours into the experiment, one of the prisoners began to exhibit extreme emotions—crying uncontrollably and going into fits of rage. Zimbardo released him from the experiment. Two days later, another participant had a breakdown and began crying hysterically because he was a "bad prisoner." Zimbardo had to remind him that it was all an experiment, and that he was free to go, at which point the "prisoner" stopped crying and said, "OK, let's go."

Although the experiment was scheduled to last two weeks, Zimbardo called an end to it after only six days when his girlfriend—and later wife—Christina Maslach, who was a graduate student in psychology, stopped by the experiment to conduct interviews. Maslach observed the prisoners being marched to the toilet with bags over their heads and chains around their ankles, and she told Zimbardo: "It's terrible what you are doing to these boys!" In a move that probably saved Zimbardo some future unhappiness in his relationship, he immediately shut down the experiment.

But Did It Matter?

Even Zimbardo was surprised by how each group of young men embraced their roles: The "guards" became more and more sadistic, while the "prisoners" became more and more subdued. Many of the prisoners said they felt like they really couldn't leave, even though they were free to go at any time. When Maslach questioned why Zimbardo had allowed the conditions within the experiment to deteriorate, he realized that he, also, had been embracing his role as "superintendent."

Many experts deem the results of the experiment mostly subjective and insignificant. Zimbardo's participation in the experiment meant he himself influenced it, instead of remaining neutral. Psychologists have also questioned whether selection bias, a small sample size, and the participants' preconceived ideas about how "guards" and "prisoners" act affected the outcome. And finally, of course, many have criticized what is seen as the unethical nature of the experiment. Since the Stanford Prison Experiment, ethical guidelines have been developed for any experiment involving human subjects.

The Kidnapping of a Publishing Magnate Heiress

In 1974, members of the Symbionese Liberation Army, a left-wing organization in the San Francisco Bay Area, kidnapped Patty Hearst. Hearst was the 19-year-old heiress to the publishing magnate William Randolph Hearst.

The SLA initially attempted to pressure the Hearst family into using their political influence to free two of their members who were in prison for murder. When they were unable to do so, the group demanded that they distribute food to needy Californians. Hearst's father donated $2 million worth of food to poor people in the Bay Area, but the SLA refused to release Patty.

The group, who subjected her to torture and intimidation, held Hearst for nineteen months. She eventually was coerced to join the SLA, and was seen participating in a bank robbery with other members of the group. The authorities no longer considered her a kidnapping victim after the robbery, and she was now a fugitive. She was arrested with another SLA member the following year and convicted of bank robbery. President Jimmy Carter commuted her sentence, and President Bill Clinton later pardoned her.

The Tailhook Scandal

The U.S. military is the largest employer in the world, with 3.2 million employees. Usually, we ponder our military with great respect, and with good reason: these men and women repeatedly put their lives on the line to protect our freedoms and way of life. But in 1991, the military was the focus of a scandal that shone a light on a darker side of its operations, and the fallout still reverberates today.

What Happens in Vegas . . .

A "tailhook" is a hook beneath the tail of a plane that lands on aircraft carriers. To arrest its momentum as it lands on the short runway, the plane's hook catches a wire on the deck of the carrier. This is where the Tailhook Association—a fraternal organization that supports sea-based aviation—got its name. The association has been around since 1956, and every year it sponsors the Tailhook Symposium—a reunion of former Navy and Marine pilots.

The 1991 symposium was held at the Las Vegas Hilton between September 8 and 12. It was the largest meeting the Tailhook Association had ever held, with more than 4,000 active, reserve, and retired personnel attending to hear about Navy and Marine Corps aviation during Operation Desert Storm. But not everything that happens in Vegas stays in Vegas, and after the symposium, disturbing reports began to surface.

Running the Gauntlet

After then-Tailhook president Captain Rick Ludwig returned to his ship, the USS Midway, he debriefed his staff on reports he received of fights in the hallways and roughhousing on the pool patio. But much more sinister complaints started to circulate in the wake of the Tailhook Symposium: 83 women and seven men came forward and stated that they'd been sexually assaulted and harassed during the course of the meeting. Many claimed that they were forced to walk past hallways filled with drunken, groping officers in order to reach their rooms. After an investigation, the United States Department of the Navy mostly shrugged off the complaints, concluding that the incident amounted to nothing more than a bunch of drunken frat boys.

Frustrated by the Navy's lack of accountability, one of these victims, Lieutenant Paula Coughlin, appeared on ABC news in 1992 and told her story of having to "run the gauntlet" as she walked back to her room. The drunken men in the hallway grabbed, groped, and even tried to undress her, all the while making frighteningly inappropriate comments.

Changing the Culture

Coughlin's story, along with prompting from Assistant Secretary of the Navy Barbara S. Pope, sparked an investigation by the Inspector General of the United States Department of Defense. This investigation uncovered 140 cases of misconduct against at least 80 women. Some defenders of the Tailhook Association attempted to question Coughlin's credibility, but she remained steadfast in her claims. She and six other victims ultimately sued the association and settled out of court.

Because of the scandal, many military officers, including those who had been in charge of the original Navy investigation, were fired, resigned, or endured damaged careers. And although progress has been made in the treatment of women in the military, echoes of Tailhook remain. As late as 2014, one in four women in the military reported sexual harassment or discrimination, and often their complaints go unheard. Writing for *USA Today* in 2017, Paula Coughlin said, "Confronting this culture of misogyny and discrimination against women is a moral obligation. It is time to show the country and the world how the U.S. military can lead."

Woody Allen's Idiosyncrasy

Director, actor, and screenwriter Woody Allen is famous for making movies that chronicle the bizarre struggles of his neurotic protagonists. But the very public personal saga that made headlines in the early 1990s tops even the most convoluted of Allen's screenplays.

Setting the Stage

Woody Allen had built a career as a respected filmmaker with movies such as *Bananas* (1971), *Sleeper* (1973), *Manhattan* (1979), and the Oscar-winning *Annie Hall* (1977). His films were recognizably his own, and announcements of new projects were greeted with anticipation among critics and the public.

In 1980, Allen began a relationship with actress Mia Farrow, best known at the time for her roles in the movie *Rosemary's Baby* (1968) and on the TV series *Peyton Place*. Farrow already had six children, both adopted and biological, from her previous marriage to pianist Andre Previn. In 1987, Allen and Farrow had a son of their own, Satchel O'Sullivan Farrow (who later changed his name to Ronan Seamus Farrow). While she was with Allen, Farrow also adopted a boy named Moses and a girl named Dylan. Allen and Farrow never married, but in 1991, Allen also adopted Dylan and Moses.

The Rising Action

Allen and Farrow spent a dozen years leading what looked like an idyllic, if somewhat peculiar, existence. The two never lived together but kept separate residences on opposite sides of New York City's Central Park. Farrow and her roster of kids would trudge across the green, armed with sleeping bags, to spend the night at Allen's place.

But that all ended in 1992, when Farrow discovered nude photos that Allen had taken of her adopted daughter Soon-Yi Previn. It turned out that Allen had been sleeping with Soon-Yi for a while—at least since her first year of college. Soon-Yi was 21 at the time of her mother's discovery, and Allen was 57.

Recognizing that Farrow was miles beyond peeved by this turn of affairs, Allen sued her for custody of their three children—Satchel, Moses, and Dylan. Farrow responded by accusing Allen of sexually abusing Dylan, who was seven years old at the time.

Not surprisingly, the press had a field day. The ensuing courtroom drama was covered daily in newspapers in the United States and around the world. It didn't hurt that the two stars of this media circus never shied away from reporters. Allen was eager to emphatically deny the accusation of molestation, and he also revealed that he didn't regret his affair with Soon-Yi. When the story of the affair first broke, Allen responded, "It's real and happily all true."

Farrow, meanwhile, was more than open to depicting Allen as a small, sniveling, neurotic, and deeply disturbed man. Regarding Allen's relationship with their daughter Dylan, Farrow testified, "He would creep up in the morning and lay beside her bed and wait for her to wake up . . . I was uncomfortable all along."

Resolution—Sort Of

In the end, Farrow was granted full custody of the three children. The judge wrote a 33-page decision in which he described Allen as a "self-absorbed, untrustworthy, and insensitive" father. He chastised Allen for not knowing the names of his son's teachers or even which children shared which bedrooms in Farrow's apartment. A state-appointed group of specialists concluded that Allen was not guilty of molesting Dylan, although the judge deemed the report "sanitized and . . . less credible."

Allen was disappointed to lose custody of his children, but he was happy to continue his relationship with their older adopted half-sister. Shortly after the conclusion of the court battle, Soon-Yi and Allen were spotted at trendy restaurants all across Manhattan. They married in 1997 and have since adopted two children of their own.

In her 1997 memoir, Farrow compared her relationship with Allen to her childhood battle with polio: "I had unknowingly brought danger into my family and . . . I might have contaminated those that I loved the most."

A Crying Shame

A popular public-service campaign from the 1970s featured a Native American man named Iron Eyes Cody whose tearful visage implored people not to litter. In truth, his heritage was fabricated.

"People start pollution; people can stop it." Although the publics service campaign was one of the most successful ever created, Iron Eyes Cody's career encompassed much more than that particular spot. He appeared in an estimated 200 movies and dozens of television shows, typically playing a Native American. Off-screen, he worked faithfully and tirelessly on behalf of the Native American community. Throughout his adult life, Iron Eyes Cody claimed to be of Cherokee/Cree lineage. However, the assertion was a lie: Cody was, in fact, a full-blooded Italian.

Of Immigrants Born

His story began in the tiny town of Kaplan, Louisiana, where he was born Espera DeCorti in 1904. His parents, Antonio DeCorti and Francesca Salpietra, had emigrated from Italy at the turn of the century. Espera—who went by the name Oscar—was the second eldest of the couple's four children.

Antonio abandoned his family in 1909 and moved to Texas. Francesca divorced him and married a man named Alton Abshire, with whom she bore five more children. While still in their teens, Oscar and his brothers, Joseph and Frank, joined their father in Texas and, like their father, shortened their last name to Corti. In 1924, following Antonio's death, the brothers moved to Hollywood, where they again changed their last name—this time to Cody—and started working in motion pictures.

Joseph and Frank managed to land a few jobs as movie extras, but they eventually gave up their acting dreams and moved on to other careers. Oscar, however, had found his niche. He quietly changed his name to Iron Eyes Cody and started passing himself off as a full-blooded Native American.

Who Knew?

At the time, no one had reason to challenge him. Cody had a distinctive Native American look, and he took great pains to embrace his new identity and false heritage. He married a Native American woman named Bertha Parker, and together they adopted several Native American children. Iron Eyes almost always wore his long hair in braids and dressed in Native American attire, including beaded moccasins.

In fact, it was Cody's appearance that made his anti-littering public service announcement such a success. Everyone who saw it assumed that Cody was a real Native American and thus felt tremendous sympathy for him when a bag of garbage was tossed at his feet. Many even thought the tear that ran down his cheek at the ad's conclusion was real, but it was really just a drop of glycerin.

The television ad made Cody a household name and brought him quite a bit of attention. In the years that followed, he repeatedly denied nagging rumors that he was not what he claimed to be, but his story finally unraveled in the mid-1990s when his half-sister sent journalists proof that he was actually Italian. Several newspapers jumped on the story, eagerly pulling back the curtain to reveal the truth behind Cody's ancestral lie. But even in the face of overwhelming evidence (including his birth certificate), Cody stuck steadfastly to his story, which he maintained until his death.

Who Cared?

Ultimately, it didn't really matter to most Native Americans that Iron Eyes Cody had lied. He had spent decades working on their behalf, drawing international attention to their concerns. In 1995, Hollywood's Native American community honored him for his many charitable endeavors.

Iron Eyes Cody—perhaps the most famous Native American who never was—died on January 4, 1999, at the age of 94.

A Senator's Lewd Bathroom Behavior

There are few things more private than a person's bathroom habits. This generally falls into the "none of your business" category. But for one United States Senator, a trip to the bathroom proved to be anything but private, and it ultimately led to his downfall.

Can I Have Some Privacy?

On June 11, 2007, U.S. Senator from Idaho Larry Craig was passing through the Minneapolis-St. Paul International Airport when he stopped for a bathroom. A short while later, he was led out by a police officer and arrested on suspicion of lewd conduct. So, what exactly happened in that bathroom?

On the day of Craig's arrest, police had planned an undercover operation after receiving complaints of sexual activity in the airport bathroom. An undercover officer waited in one of the stalls, and after about 15 minutes, he noticed Craig loitering just outside, occasionally peeking through the partition between doors. The senator then went into the adjacent stall, and after a few moments, began tapping his foot. This tapping gesture was, according to the arresting officer, "a signal used by persons wishing to engage in lewd conduct." Craig then slid his foot over until it was touching the officer's foot in the next stall, and then waved his hand under the stall divider several times.

Wide Stance

Craig's actions were allegedly well-known signals that implied a solicitation for anonymous sex. But instead of agreeing to a rendezvous, the officer in the next stall showed Craig his police identification and escorted him out of the bathroom. He was interviewed in the airport police station, and he denied that his actions had any particular meaning. When asked about moving his foot into the next stall, he said, "I'm a fairly wide guy," and Craig claimed that he had merely "positioned" himself in the stall. As for the hand underneath the partition, Craig insisted that he was simply reaching down to the floor to pick up a piece of paper, but the arresting officer stated that "there was not a piece of paper on the bathroom floor."

Accusations and Denials

On August 8, Craig pleaded guilty to disorderly conduct and paid a $500 fine; but he later stated that he regretted ever pleading guilty. "At the time of this incident, I complained to the police that they were misconstruing my actions. I was not involved in any inappropriate conduct," he asserted. But after the scandal broke, several men came forward claiming to have had sexual contact with the senator. Again, Craig vehemently denied the accusations, telling a reporter for the *Idaho Statesman* that "I don't go around anywhere hitting on men, and by God, if I did, I wouldn't do it in Boise, Idaho!"

The senator stated that his reasons for pleading guilty stemmed from being "relentlessly and viciously harassed" by the *Idaho Statesman*, which began investigating claims of Craig's homosexuality shortly after his arrest. He stated that he made the "poor decision" to plead guilty "in hopes of making it go away." Unfortunately for the senator however, things just got worse: Craig resigned from Mitt Romney's 2008 presidential campaign, with Romney stating, "He's disappointed the American people." Members of Craig's Republican Party began demanding that he resign, and a complaint was filed with the Senate Ethics Committee.

On September 1, 2007, Craig announced that he would resign at the end of the month; however, within a few weeks he'd changed his mind, saying that he would serve out his term in an effort to "clear my name in the Senate Ethics Committee. He left office on January 3, 2009, and did not run for reelection, bringing his political career to an end. He unsuccessfully attempted to get his guilty plea reversed several times, which led to one more giant misstep for the former senator: to pay for all of his appeals, Craig dipped into his campaign funds, and he was subsequently ordered to pay back $242,000 to the U.S. Treasury Department.

A Private Matter Becomes a Public Spectacle

The decade and a half leading up to 2009 seemed to be the best years of golfer Tiger Woods's life. The once child-prodigy—who was introduced to the game of golf as a toddler by his father, Earl—had already signed advertising deals with huge companies like Nike and Titleist, became the youngest ever Masters Tournament winner at the age of 21, had a total of 14 major championship wins, and was the top-ranked golfer in the world for a total of 545 weeks. Not to mention the fact that he married a beautiful Swedish model named Elin Nordegren, had two equally beautiful children, and became the world's first athlete to earn a billion dollars in his career. But Woods's fairytale life wasn't as perfect as it seemed. And when it came crashing down, it did so in a spectacular fashion.

A Mysterious Crash

Just before Thanksgiving of 2009, Woods returned home to Florida after winning the Masters in Australia. The day before the holiday, the new issue of the *National Enquirer* was published, with a headline proclaiming, "Tiger Woods Cheating Scandal." The magazine alleged that Woods had been having an affair with a nightclub hostess named Rachel Uchitel, who had been photographed checking into Woods's hotel in Australia. Woods insisted the story was untrue, even calling Uchitel and allowing Nordegren to speak to her in an effort to convince her of his innocence.

Two days later, at 2:30 a.m., Woods pulled his Cadillac Escalade SUV out of his driveway and erratically careened down the street, where he eventually hit a fire hydrant and ran into a tree. Immediately, the media began to speculate about the cause of the crash, but Woods would only say that it was a "private matter" and that he would need to pull out of the rest of his 2009 tournaments due to his injuries.

Out of the Woodwork

Over the next few days, Woods's life began to unravel. *Us Weekly* reported on another alleged mistress and a voicemail Woods had left for her, and suddenly, women were popping up everywhere with claims of affairs with the golfer. More than a dozen women came forward, and Woods released a statement admitting that there were "transgressions" and apologized to his fans. He decided to take an "indefinite" break from golf, and companies that had given him lucrative advertising deals began to sever ties. By February 2010, Woods announced that he had been in a therapy program, and was hoping to return to golfing for the 2010 Masters Tournament.

Unfortunately, the damage to his marriage was done, and he and Nordegren divorced on August 23, 2010. So, what actually happened the night of Woods's car accident?

A Woman Scorned

That night, after Thanksgiving dinner with his family, Woods took an Ambien to help him fall asleep. Once he was out like a light, Nordegren found his phone and scrolled through his text messages until she found one he'd sent to Uchitel: "You are the only one I've ever loved," it said. Damning evidence, certainly. But just to be sure, Nordegren began texting Uchitel, pretending to be Woods, and then called the mistress, telling her, "I know everything." Having worked up quite a bit of anger toward her husband, Nordegren's screaming woke Woods, and the two began to argue, Nordegren hitting and scratching Woods as he ran for his car.

After that, Nordegren picked up the first weapon she could find—a golf club, of course—hopped into a golf cart, and pursued Woods's Escalade. Woods, groggy and disoriented from the Ambien and his wife's wrath, had trouble controlling the car and sailed over a hydrant and into a tree. After help arrived, onlookers noticed that Nordegren was standing nearby, holding a golf club, and the SUV's back windows were smashed. But can anyone really blame her?

Woods's career has never fully recovered, and he's been plagued with back injuries and surgeries in recent years. But he's still considered the highest-paid golfer in the world and is ranked ninth on *Forbes's* list of the world's highest paid athletes. Even with all his problems, it's safe to say no one is feeling sorry for Tiger Woods.

When Teachers Become Cheaters

If there's one thing you learn quickly in school, it's that cheating is always unacceptable. Students have been given failing grades, suspended, or even expelled for participating in cheating practices. And teachers are charged with holding their students accountable—after all, cheating benefits no one. So it came as a shock when, in 2009, the very people who were supposed to prevent cheating became cheaters themselves.

A Model District?

In February 2009, Beverly Hall, who had been the Atlanta Public Schools superintendent for 10 years, was named Superintendent of the Year, partly due to the rising scores exhibited on standardized tests in Atlanta schools. Between 2002 and 2009, students' scores on Criterion-Referenced Competency Tests (CRCT) rose 14 points, the highest jump of any urban area. The American Association of School Administrators, who bestowed the honor upon Hall, called Atlanta a "model of urban school reform." It would have been something to be proud of, had it been true.

Suspicious Scores

The same year, the *Atlanta Journal-Constitution* began investigating the test scores. The newspaper discovered that many districts in Atlanta were showing "statistically improbable" increases in scores on the CRCT. But Hall claimed that she didn't know of any cheating and agreed to allow national experts to review test scores at schools that showed marked improvement. The findings were troubling, and by October 2010, the Georgia Bureau of Investigation sent 50 agents to Atlanta to question teachers and administrators. Their conclusions raised questions about what role standardized testing should have in schools and whether teachers should be held accountable for their students' scores.

A Pattern of Deception

After reviewing more than 800,000 documents, GBI investigators concluded that 44 of the 58 schools in Atlanta had participated in cheating on CRCT tests. Investigators found that in 2009, there were 256,779 answers on tests that had been wrong, erased, and changed to correct answers. The probability of this being a random occurrence was a nearly impossible one in a quadrillion.

State investigators also discovered that school employees who reported cheating were often intimidated and threatened, and a high-ranking district official told the *Atlanta Journal-Constitution* that Hall had ordered documents detailing the cheating be destroyed.

In July 2012, a report was issued that detailed the GBI's findings, which implicated 178 teachers in 44 districts. The cheating was said to have possibly dated all the way back to 2001, when the No Child Left Behind Act was created and required states receiving federal funding to administer basic skills tests. But from at least 2005 to 2009, test answers in Atlanta public schools were altered, fabricated, or falsely certified. Teachers cheated to earn bonuses, get promotions, or to keep their jobs, saying they felt enormous pressure to have a classroom full of high-scoring students.

Ultimately, about 150 educators resigned or lost their jobs due to the scandal, and only 21 were reinstated. Hall was indicted for her role in the debacle, but she was gravely ill with stage IV cancer and unable to stand trial. Twelve others were indicted, with 11 convicted of racketeering. They were given sentences ranging from five years' probation to a stunning 20 years in prison. It's true: cheaters never win.

Anything but a Shining Example

College football has produced some notable coaches throughout the history of the game, like Pop Warner, Barry Switzer, and of course the incomparable Bear Bryant. But in 2011, the football program at Pennsylvania State University came under scrutiny for a disturbing and horrifying reason, and the names of Jerry Sandusky and Joe Paterno would be remembered for deeds that were anything but an innocent game.

A Shining Example

Sandusky married his wife, Dottie, in 1966. The couple adopted six children, and also occasionally served as foster parents. By all appearances a man who cared for troubled kids, Sandusky founded "The Second Mile"—a charity that helped children in need and provided care for foster children—in 1977. The charity provided services to 100,000 kids every year, and donors included major companies like Walmart, Bank of America, and PepsiCo. President George H.W. Bush even praised The Second Mile, calling it a "shining example" of charity work.

Professionally, Sandusky was an assistant coach for the Penn State Nittany Lions from 1969 until 1999, and after he retired he became a coach emeritus, with an office at Penn State and access to all the football facilities. He also remained active in The Second Mile, hosting summer football camps every year.

Disturbing Allegations

Then, in 2008, almost a decade after his retirement, a student at Central Mountain High School in Mill Hall, Pennsylvania, made an allegation of abuse against Sandusky. The student claimed that he and Sandusky had met through The Second Mile program, and

Sandusky had been molesting him since he was 12 years old. As the Pennsylvania attorney general's office looked into the claim, they began to discover an unsettling number of new complaints against the former coach and revealed the shocking truth about Sandusky's image as a fatherly caretaker.

Over the next three years, Pennsylvania Attorney General Linda Kelly gathered enough evidence to indict Sandusky on 52 counts of sex crimes against boys, with some of the victims being as young as seven years old. As details came to light, the public was sickened by the manipulative, deviant actions of a man who took advantage of children he supposedly cared for. Sandusky would choose his victims from The Second Mile charity, looking for boys who lacked a father figure in their life. He would then employ a tactic common with pedophiles called "grooming," where he would buy the children gifts and take them to football games to earn their trust, all the while engaging in increasingly inappropriate touching and behavior.

Locked Away for Life

In addition to Sandusky's crimes, an independent investigation by former FBI director Louis Freeh concluded that several Penn State school officials—including coach Joe Paterno, athletic director Tim Curley, school president Graham Spanier, and school vice president Gary Schultz—knew about the abuse and did nothing to stop it. Paterno's contract was immediately terminated, and Curley, Spanier, and Schultz were found guilty of child endangerment.

The Penn State football program was also punished, with the NCAA imposing a $60 million fine, a four-year post-season ban, scholarship reductions, and a forfeit of all victories between 1998 and 2011. The Big Ten Conference also imposed an additional $13 million fine. As for Sandusky, he was found guilty on 45 of the charges against him and sentenced to a minimum of 30 years in prison. Because of Sandusky's age, the judge who presided over the case was satisfied that the disgraced football coach would be imprisoned for the rest of his life.

United's Public Relations Nightmare

The advantages of flying are hard to beat: no other mode of transportation can get you from point A to point B as quickly. But very few of us actually enjoy the airline experience. We drag our luggage through crowded airports, wait in seemingly endless lines, and endure delays, only to wind up crammed inside a metal tube with a hundred other passengers, stuck in an uncomfortable seat for hours on end. Only in an airport, too, can you be made to feel like a criminal for possessing a bottle of water.

But even with the hassles, millions of us use air travel every day, and the more passengers who use airlines, the more complaints are filed against those airlines. More than 18,000 complaints were filed against airlines in 2017, for everything from lost luggage to excessive delays to customer service problems. But on April 9, 2017, one United Airlines passenger had more reason to complain that any of his fellow passengers.

Involuntary Volunteers

The trouble began at Chicago O'Hare International Airport after all of the passengers on United Express Flight 3411 were seated, with less than 20 minutes to go before its departure to Louisville, Kentucky. That's when an airline employee announced that four crew members needed to board the full flight to cover an unstaffed flight at another location. The employee asked four passengers to voluntarily deplane, offering $400 vouchers, a hotel stay, and a seat on a flight the next day. When no one volunteered, the offer was upped to $800 in vouchers.

And when that didn't entice anyone, a supervisor announced that four people would be chosen by computer.

The first three passengers who were chosen left without incident, but the fourth passenger—pulmonologist David Dao—refused to leave, saying he needed to see patients at his clinic the next day. The situation quickly escalated from there: employees called Chicago Department of Aviation security officers, who also demanded Dao leave. When he refused, the officers began to forcibly remove the 69-year-old from his seat. According to passengers who witnessed the incident, as Dao was struggling to remain in his seat, officers threw him against an armrest. They then dragged Dao down the aisle by his arms. Somehow, the battered man managed to reboard the plane, and dazedly ran down the aisle repeating, "I have to go home." He collapsed into a seat, and he was removed from the plane on a stretcher.

A Viral Video Causes Backlash

Several passengers on their phones recorded the entire event, and the video immediately went viral. The footage shows Dao screaming as officers aggressively pull him out of his seat, and he appears disheveled and bloody as he is dragged away. Dao suffered a broken nose, broken teeth, and a concussion as a result of his treatment.

The backlash against United Airlines was swift. Passengers who were on the flight were disgruntled before the plane even left the ground: The four employees who boarded in place of the removed passengers were reviled by fellow travelers and told they should be ashamed to work for United. Calls for boycotts went out on social media, and online petitions called for United Airlines CEO Oscar Munoz to resign. Munoz released a statement that insisted Dao had been "belligerent" and "disruptive," and he praised United staff for following procedure. But when he was widely criticized for his words, he backtracked, saying,

"No one should ever be treated this way," and he admitted that Dao was not at fault. The Chicago Department of Aviation also released a statement saying that the actions of its officers were "not in accordance with our standard operating procedure." Two of the officers who dragged Dao off the plane were later fired.

Perhaps the most troubling part of Dao's story is that technically, United was within their rights to ask passengers to leave. Overbooking a flight is not illegal, and airlines are allowed to remove paying customers if they need an extra seat. But the Dao incident proves that within the airline industry, there is room for improvement.

PepsiCo's Epic Facepalm

If there's one American family that is no stranger to scandal and controversy, it's the Kardashian/Jenner clan. You name it, they've probably done/said/dated it. But out of the whole family, Kendall Jenner is perhaps the least controversial of the bunch, often keeping a much lower profile than her social media-obsessed sisters. She even describes herself as having a "shy personality," and says that she prefers to keep her love life out of the public spotlight, unlike the rest of her family. The model, entrepreneur, and photographer has managed to make a name for herself based mostly on her merits, without drawing too much negative attention. But that all changed in 2017, when Jenner starred in an ill-conceived commercial that had the internet in an uproar.

An Old Idea with a New Twist

Many of us remember the old Coca-Cola ad that debuted in 1971, which featured an internationally diverse group of people on a hilltop, singing, "I'd like to buy the world a Coke." The ad was a huge hit for Coca-Cola, and it has often been referenced and reused throughout the decades since it first aired. But its message of peace and inclusion was not appreciated universally. The then-apartheid South African government asked Coke to make a version of the ad without black singers. Coca-Cola refused, and the company later sold all of its holdings in South Africa. This little commercial became a symbol not only of hope for all mankind, but of standing up against injustice.

So, it's understandable that Coca-Cola's rival, PepsiCo, would want to try their own hand at releasing a commercial full of messages of hope and inclusion. And they attempted to do just that in April 2017, with an ad titled, "Live for Now." The commercial features a crowd of generic "protestors" flashing peace signs and holding placards that read, "Join the Conversation." Jenner's character—a model at a photoshoot—notices the marchers passing by and eventually decides to join them. The diverse group of protestors laughs, dances, and seems to have a good time, until they reach a line of police officers. Jenner then walks forward with a can of Pepsi, hands it to an officer, and when he drinks it, the crowd cheers, hugs, and high-fives. The ad ends with the phrases, "Live Bolder, Live Louder, Live for Now."

Social Media Backlash

The negative reaction to the ad was immediate, with many saying it co-opted imagery from protests like Black Lives Matter, women's marches, and travel ban protests and trivialized them. Others felt that the commercial brazenly stole ideas from BLM marches, including an iconic photo of Ieshia Evans standing before police in riot gear at a protest in Baton Rouge, Louisiana. The image of Jenner handing a police officer a can of Pepsi was strikingly similar. And still other viewers felt the commercial was merely silly, making light of serious issues and suggesting that race relations, violence, and argumentative views can find harmony through cans of soda.

Social media exploded with opinions and memes. Martin Luther King Jr.'s daughter Bernice tweeted, "If only Daddy would have known about the power of #Pepsi" alongside a photo of her father being held back by a police officer. And *HuffPost* editor Taryn Finley posted, "Y'all can go somewhere with this tone-deaf, shallow, and over-produced ad." Others criticized Jenner herself, such as Eric Thomas, a senior partner at Saga Marketing, who said, "A Caucasian, blond, classically beautiful, affluent kid born into celebrity probably isn't the person you need to represent struggle and civil unrest."

Jenner eventually addressed the controversy, saying she felt "stupid" for making the ad and insisting that she'd "never purposely hurt anyone." PepsiCo pulled the ad after a single day and released a statement expressing regret for the commercial, stating, "Pepsi was trying to project a global a message of unity, peace, and understanding. Clearly, we missed the mark, and we apologize. We did not intend to make light of any serious issue. We are pulling the content and halting any further rollout. We also apologize for putting Kendall Jenner in this position."

CHAPTER 7

CHEATERS, DOPERS, AND FIXERS

1919 World Series: It Ain't True, Is It?

Baseball's Golden Age was preceded by its darkest hour: the 1919 World Series fixing scandal in which Shoeless Joe Jackson emerged as a shameful symbol. Though acquitted by a jury, Jackson and his coconspirators were convicted in the court of public opinion and banned from baseball for life.

The *Chicago Herald and Examiner* described him as "a little urchin," the young lad who emerged from the crowd outside a Chicago courthouse on that September day in 1920 and was said to have grabbed Joe Jackson by the coat sleeve. The newspaper's report of the exchange went on:

"It ain't true, is it?" the lad said.

"Yes, kid, I'm afraid it is," Jackson replied.

"Well, I'd never have thought it," the boy exclaimed.

Nowhere did the newspaper report that the boy demanded, "Say it ain't so, Joe," although this version of the story became the standard that was passed down through the years among generations of baseball fans. Almost three decades later, a few years before his 1951 death, Jackson told *Sport Magazine* that the entire story was a fictional account, made up by a sportswriter. He said the only words exchanged on the way out of the courthouse that day were between him and a law enforcement officer. Had there been such a boy, Jackson added, he would have told him, "It ain't so, all right, just like I'm saying it now."

What is so is this: Members of the 1919 Chicago White Sox committed baseball's cardinal sin, deliberately losing the World Series to the Cincinnati Reds for pay. Eight members of that team, including the great and graceful "Shoeless" Joe Jackson, were banned from baseball for life for their part in the scandal.

Whispers Become a Roar

Two years after their 1917 world championship, the White Sox fielded a powerful team that took the American League pennant. The White Sox were favored to defeat Cincinnati in the World Series.

By all accounts, Sox infielder Chick Gandil was the ringleader among the "Black Sox"—the man who made contact with known gamblers and indicated that the Series could be thrown. He immediately involved 29-game-winner Eddie Cicotte, and others followed: Jackson, pitcher Claude Williams, infielders Buck Weaver and Swede Risberg, outfielder Oscar "Happy" Felsch, and utility man Fred McMullin. Some of the players would play lead parts in the fixing of games. Others, notably Weaver and some say Jackson, had knowledge of the plan but were not active participants.

When the Series began, the players were promised a total of $100,000 to throw the games. But by the time the Reds won the Series in eight games, the payout was considerably less, and whispers about what had taken place began swelling to a roar. Sportswriters speculated in print about a possible fix even before Cincinnati wrapped up the Series, but nobody wanted to believe it could be true. No official action was taken, however, until the following September.

The 1920 season began with rumors about gambling in other big-league dugouts. Something had to be done, and in September a grand jury convened to examine allegations of other instances of gambling in the game—and soon looked at the 1919 World Series as well. Eight White Sox players were called to testify, and several, including Jackson, admitted knowledge of the fix. All eight were indicted for conspiracy to defraud the public and injure "the business of Charles Comiskey and the American League." Although the group was acquitted due to lack of evidence when Jackson and Cicotte's testimony "disappeared," the damage had already been done in the form of huge black headlines across the country. Baseball, America's game, was facing its darkest hour.

A Crushing Blow

The Black Sox were not as fortunate on the scales of baseball justice as they had been in the court of law. Kenesaw Mountain Landis, baseball's newly appointed commissioner, suspended all eight players for life in an effort to restore credibility to the game. It was a crushing blow for Chicago and for Weaver and Jackson. While Gandil had received $35,000 and Cicotte $10,000 for the fix, Weaver received nothing. Actually, it was proven that he had turned down an invitation to participate in the scam. And Jackson, considered one of the greatest outfielders and hitters—and certainly one of the most sympathetic figures—in the history of the game, hit .375 with six RBI in the 1919 Series while playing errorless defense.

Many still clamor for Shoeless Joe to be enshrined in the Hall of Fame, arguing that his numbers support the claim that he did nothing to contribute to the fixing of the 1919 World Series. The $5,000 he accepted from the gamblers, however, nearly matched his $6,000 salary during that campaign and sealed his fate as a tragic figure in baseball's most infamous twentieth century scandal.

Say it ain't so, Joe.

Pete Rose: From Highest-Paid to Prison

The name Pete Rose is synonymous with the Cincinnati Reds, the team he managed and played with throughout most of his career. It's also synonymous with record-breaking feats: Rose holds Major League Baseball records for most career hits, singles, games played, at-bats, and plate appearances. He also earned three World Series rings, three batting titles, two Gold Glove awards, and 17 All-Star appearances. But there's one other word often associated with Pete Rose: gambling. And unfortunately, this is the legacy that frequently overshadows the player's athletic accomplishments.

A Stellar Career

Pete Rose played his first professional season with the Cincinnati Reds in 1963, when he was voted the National League Rookie of the Year. He was batting .312 by the 1965 season, and he spent 16 seasons batting at least .300. In 1979 he became the highest-paid athlete in team sports when the Philadelphia Phillies signed him to a four-year, $3.2 million contract, and in 1984 he briefly joined the Montreal Expos. It was during his stint with the Expos, on April 13, 1984, that Rose got his 4000th career hit.

After only 95 games with the Expos, Rose was traded back to the Reds, where he was named player-manager. He retired from playing in 1986, but he continued to manage the Reds for another three years, ending with a career managerial record of 412 wins and 373 losses.

A Career Gamble

In February 1989, Commissioner of Baseball Peter Ueberroth and National League President Bart Giamatti began questioning Rose about rumors that he had made bets on baseball. Rose denied the allegations, but in March of that year, *Sports Illustrated* published a detailed account of the unfolding scandal, and soon lawyer John M. Dowd was hired to conduct a formal investigation into the matter.

On June 27, 1989, the *Dowd Report*, a 225-page summary of the lawyer's findings, was published.

Along with the report, Dowd submitted bank and telephone records, betting records, expert testimony, and transcripts of interviews with Rose and other witnesses to Giamatti, who had replaced Ueberroth as Commissioner of Baseball. The report detailed Rose's alleged gambling activities between 1985 and 1987, including 52 games in 1987 where Rose bet between $2,000 and $10,000 a day. Even after the report's release, Rose continued to deny any wrongdoing; however, on August 24, he agreed to be placed on baseball's ineligible list. In return, the MLB agreed not to issue a formal finding regarding the gambling allegations. Tommy Helms replaced Rose as Reds manager, and soon after he began therapy for treatment of a gambling addiction.

One year later, Rose found himself in hot water again, this time for tax evasion. Rose was charged with filing false income tax returns that did not report income from selling autographs and memorabilia and from horse racing winnings. The ex-MLB star was sentenced to five months in prison and fined $50,000.

Coming Clean

It wasn't until Rose published his autobiography, *My Prison Without Bars*, that he finally admitted what seemed to be clear all along: he bet on baseball games while playing with and managing the Reds. He emphasized that he never bet *against* his team—he only bet for the Reds to win. Some fans felt that this was excusable; after all, he wasn't trying to throw games like the 1919 White Sox World Series scandal. He only wanted his team to win. But experts point out that even betting on a team to win can damage the integrity of the game. Especially since Rose did not bet on every single game—he bet on games in which he had the most confidence. Which meant that when he *didn't* bet on a game, it was a signal to other gamblers to bet against the Reds. And when he did bet on his team, he was more apt to change his managerial style for that particular game, in order to give himself the best chance of winning.

Over the years, Rose has made repeated attempts to be reinstated into MLB, but he so far has been denied. And because he is on the permanent ineligible list, he may not be inducted into the Baseball Hall of Fame, despite his many records. He was, however, inducted into the Cincinnati Reds Hall of Fame in 2016.

Southern Methodist University's Death Penalty

In the early 1980s, the Southern Methodist University Mustangs were a football powerhouse. Between 1981 and 1984, they had an impressive record of 41 wins, five losses, and one tie. This feat would've been admirable for any school, but it was especially notable for SMU, a tiny private school in Dallas with a total enrollment of less than 10,000 students. The university was seemingly undeterred by its small stature, holding its own against Southwest Conference giants like Texas and Arkansas. But the football world was about to find out that SMU's prowess wasn't created by chance, but rather by deliberate—and illegal—action.

The J.R. Ewing of Football

In the 1970s, SMU was popular enough—they attracted plenty of fans to their games, but the team wasn't taken as seriously as they wanted to be. So they hired Ron Meyer, the previous coach at the University of Nevada, Las Vegas. While at UNLV, Meyer had accrued a respectable 27-8 win-loss record. He was also determined and flashy, which SMU hoped would work in their favor.

And it certainly did: Meyer's aggressive recruiting strategy helped him procure some of the best football players in Texas. His brash but charming manner earned him many comparisons to *Dallas's* J.R. Ewing, and one after another, talented players signed on to the unassuming SMU. Former quarterback Lance McIlhenny has stated that Meyer was the "greatest salesman" he ever knew.

But the best college players in the state weren't necessarily signing up for SMU because of great sales tactics. Meyer's recruiting staff would often pay players, while Meyer looked the other way. Small incentives of $10 or $20 soon turned into hundreds of dollars, with some recruiters handing prospective players $100 dollar bills when meeting them for the first time.

Payments and Probation

In 1982, Meyer moved on to coach the New England Patriots, but his recruiting tactics were well established within the school by then. Eventually, the fact that unusually good players were signing on to SMU did not go unnoticed, and by 1985, investigations into recruiting practices resulted in three years' probation for the Mustangs. Probation was nothing new for the team: SMU had faced probation seven times—more than any other school in their division.

But the worst was yet to come for SMU: Two former Mustangs players—Sean Stopperich and David Stanley—came forward with information about SMU's recruiting methods, claiming that not only had they both been paid large sums of money but also that SMU maintained a "slush fund" to quietly pay players. The National Collegiate Athletic Association (NCAA) launched an investigation and discovered that between 1985 and 1986—while the school was in the midst of a three-year probation—SMU paid 13 players a total of $61,000 from this fund. The athletic department was well aware of this fund, but it allowed it to continue unabated, planning to secretly phase it out once the 13 players graduated.

Laying Down the Law

Due to SMU's repeat violations, they were shown no mercy by the NCAA, which instituted the "death penalty": this harsh penalty bans a school from competing in a sport for at least one year. The university's entire 1987 season was cancelled, and all of SMU's home games for 1988 were cancelled. In addition, their probation was extended until 1990, and the team was banned from bowl games and live television until 1989.

The scandal—and its death penalty—greatly damaged SMU's football program, leading to years of repairing and reworking the once mighty Mustangs. In 2009, the school won its first bowl game since 1984, with a 45-10 victory over the University of Nevada, Reno, in the Hawaii Bowl. Since then, they've appeared in a handful of bowl games over the years, as the modest little school slowly and steadily tries to rebuild itself to its former glory.

A Plot for Naught

January 6, 1994 started out as a normal day for figure skater Nancy Kerrigan. Preparing to skate at the U.S. Figure Skating Championships in Detroit, she put in some practice time on the rink at Cobo Arena and then left, walking out through a corridor. Suddenly, her "normal" day was anything but: an attacker viciously hit her in the leg with a metal baton, leaving her on the floor clutching her knee and wailing, "why?" And it was a good question: Why would anyone want to attack America's skating sweetheart?

Fierce Rivals

Kerrigan wasn't the only top skater in 1994. Her main rival was Tonya Harding, who'd been climbing the ranks in the skating world since the mid-1980s. Her defining year was 1991, when she became the first woman to land a triple axel in competition. Over the next few years, she developed a fierce rivalry with Kerrigan, and by 1994, the two were favored to be chosen for the Olympic team set to compete in Lillehammer, Norway. Was the attack on Kerrigan an attempt to knock her out of Olympic contention?

What Did Harding Know?

It didn't take long for investigators to find Kerrigan's attacker. He was identified as Shane Stant, who had followed Kerrigan to Detroit and waited for her in the arena corridor, ready to ambush. Soon after, it was discovered that Harding's ex-husband, Jeff Gillooly, and her bodyguard, Shawn Eckhardt, had hired Stant to carry out the attack on Kerrigan. At first, Harding insisted that she knew nothing about her ex-husband's plans, but Gillooly had another story to tell. He claimed that Harding was in on the plot from the beginning, and she even helped to schedule the attack. He showed authorities a scrap of paper on which Harding had written some of Kerrigan's practice times and locations, presumably to help Stant know exactly where he needed to go.

Even after the information came to light, Harding denied involvement in the attack. She did, however, change her story to say that she found out about Gillooly's actions *after* the fact and failed to report anything to authorities. On March 16, 1994, she pleaded guilty to conspiring to hinder prosecution of the attackers, and she received three years' probation, a $100,000 fine, and 500 hours of community service. She was also forced to resign from the U.S. Figure Skating Association, which banned her for life.

A Foiled Plot

After the investigation, one thing was clear: the attack on Kerrigan was meant to remove her from competition. Kerrigan's doctor told the *New York Times* that Stant "was clearly trying to debilitate her." Years after the attack, Stant was interviewed for sports site *Bleacher Report*, where he described how bodyguard Eckhardt's original plan involved cutting Kerrigan's Achilles tendon. Fortunately, Stant—who apparently had a bit of a conscience—refused to cut her, and instead decided on the "whack heard 'round the world."

While Kerrigan recovered from the attack, Harding won the U.S. Figure Skating Championships. And because the investigation into the Kerrigan attack was still ongoing, she secured a spot to the Olympics and was allowed to compete. But Kerrigan, who suffered only bruising to her knee, recuperated in time to take the second spot, and she ultimately won the silver medal that year. And Harding? A disappointing eighth place. What's more, she was forced to give up her 1994 U.S. Champion title. The entire plot, it turned out, was all for naught.

Mark McGwire and the Steroids Era

In 1961, Roger Maris of the New York Yankees hit 61 home runs in a single season, breaking Babe Ruth's 1927 record of 60. Maris's record would stand for the next 37 years, until two players—Mark McGwire of the St. Louis Cardinals, and Sammy Sosa of the Chicago Cubs—would race to become the new all-time leader. Both players broke Maris's record that year; but ultimately, it would be McGwire, with 70 home runs, who would claim the top spot.

But not long after McGwire's impressive feat, journalist Steve Wilstein wrote a story for the Associated Press that called McGwire's integrity into question and ended up turning the game of baseball on its head.

The Steroids Era

Wilstein's story, which was written with help from his colleague Nancy Armour, revealed that McGwire had been using a hormone called androstenedione during his years with Major League Baseball. The product was available over-the-counter as a "dietary supplement" and, at the time, was not prohibited by the MLB—although it was banned by the World Anti-Doping Agency, the NFL, and the International Olympic Committee. McGwire admitted to using the substance, but when questioned about other banned substances, he denied using anything illegal.

But Wilstein's story touched off an investigation into the use of performance-enhancing substances in the game of baseball, ushering in what would be known as the "Steroids Era." He continued to report on various allegations, and the information he uncovered eventually led to drug testing in the MLB for the first time. The U.S. Food and Drug Administration also banned androstenedione, and Congressional hearings resulted in the Anabolic Steroid Control Act of 2004.

An Apologetic Admission

Throughout it all, McGwire continued to insist that he had only taken androstenedione, and since it was perfectly legal at the time, he had done nothing wrong. In 2005, he was one of 11 baseball players subpoenaed to testify at a congressional hearing on steroids. McGwire declined to answer specific questions about his own steroid use, however, saying, "My lawyers have advised me that I cannot answer these questions without jeopardizing my friends, my family, and myself."

It wasn't until 2010 when McGwire decided to accept a position as hitting coach for the St. Louis Cardinals that his conscience caught up to him. He finally admitted to using illegal steroids on and off for a decade. Feeling remorseful, the former slugger personally called Commissioner of Baseball Bud Selig and Cardinals manager Tony La Russa to confess and apologize. He also made what must have been a difficult call to Roger Maris's widow, Pat Maris, to admit his wrongdoing.

McGwire is adamant that he still would have hit all of those home runs without the help of steroids, telling sportscaster Bob Costas during a 2010 interview that he "was given a gift to hit home runs." Still, when Costas pointed out that many members of Roger Maris's family still consider his 61 home runs the official record, a remorseful McGwire admitted, "They have every right to."

From Cheating Death to Cheating in Sport

If there's one thing that sports fans love, it's a good comeback story. So when cyclist Lance Armstrong fought his way back from a frightening cancer diagnosis and went on to win seven consecutive Tour de France races, even those who rarely watch the sport were cheering him on. His seemingly superhuman strength and indestructible spirit inspired fans around the globe. But as is often the case, things that seem too good to be true often are.

A Scary Setback

Armstrong began cycling at the age of 16, and he launched his professional career in 1992 when he joined the Motorola cycling team. He had some modest success over the next few years, winning individual stages in several Tour de France races, and coming in 36th in his first finished race. But in 1996, at the age of 25, Armstrong's career came to a sudden halt when he was diagnosed with an aggressive form of testicular cancer. By the time he was diagnosed, the disease had already spread to his lungs, abdomen, and brain, and it was so advanced that oncologists believed there was "almost no hope" that he could recover.

Armstrong immediately began treatment at the Indiana University medical center, which included strong chemotherapy drug cocktails and surgery to remove the lesions in his brain. Amazingly, after only a few months of treatment, Armstrong was declared cancer-free.

On Top of the World

In January 1998, less than a year after recovering from cancer, Armstrong was back to training, and he had a contract to cycle for the U.S. Postal team. He finished fourth in the Vuelta a Espana race that year, and he then headed strong into the 1999 Tour de France. In a foreshadowing of what was to come, Armstrong tested positive for a corticosteroid before the race; however, he was able to produce a doctor's certificate showing that the substance was an approved skin cream, and he was allowed to race. He won his first Tour de France that year.

The years that followed were the highlight of Armstrong's career, netting him seven consecutive Tour de France wins and a bronze medal at the 2000 Sydney Olympic Games. These would be impressive accomplishments for any athlete; but for Armstrong, who had at one time been at death's door, the wins seemed even more significant. His Lance Armstrong Foundation (now know as the Livestrong Foundation), which he established in 1997, inspired cancer survivors and athletes with its messages of strength and hope. The cyclist was a hero and a champion to millions.

Fallen from Grace

Armstrong's untarnished image would not last, however. In 2004, suspicions began to rise over his use of illegal substances when sports journalist Pierre Ballester and the *Sunday Times* correspondent David Walsh published a French-language book entitled *L.A. Confidential*. The book detailed allegations by Armstrong's former masseuse, Emma O'Reilly, who claimed that she was often sent on trips to pick up drugs and was asked to hide needle marks on his arms.

Armstrong retired from cycling in 2005 in order to spend more time with his family, but perhaps to also hide from the limelight. But it was no use: *L.A. Confidential* served to set off a chain reaction, as accusations of doping began to hit the cyclist from all sides. Multiple publications in the U.S. and France quoted sources as saying Armstrong used banned substances, which he repeatedly denied. But as the noose tightened, even Armstrong's former teammates began to share troublesome stories. His U.S. Postal teammate Floyd Landis said he witnessed Armstrong receiving blood transfusions and using testosterone patches. Another teammate, Tyler Hamilton, claimed that he and Armstrong had both taken a banned substance called erythropoietin. By 2012, the U.S. Anti-Doping Agency was investigating the claims against Armstrong, and after a long inquiry, they concluded that the cyclist was part of "the most sophisticated, professionalized and successful doping program that sport has ever seen."

Humiliated, Armstrong could do nothing but admit that the allegations were true. In January 2013, he appeared in an interview with Oprah Winfrey where he came clean about his doping past, even acknowledging that performance-enhancing drugs helped him win all seven Tour de France titles. The disgraced athlete was stripped of his seven titles and his Olympic bronze medal and banned for life from the sport he once loved. If Armstrong wanted to cheat, he should've stuck to cheating death.

Spygate

After the New England Patriots' "Deflategate" scandal in 2015, some football fans felt the controversy was (pardon the pun) overblown. Was it overkill to fine the team a million dollars and to suspend Tom Brady for four games? After all, it would seem that the final result would've been the same either way: the Patriots would win the game.

But some fans believe that the harsh penalties imposed for Deflategate were really more of an ongoing reminder to the Patriots that cheating of any kind will not be tolerated. Because eight years earlier, the New England Patriots were entangled in another cheating scandal—and this time, their actions could've clearly given them the upper hand.

Someone Is Watching Me

During a Sept. 9, 2007 game between the Patriots and the New York Jets, Jets head coach Eric Mangini told NFL security that he observed the Patriots filming from the sidelines during the game. Filming an opposing team's offensive or defensive signals is a violation of league rules, but Patriots head coach Bill Belichick claimed that he thought it was legal to film an opposing team as long as the film wasn't used during the game.

But the Patriots' methods went far beyond casual observation: according to an ESPN report, the team had an intricate system in place for spying on their opponents. Players were told to watch films of opposing teams' signals and memorize them, then watch the sidelines during a game and relay to coaches which signals were used. Some people within the Patriots organization would pose as members of the media and go to upcoming opponent's games to film from the sidelines, with excuses at the ready in case security got suspicious.

There were also allegations of Patriots employees stealing opposing teams' play sheets and playbooks, a practice which become so common that teams would often leave fake play sheets lying around. Even superstar quarterback Peyton Manning distrusted the Patriots: when playing on the Patriots' home turf at Gillette Stadium, Manning would leave the visitor's locker room to discuss any kind of plays or plans, for fear the room might be bugged.

Aftermath

Once Mangini helped to break the scandal, NFL Commissioner Roger Goodell fined Belichick $500,000 and the Patriots $250,000—a far cry from the cool million they'd later pay for Deflategate. Investigators then went to Gillette Stadium and found a room with "a library of scouting material containing videotapes of opponents' signals" plus "notes matching signals to plays." According to investigators, the library contained seven seasons of documentation. Strangely, though, Goodell had all of the evidence destroyed, a decision that some believed was to help out his good friend, Patriots owner Robert Kraft.

As with many NFL controversies, the wrongdoing may not be isolated to one team. Former Dallas Cowboys head coach Jimmy Johnson claims "a lot of teams are doing this." But the Patriots seem to have a penchant for getting caught with their hand in the cookie jar, so to speak. And while Patriots fans may find it unfair, other football fans just sit back and enjoy the show.

Bountygate

For sports stars, it's bad enough to cheat during games and events; using performance-enhancing drugs, illegal equipment, or running shady plays that escape the notice of referees can end up ruining careers and disappointing loyal fans. But between 2009 and 2011, the New Orleans Saints took cheating to a much more sinister level.

A Bounty of Suspicion

In the NFL, non-contract bonuses are referred to as "bounties"; but paying them out is frowned upon, and the NFL constitution specifically forbids bounties that are paid for on-field misconduct or any actions against individual players or teams. Supposedly, however, many teams maintain bounty programs anyway. Former NFL players claim that these programs have been around for decades, with anywhere from 30 to 40 percent of players participating at any given time. But for the most part, the players themselves maintain these bounty programs—a sort of informal betting system to which team coaches turn a blind eye.

But in 2009, after the Saints defeated the Minnesota Vikings in the National Football Conference (NFC) Championship game, Vikings players and coaches began voicing concerns that Saints players were deliberately attempting to injure Vikings quarterback Brett Favre. In fact, Vikings coach Brad Childress recalled at least 13 instances where he felt that Saints players had hit Favre harder than necessary. There was also some concern that the same thing had happened to Arizona Cardinals quarterback Kurt Warner a week earlier. The Saints went on to win the Super Bowl that year, but seeds of suspicion about the team's integrity had been planted.

Cheaters Never Win

During the 2010 offseason, an anonymous source contacted NFL officials and revealed that the suspicions were well-founded: not only had the Saints players been targeting Favre and Warner, but their attempts to knock the quarterbacks out of the game were part of a bounty program organized by Saints defensive coordinator Gregg Williams.

After a yearlong investigation, the NFL concluded that Williams had, in fact, created a bounty program when he joined the Saints in 2009, in an effort to make the team's defense more aggressive. There was also evidence that head coach Sean Payton knew about the program and tried to cover it up. The details of the program were disturbing: Williams and 22 of 27 Saints players took part, by pooling cash into a pot that was doled out depending on each player's performance. Knocking down a kick returner could earn a player $100. Causing an injury that resulted in an opposing player being carted off or carried away by a stretcher was worth $1,000. And if a player was so injured that they were unable to return for the rest of the game, whoever caused the injury was awarded $1,500. In a memo sent by the NFL to all 32 teams in the league, it was even revealed that Saints linebacker Jonathan Vilma offered $10,000 cash to any player who could knock Brett Favre out of the NFC Championship game. And Favre and Warner weren't the only specific players targeted: others included Green Bay Packers quarterback Aaron Rodgers and Seattle Seahawks quarterback Matt Hasselbeck.

Williams eventually issued a statement calling the bounty program "a terrible mistake," and he was indefinitely suspended. Payton was suspended for the entire 2012 season. And the New Orleans Saints were fined $500,000, hopefully convincing other teams to avoid negative controversy in the future.

Deflategate

Fans of football generally fall into one of two camps: New England Patriots fans, and fans who hate the New England Patriots. So when the Patriots played the Indianapolis Colts in an American Football Conference (AFC) Championship game in 2015, those in the former camp were thrilled with the Patriots' 45-7 win over the Colts. Those in the latter camp, however, smelled something fishy about the New England Patriots, and it wasn't the region's famed clam chowder.

Rules of the Game

First, a few details about NFL rules: Each team provides a dozen balls to the referee two hours and fifteen minutes before the game. The home team also provides 12 backup balls, and the visiting team can bring an extra dozen if the game is played outdoors. There are also eight balls sent directly from Wilson, the ball manufacturer, to the referee, which are each marked with a "K" and used for kicking. The balls should be inflated to a pressure of between 12.5 and 13.5 pounds per square inch, and should weigh between 14 and 15 ounces. Oh, and each ball should be a natural tan-colored prolate spheroid—which basically means that they should be brown and shaped like footballs.

Prior to 2006, NFL rules stated that the home team provided all of the footballs used in a game. Now, however, each team uses its own balls, and the only time an opposing team handles the other team's football is in the case of recovering a fumble or interception.

Letting the Air Out

And it was an interception that launched the Deflategate controversy: Colts linebacker D'Quell Jackson intercepted a ball thrown by Patriots quarterback Tom Brady, and he gave the ball to an equipment manager so he could later keep it for a souvenir. What happened next isn't entirely clear, but in the vein of "heard it from a friend of a friend" the officials on the field were informed—possibly by NFL director of football operations Mike Kensil, who heard it from Colts general manager Ryan Grigson, who heard it from head coach Chuck Pagano—that some of the Patriots' footballs were underinflated. During halftime, the referees tested the balls, and 11 of the 12 Patriots' footballs were found to be about two pounds per square inch under regulation. The balls were then inflated to their proper pressure, and the game continued.

But that didn't stop the controversy. The media had a field day once it caught wind of the deflation allegation, and football fans across the country decried the suspected cheaters. Patriots players and coaches, including Brady and head coach Bill Belichick, insisted they knew nothing about the air pressure in the footballs and found the accusations "ridiculous." But after an investigation, the NFL decided that there was enough evidence to show that Brady and others within the organization knew about the deflated footballs. The Patriots were fined $1 million, and Brady was suspended for four games.

Did It Really Matter?

So what's the big deal about underinflated footballs, anyway? Supposedly, a football with less air in it is easier to grip and throw than a fully inflated ball. And the AFC Championship game was played in cold and rainy weather, which would have made an easier-to-handle ball even more advantageous. However, 28 of the Patriots' 45 points in the AFC Championship game came in the second half, after the balls had been re-inflated, so ultimately, it didn't seem to make a difference. Interestingly, even Jackson, who caught the original ball that launched the controversy, said he didn't even notice that anything was off about the football. "I definitely wouldn't be able to tell if one ball had less pressure than another," he said. "I wouldn't know how that could even be an advantage or a disadvantage." But to those fans eager to watch the downfall of the New England Patriots, their guilt is clear.

CHAPTER 8

HOLLYWOOD HEADACHES AND HEARTBREAKS

When Celebs Go Bad!

Back in the day, celebrities were publicly pilloried for their bad behavior. Today, a well-publicized arrest and brief stint in jail might seem like a smart career move. Here are just a few of the rich and famous who have had brushes with the law.

Ozzy Osbourne

In 1982, the Black Sabbath front man and reality TV superstar angered Texans everywhere by drunkenly urinating on a wall at the Alamo. Osbourne was banned from the city of San Antonio for a decade but later made amends by donating $20,000 to the Daughters of the Republic of Texas to help restore the fabled landmark.

Matthew McConaughey

In October 1999, following a noise complaint, McConaughey was found by police sitting naked in his home playing the bongos. The cops also found the actor's stash, which led to McConaughey being arrested for marijuana possession and resisting arrest. The drug charges were dropped, and the actor was fined $50 for violating a municipal noise ordinance.

Winona Ryder

In December 2001, Ryder was nabbed for shoplifting merchandise at the ritzy Saks Fifth Avenue store in Beverly Hills. She was convicted of grand theft and vandalism but received a relatively light sentence: three years probation and 480 hours of community service and restitution.

Nicole Richie

In February 2003, the daughter of singer Lionel Richie was charged with heroin possession and driving with a suspended license. Three years later, she was arrested again for driving under the influence. Her sentence: four days in jail. Actual time served: 82 minutes.

Natasha Lyonne

Known for such films as *Slums of Beverly Hills* (1998) and *American Pie* (1999), Lyonne was arrested in December 2004 after verbally attacking her neighbor, breaking the neighbor's mirror, and threatening to harm the neighbor's dog. A warrant was issued for the troubled actress in April 2005 for failure to appear before a judge, and a second warrant was issued in January 2006. In December 2006, Lyonne was finally sentenced to a conditional discharge.

Paris Hilton

Over the years, Hilton has been charged with a variety of crimes, including driving under the influence of alcohol and driving with a suspended license (twice). In June 2007, the hard-partying hotel heiress finally received her due when she was sentenced to 45 days in jail, though she was quickly released because of an undisclosed medical condition. Instead of doing her time in the slammer, Hilton was given 40 days house arrest with a monitoring device.

Lindsay Lohan

In July 2007, police found the former child star in a Santa Monica parking garage engaged in a heated argument with a former assistant.

She failed a sobriety test, and police also found a small amount of cocaine on her person. Lohan pleaded guilty to cocaine possession and driving under the influence and was sentenced to one day in jail, community service, and three years probation. Actual time spent behind bars: 84 minutes.

Bill Murray

In 2007, during a trip to Sweden, the former *Ghostbuster* and *Saturday Night Live* funnyman was charged with driving under the influence—while driving a golf cart. He refused to take a breath test but signed a document saying he had been driving drunk. He was allowed to leave the country without punishment.

The Hollywood Sign Girl

In the 1930s, Millicent Lilian "Peg" Entwistle was a young, aspiring actress in New York when she was lured to Hollywood by two West Coast producers, Homer Curran and Edward Belasco, who asked Entwistle to costar in their play, *The Mad Hopes*. With dreams of finally hitting the big time, Entwistle moved to Hollywood. Although the play was a success, it closed on schedule on June 4, 1932, at which time Entwistle signed a one-movie deal with RKO Pictures and began working on the film *Thirteen Women* (1932).

Several months later, test screenings for the film produced very negative comments, many of which were directed at Entwistle. RKO held back the film from general release while the director heavily edited the movie, deleting many of Entwistle's scenes in the process. According to those close to her, Entwistle took this to mean that she was a failure and would never succeed in Hollywood.

On Friday, September 16, 1932, Entwistle said she was going to meet some friends, but instead, she made her way to the top of Mount Lee. After placing her personal belongings at the base of the Hollywood sign, she used a workman's ladder to climb to the top of the "H" and jumped to her death. She was only 24 years old. The suicide note found in her purse read simply:

"I am afraid I am a coward. I am sorry for everything. If I had done this a long time ago, it would have saved a lot of pain. P.E."

Thirteen Women officially opened after Entwistle's death, and while it did not get good reviews, her name was never mentioned. Her uncle speculated to the press after her death that she was disappointed by not being able to impress the movie industry, and the rumors spiraled from there. The real cause of her decision to end her life remains a mystery, but to this day, Entwistle's suicide symbolizes Hollywood's ability to smash the dreams of so many aspiring actors and actresses.

A Law for the Future Uncle Fester

As the bizarre and bald member of *The Addams Family* TV series (1964—1966), the frighteningly adorable Uncle Fester charmed fans young and old. This was nothing new; actor Jackie Coogan had been wowing audiences since childhood.

Born John Leslie Coogan, little Jackie was the son of vaudevillians, who, like many, spent their careers on the road, families in tow, traveling the different theater circuits, much like musical acts do today. Many vaudevillian families incorporated their children into their acts, with little thought to their suitability for such a life or their long-term educations. Charlie Chaplin caught Jackie's act in Los Angeles and was so impressed that he cast the boy in a comedy short called *A Day's Pleasure* (1919). This association with Chaplin led to his first feature role in the classic *The Kid* (1921).

Appearing in popular silent films such as *The Kid and Oliver Twist* (1922) cemented the child actor's status. The cute kid with the pageboy haircut raked in a whopping $4 million before his 18th birthday, making him one of Hollywood's highest paid performers of the time. Clearly, the only thing small about Coogan was his stature.

Despite ruling the popularity roost, Coogan found his financial state far from secure. His parents had complete control of his holdings, but tragically for Jackie, his parents didn't have his best interests in mind. Through a combination of greed and ineptness, the dastardly duo drove Jackie Coogan Productions straight into the ground. After a 1935 accident claimed the life of his father, a grown-up Coogan realized what had happened, but the damage had already been done. After suing the family company to reclaim his earnings in 1938, Coogan would recoup just $126,000. The sum represented one-half of the floundering firm's remaining value.

Coogan's predicament made headlines and caused people to question how such a travesty could happen. To spare other child actors a similar plight, in 1939, California enacted the California Child Actor's Bill (aka the Coogan Act), which directs a portion of a child actor's earnings into a trust fund. The sweeping law came too late for a young Jackie Coogan, but at least the child star's loss had not been in vain.

The Sex-sational Trial of Errol Flynn

When a handsome leading man was charged with rape, his status in Hollywood was in doubt. But rather than signaling his end in the business, his popularity soared ever higher.

The saying "In like Flynn" means little these days, but during the 1940s, it was used to compliment one who was doing exceedingly well. More to the point, it usually referred to sexual conquests made by a lucky "man about town."

The saying originated with Hollywood heartthrob Errol Flynn (1909—1959), the swashbuckling star of *Captain Blood* (1935) and *The Adventures of Robin Hood* (1938). A "man's man" in the most cocksure sense, Flynn was known for his barroom brawls and trysts both on camera and off, which became part of his star image. He wore this colorful mantle like a badge of honor, but he did hit a rough patch in life when he was charged with two counts of statutory rape.

Swashbuckling Seducer

The alleged crimes took place during the summer of 1942. In one instance, 17-year-old Betty Hansen claimed that Flynn had seduced her after she became ill from imbibing at a Hollywood party. In the other, 15-year-old Peggy Satterlee insisted that Flynn took advantage of her on his yacht, *The Sirocco*, during a trip to Catalina Island. Both women claimed that he referred to them by the nicknames "S.Q.Q." (San Quentin Quail) and "J.B." (Jail Bait), thereby suggesting that Flynn knew that they were under age. Flynn was arrested that fall and charged with two counts of rape. Proclaiming his innocence, he hired high-powered attorney Jerry Giesler, who called the women's motives and pasts into question and stacked the jury with nine females in the hopes that Flynn's considerable charm might win them over. The move would prove prophetic.

Women of Questionable Character

When the defense presented its case, Giesler went directly for the jugular. His cross-examination revealed that both women had engaged in sexual relations before the alleged incidents with Flynn and that Satterlee had even had an abortion. Even more damning, Satterlee admitted to frequently lying about her age and was inconsistent in a number of her answers. Suddenly, the veneer of innocence that the women had hoped to project was stripped away.

There was also Satterlee's claim that Flynn had taken her below deck to gaze at the moon through a porthole. Giesler challenged the expert testimony of an astronomer hired by the prosecution, getting the man to admit that, given the boat's apparent course, such a view was physically impossible through the porthole in Flynn's cabin.

The Verdict

By the time Flynn took the stand, the members of the all-female jury were half won over by his charm. By the time he finished arguing his innocence, their minds were made up. The effect was not at all surprising for a man whom actress and eight-time costar Olivia de Havilland once described as " . . . the handsomest, most charming, most magnetic, most virile young man in the entire world."

When a verdict of "not guilty" was read, women in the courtroom applauded and wept. Afterward, the jury forewoman noted: "We felt there had been other men in the girls' lives. Frankly, the cards were on the table and we couldn't believe the girls' stories."

Continued Fortune in a Man's World

Cleared of all charges, Errol Flynn continued to make movies, resumed his carousing ways, and grew even more popular in the public eye. Many felt that, despite the verdict, Flynn had indeed had sexual relations with the young women, but most were willing to forgive the transgression because the liaisons seemed consensual and the allegations of rape looked like little more than a frame job.

Young men would regard the amorous actor as an ideal to emulate, and women would continue to swoon as always. But years of hard living eventually took their toll on Flynn. By the time he reached middle age, his looks had all but vanished. At the age of 50, Flynn suffered a massive heart attack and died. Death only served to cement Flynn's legendary status amongst Hollywood's great actors and its rapscallions alike.

Trouble for the Prince of Noir

Robert Mitchum was the original off-screen bad boy before James Dean ever appeared on the scene. He defined cool before Hollywood knew the hip meaning of the word. He was rugged, handsome, and jaunty. A hobo turned actor, he was the antithesis of the typical movie hero—and he was on his way to becoming a star, primarily in film noir. Then it happened: A drug bust with a buxom blonde, and Mitchum was in the headlines in a way he never intended. Ironically, this incident accelerated his stardom.

In August 1948, Hollywood tabloids were emblazoned with headlines proclaiming the scandalous drug bust (for possession of marijuana) of actor Robert Mitchum, who was in the company of 20-year-old aspiring actress Lila Leeds. This was the era of marijuana frenzy: The government was at war with marijuana users, and propaganda, entrapment, blatant lies, and excessive punishments were just a few of the weapons they used. Mitchum was the perfect whipping boy. The actor was no stranger to pot and hashish, having experimented with both as a teenage hobo riding the rails. He was also a fugitive from the law, having escaped from a Georgia chain gang after being arrested for vagrancy in Savannah at age 16. Despite hiring Jerry Giesler, Hollywood's hottest defense attorney, Mitchum was found guilty and was sentenced to 60 days on a prison farm. His "I don't give a damn" smirk when his sentence was pronounced would define the attitude of the drug culture that burst upon the scene as the 1940s came to a close.

A Career Ruined?

When Mitchum was sentenced, he was earning $3,000 a week—a princely sum at the time. He was married to his childhood sweetheart, Dorothy Spence, and was in the midst of a seven-year contract with RKO studios. When the tabloids ran a picture of inmate 91234 swabbing the jail corridors in prison attire, Mitchum anticipated it would be "the bitter end" of his career and his marriage. In reality, the publicity had the opposite effect. With the exception of becoming a small embarrassment to the studio and causing the cancellation of a speech Mitchum was scheduled to deliver to a youth group, the actor's off-screen bad-boy persona had little negative effect on his career or personal life. If anything, it only added to his counterculture, tough-guy, antihero image.

Great PR

While Mitchum served his 60-day sentence on the honor farm (which he described as "Palm Springs without the riff-raff"), RKO released the already-completed film *Rachel and the Stranger* (1948). Not only did movie audiences stand and cheer when Mitchum appeared on the screen, the low-budget movie also became the studio's most successful film of the year.

In 1950, another judge reviewed Mitchum's conviction and reversed the earlier court decision because the arrest smelled of entrapment: Leeds's Laurel Canyon bungalow had been bugged by two overly ambitious narcotics agents. The judge changed Mitchum's plea to not guilty and expunged the conviction from his records—not that Mitchum appeared to care one way or the other. By then, he was a bona fide Hollywood star.

A Long and Successful Livelihood

Mitchum enjoyed an illustrious career, making more than 70 films, some to critical acclaim. He also enjoyed success as a songwriter and singer, with three songs hitting the best-seller charts. His marriage remained intact for 57 years, possibly a Hollywood record. He earned a star on the Hollywood Walk of Fame along with several other prestigious industry awards. Not a bad lifetime of achievements for a vagabond fugitive from a chain gang. Often seen with a cigarette dangling from his sensual lips, Mitchum died of lung cancer and emphysema on July 1, 1997, at his home in Santa Barbara, California. He was 79 years old.

Love on the Set: The Bergman-Rossellini Scandal

It didn't take much to rock the staid conventions of society in the 1950s. A director and his leading lady found that out the hard way.

It began with a fan letter sent in 1949. "I saw your films . . . and enjoyed them very much," the letter began. It was addressed to Italian filmmaker Roberto Rossellini and was written by none other than actress Ingrid Bergman, who wrote it after seeing his movie *Open City* (1945). Bergman's letter also suggested that he direct her in a film. Their resulting collaboration was 1950's *Stromboli*, but the movie was eclipsed by the controversy that swirled around the couple when word got out that the married Bergman was having a baby by Rossellini, who was also married. The ensuing scandal engulfed Bergman in a scarlet torrent of hatred so vitriolic that she would find herself branded on the floor of the U.S. Senate as "a horrible example of womanhood and a powerful influence for evil."

A Hollywood Success Story

Since taking America by storm in *Intermezzo: A Love Story* (1939), the talented Swedish-born Bergman had costarred with Humphrey Bogart in *Casablanca* (1942), been menaced by Charles Boyer in *Gaslight* (1944), and been romanced on-screen by Cary Grant, Gary Cooper, and Gregory Peck. Audiences loved her in strong but pious roles such as the nun in *The Bells of St. Mary's* (1945). In fact, Bergman had been Hollywood's top box office female draw three years in a row. To the public, the beautiful actress with the sunny smile had it all: a fabulous career, an adoring husband, and a devoted daughter. But privately, Bergman's marriage had entered rocky shoals, and she was looking for new acting challenges after the failure of her pet film project, *Joan of Arc* (1948). Consequently, the idea of working with Rossellini—a director being hailed for his mastery of what would come to be called

Italian neorealist cinema—was appealing. Bergman later admitted, "I think that deep down I was in love with Roberto from the moment I saw *Open City*."

On Location

Stromboli was filmed on location in Italy, and rumors of an affair between Bergman and Rossellini soon reached America. During filming, Bergman received a letter from Joseph Breen, head of America's stentorian Production Code office—which enforced morality in motion pictures—asking her to deny rumors of the affair. Instead, on December 13, 1949, the woman who had played a nun and other saintly figures admitted she was carrying Rossellini's love child. A firestorm of negative publicity followed the announcement.

Bergman was reproached by Roman Catholic priests and received thousands of letters denouncing her; she was even warned not to return to America. On February 2, 1950, Bergman and Rossellini's son, Robertino, or Robin, was born. Less than two weeks later, *Stromboli* was released in the United States to disastrous reviews and very little business.

The Storm Grows

The scandal reached critical mass (and the height of lunacy) on March 14, when Senator Edwin C. Johnson railed against Bergman on the Senate floor. Johnson proposed a bill that would protect America from the scourge that film stars of questionable "moral turpitude," such as Bergman, threatened. He suggested future misconduct could be avoided if actors were required to be licensed, with the license being revoked for salacious behavior. Though this idea was met with derision, Bergman's career in Hollywood was all but dead.

After divorcing their spouses, Bergman and Rossellini wed in Mexico on May 24, 1950. The couple continued to make films together in Italy and had twin girls Isabella (who went on to her own film stardom) and Isotta Ingrid in 1952. By the time Bergman was hired to star in *Anastasia* in 1956, America was ready to forgive her, and the actress was rewarded with both the New York Film Critics Award and her second Best Actress Oscar. By that point, her marriage to Rossellini—tested by financial problems and the director's affair while making a film in India—was nearing an end.

Bergman would go on to another marriage and further acclaim in her career, but she was always quick to point to the importance of her relationship with Rossellini, and the two remained devoted. Bergman died of breast cancer in 1982 on her 67th birthday.

Scandalous Hollywood: Roman Polanski

In 1969, director Roman Polanski was in the news when his pregnant wife, actress Sharon Tate, was brutally murdered by the followers of Charles Manson. Eight years later, Polanski made headlines again, this time for a scandal of his own.

In 1977, the famed director of movies such as *Rosemary's Baby* (1968) and *Chinatown* (1974) was hired to photograph 13-year-old aspiring model Samantha Geimer for *Vogue* magazine. Allegedly, 43-year-old Polanski plied the girl with champagne and anti-anxiety medication and then had sex with her. As part of a plea bargain, Polanski pleaded guilty to unlawful sexual intercourse, and, in exchange, prosecutors dropped other charges such as furnishing a controlled substance to a minor.

Initially, the judge ordered a 90-day jail term for the director to undergo a psychiatric evaluation. He was officially released after 42 days. Polanski's lawyers expected he would receive probation at sentencing, but they got wind that the judge was going to suggest imprisonment and possible deportation. So prior to sentencing, where he faced up to 50 years in jail, Polanski skipped bail. The filmmaker, who was still a French citizen, relocated to Paris, where under French law he was safe from extradition to the United States. Because he fled before sentencing, the original charges remained pending.

Despite frequent legal attempts to dismiss the case, Polanski remained a fugitive and lived in self-imposed exile from the United States for more than 30 years. When he won the Best Director Oscar for *The Pianist* in 2003, actor Harrison Ford collected the award at the ceremony on his behalf.

Then in September 2009, Polanski was arrested when he entered Switzerland to accept a lifetime achievement award at the Zurich International Film Festival. He spent two months in a Swiss jail, until late November when he was released after paying $4.5 million bail. Polanski was placed on house arrest at his luxurious Swiss chalet and was required to wear a monitoring bracelet. U.S. authorities continue their efforts to get Polanski extradited, while his lawyers attempt to get the case dismissed.

A Comedian's Tragic End

John Belushi was a 1970s comedy icon. An alumnus of Chicago's Second City comedy club and one of the original cast members of *Saturday Night Live*, he is probably best known for his partnership with Dan Aykroyd and their characters Jake and Elwood Blues. Their soul music band, The Blues Brothers, started out as a musical sketch on *SNL* but later took on a life of its own, eventually spawning the cult classic movie *The Blues Brothers*. But Belushi was known for more than just his comedic timing and singing ability. A heavy drug user, he was fired and rehired from *SNL* several times due to his unpredictable behavior, and his partying and drug use often caused delays and tensions on movie sets.

Gone too Soon

On March 5, 1982, Belushi's personal trainer, Bill Wallace, arrived at the Chateau Marmont Hotel in Hollywood for a scheduled workout with the star, but Wallace tragically found the 33-year-old dead from a drug overdose. Belushi had cocaine and heroin in his system—a concoction known as a "speedball"—and his death was officially ruled an accident. But was there more to the story?

In the early morning hours before he died, Belushi had several visitors, including actors Robin Williams and Robert De Niro and a friend named Catherine Evelyn Smith. Smith was not only a heavy drug user herself, but she also provided drugs to some big names in the entertainment industry, including Keith Richards of the Rolling Stones. Belushi asked Smith to bring the drugs that night, and she obliged. Reportedly, Robin Williams was still in Belushi's bungalow when Smith arrived, and the actor was unsettled by her presence, calling her a "lowlife."

A Shocking Admission

After Belushi's death, police questioned Smith, and she even voluntarily turned over drug paraphernalia, but she was later released. Her lawyer then advised her to hide out in St. Louis to avoid the press. But when reporters managed to track her down, she flew back to Los Angeles, and she eventually fled to her hometown of Toronto. It was there, as she tried to lay low in another country, that Smith spoke with two *National Enquirer* reporters, Tony Brenna and Larry Haley. The journalists published an article in which they quoted Smith as saying, "I killed John Belushi. I didn't mean to, but I am responsible."

Smith admitted that she not only supplied the drugs that killed Belushi, but she herself injected him with 11 speedballs. According to the medical examiner, this was enough to kill even a healthy man, and Belushi was far from healthy—the comedian suffered from pulmonary congestion, a swollen heart, a swollen liver, and obesity, just to name a few of his many ailments.

Lesson Learned?

The *Enquirer* story caught the attention of Los Angeles police, who reopened the Belushi case. Smith was extradited from Canada and charged with second-degree murder, but she accepted a plea bargain that brought the charges down to involuntary manslaughter and drug charges. She served 15 months in prison and afterwards was deported to Canada, where she spent time lecturing school kids on the dangers of drugs. Unfortunately, she didn't take heed of her own lesson, and in 1991 was arrested in Vancouver, British Columbia, when she was found to have heroin in her purse.

Madonna's 1989 Hit: Brilliance or Blasphemy?

Burning crosses, saintly eroticism, stigmata, and scandalous dancing: Madonna's 1989 music video had it all.

That video in question, "Like a Prayer," would go on to become one of the most successful—and controversial—music videos of all time. It would also help cement the pop star's reputation as a legendary cultural icon. But it would take a helping of raised eyebrows and moral outrage from some quarters before Madonna crossed the bridge of musical immortality.

Brilliance or Blasphemy?

Madonna debuted the song "Like a Prayer" in a two-minute television commercial in March 1989. PepsiCo paid the star $5 million to appear in the commercial where Madonna travels back to her eighth birthday. The next day, Madonna released the music video to the song.

In the video, Madonna witnesses the robbery and murder of a woman by a group of men. Police mistakenly arrest an African American man for the murder after the men flee the scene. Madonna enters a church and finds a caged saint statue that resembles the innocent man; the statue then metamorphoses into him. He kisses Madonna's forehead and leaves the church. Dreamy images of burning crosses and risqué dancing follow, and Madonna ultimately finds the courage to enter the jail and secure the man's release.

The video, unsurprisingly, drew outrage from religious organizations, including the Vatican, which called it "blasphemy." Pepsi executives were not aware about the video's eroticism, and the ensuing controversy prompted Pepsi to cancel the $5 million ad campaign featuring the song and pop singer.

Pepsi said it canceled the commercial because consumers thought the video was part of the Pepsi ad, not because of boycott calls from religious groups. "When you've got an ad that confuses people or concerns people, it just makes sense that that ad goes away," a company spokesperson said.

A Case for Controversy

Madonna, however, still kept her money. And the video—and Madonna's reputation—ultimately succeeded.

"When I left home at 17 and went to New York, which is the city with the most sinners, I renounced the traditional meaning of Catholicism in terms of how I would live my life," Madonna told the *New York Times* in March 1989, shortly after the video's release.

Rolling Stone's J.D. Considine said the song "seems at first like a struggle driven by a jangling, bass-heavy funk riff and framed by an angelic aura of backing voices." The pop singer, Considine said, "stokes the spiritual fires with a potent, high-gloss groove that eventually surrenders to gospel abandon."

And writing about the song and video for the *Los Angeles Times*, Chris Willman said Madonna "wants to show that she can amply display her hourglass figure and still be a complete innocent, guiltlessly joining a choir in a place of worship at the happy finale with a childlike glee."

Madonna summarized her view about art and commerce in that March 1989 interview with the *Times*.

"Art should be controversial, and that's all there is to it."

And the Oscar Goes to . . . ?

In 1992, when the relatively unknown Marisa Tomei won an Oscar for Best Supporting Actress, she had little reason to celebrate. The media reported that she'd received it by mistake.

Poor Marisa Tomei. Winning an Academy Award is supposed to be the highlight of any actor's career. But when she picked up the 1992 Oscar for her portrayal of Mona Lisa Vito in the comedy *My Cousin Vinny*, rumors immediately began to circulate that presenter Jack Palance had read the wrong name at the podium.

A Peculiar Presenter

Palance has a peculiar history at the Oscars. In 1991, at the age of 73, he won the Best Supporting Actor award for his role as Curly in the Billy Crystal comedy *City Slickers*. Up on stage, he memorably celebrated the win by dropping to the floor and performing one-handed push-ups. Such eccentric behavior probably contributed to the idea that, when asked to return the following year as a presenter, he could have announced the wrong person as the winner. In fact, when he read the names of nominees for the Best Supporting Actress category, he mistakenly called Judy Davis "Joan" Davis.

Upset about the Upset

Tomei, though inexperienced, was up against acting stalwarts who were nominated for their roles in much more critically acclaimed films. Along with Judy Davis in *Husbands and Wives*, the nominees were Joan Plowright for *Enchanted April*, Vanessa Redgrave for *Howards End*, and Miranda Richardson for *Damage*. It was understandably perceived to be a huge upset when Tomei won. But it wasn't a mistake. At every Oscar ceremony, the accounting firm

PricewaterhouseCoopers (which collates the results) stations two employees in the wings with instructions to immediately correct a presenter if an error is made.

The Curse of Billy Bob Thornton

By and large, actors tend to be a pretty superstitious bunch. Even so, if you're an aspiring actor and are offered a role in a Hollywood movie, you might want to scan the cast list just to make sure Billy Bob Thornton's name isn't on it. If it is, consider passing on the role because, according to a bizarre legend, Billy Bob Thornton is cursed, and sharing a scene with him might cause injury and even death.

Origins of a Curse

No one's really sure when the Billy Bob curse originated, but most believe it first reared its ugly head right around the time Thornton hit it big in the film industry with the release of *Sling Blade* (1996), which he wrote, directed, and starred in. On February 27, 1998, less than two years after costarring in the hit film with Thornton, actor J. T. Walsh died suddenly of a heart attack at age 54.

Though many knew him only as a character named Ernest, actor Jim Varney was always looking for roles that would expand his acting repertoire. And so, in the late 1990s, Varney signed on for a role in *Daddy and Them* (2001), another film that Thornton wrote, directed, and starred in. Varney completed the film but died of lung cancer on February 10, 2000, before the movie was released.

Curse Schmurse

Curse or no curse, as the twenty-first century began, Thornton decided to focus on his acting and put writing and directing on the back burner. In late 2002, he took the lead role in *Bad Santa*, which was set for a

Christmas 2003 release. John Ritter, one of Thornton's costars in the movie, would not live to see its debut, though, as he died unexpectedly from an aortic dissection on September 11, 2003.

On January 22, 2008, the world mourned the loss of 28-year-old actor Heath Ledger, who died tragically of an accidental drug overdose. Curse believers were quick to point out that Ledger and Thornton had worked together on the Oscar-nominated movie *Monster's Ball* (2001).

Then, in the summer of 2008, *Bad Santa* became the first movie to claim two victims from the alleged curse when, in addition to John Ritter, actor Bernie Mac died at age 50 from complications from pneumonia.

Another recent victim of the Billy Bob curse was actress Natasha Richardson, who costarred with Thornton in 2002's *Waking Up in Reno*. On March 18, 2009, Richardson died suddenly of an epidural hematoma after falling while skiing. She was 45 years old.

Last and certainly not least is actor Patrick Swayze, who also shared the screen with Thornton in *Waking Up in Reno*. Swayze passed away on September 14, 2009, at age 57, after a battle with pancreatic cancer.

Is the Curse Losing Strength?

Obviously, not everyone who has been involved in a Billy Bob Thornton movie has met an untimely death. So even if Thornton is indeed cursed, a few lucky actors have managed to work with him and live to tell the tale.

For example, in July 2008, rising star Shia LaBeouf—Thornton's costar in *Eagle Eye* (2008)—was involved in an auto accident during which the vehicle he was traveling in flipped upside down and landed on its roof. LaBeouf walked away from the accident with only minor injuries.

The following month, actor Morgan Freeman, who costarred with Thornton in the film *Levity* (2003), was involved in a serious car accident in Mississippi. Freeman's injuries were critical enough that he had to be airlifted to a hospital, but he made a full recovery.

So what does Billy Bob think of this alleged curse? So far, he isn't talking, but he's probably not worried about it. After all, the curse would have to be pretty powerful to shake a man who survived a marriage to Angelina Jolie.

During his short-lived romance with Angelina Jolie, Thornton and his beloved actually wore vials of each other's blood around their necks as a symbol of their devotion to each other.

Hollywood Drops the Ball

It's hard not to like a sports movie, even if you're not into sports. However, when a movie is based on a historic sporting event or a real athlete, sometimes the filmmakers take dramatic license to make a more logical story, to suggest a moral, or even for legal reasons. Here are some all-star sports movies that stand out for fumbling a few details.

Knute Rockne All American (1940)

Remembered for Ronald Reagan's portrayal of George "The Gipper" Gipp and Pat O'Brien's performance as Knute Rockne, this one has plenty of heart, even if some of the facts are a bit clouded, such as Rockne's role in developing the forward pass. Although he may have popularized it, it had been used before Knute hit the gridiron. Likewise,

Gipp's famous deathbed speech, in which he urges Rockne to "Tell them to win one for the Gipper," was most likely an inspiring fabrication.

Pride of the Yankees (1942)

Long before the TV movie Brian's Song made it OK for men to cry during a movie, the story of Lou Gehrig told what it was like to be "the luckiest man on the face of the earth." This film also went to great lengths to get the facts straight, including having right-handed Gary Cooper wear a uniform with the letters reversed to depict the lefty slugger Gehrig and then reversing the film during processing. However, there were notable departures, including the fact that the final speech was heavily rearranged for dramatic effect. In reality, Gehrig ended with the famous line rather than beginning with it.

Chariots of Fire (1981)

This film took the Oscar for Best Picture for its portrayal of the 1924 Summer Olympics in Paris, but it also took liberties with the accuracy of events. In real life, Eric Liddell knew months in advance that the preliminary heats in his main event would be held on a Sunday, and teammate Harold Abrahams competed and lost in the 1920 Olympics. Also, the two were not rivals as the film depicts. Instead, the experiences of these two athletes, whose religions defined them, are used to weave a timeless story of religious tolerance and the power of faith.

Eight Men Out (1988)

This film captures the darkest days of baseball (at least until the recent steroid scandals), but there are a few details that are totally off base—such as southpaw pitcher Dickie Kerr being right-handed in the movie. The film recounts the story of the 1919 World Series between the Chicago White Sox and the Cincinnati Reds, after which eight White Sox players were accused of accepting bribes to lose the series. The players were accurately depicted as victims caught between organized gambling syndicates and team owners (and their selfish agendas), but the film does take liberties with some facts. For example, Chick Gandil's pro career did not end because of the scandal. He had already retired before the scandal was exposed because Sox owner Charles Comiskey would not give him a $1,000 raise. At least this one, while making it hard to root, root, root for the home team, shows that the villains weren't just those who took the money.

Rudy (1993)

The true story of Daniel "Rudy" Ruettiger was the first film given permission to shoot on the campus of the University of Notre Dame since *Knute Rockne All American*. And while this true story is proof that dreams do come true in the world of sports, the film's low budget did allow for some inaccuracies to creep in. For example, cars in street scenes were of later models than those of the era in which the film was set, and a New York City scene set in the late 1960s included the World Trade Center towers, which were not completed until the early 1970s. The film also portrays Ruettiger's high school as coed years before it was in real life. One scene that took a great deal of dramatic license sees a player set his shirt on Coach Dan Devine's desk to sacrifice his place on the "dress list." It never happened. In fact, Devine had planned to put Ruettiger in the game all along. But for the sake of a dramatic story line, Devine agreed to be painted as the villain in the film.

Invincible (2006)

It's a fantasy that every Monday morning quarterback dreams about: playing for his favorite professional football team. This film, starring Mark Wahlberg, captured the look and feel of the 1970s authentically enough, but it fumbled badly on a few key points, notably that the real Vince Papale wasn't a complete unknown when he tried out for the Philadelphia Eagles in 1976. In fact, Papale had played for the World

Football League's Philadelphia Bell for two seasons before trying out for the Eagles.

The Non-Scandal: Hollywood Does Good

Hollywood celebrities tend to make the tabloid pages for all the wrong reasons. Every now and then, though, they find themselves in the headlines for heroic deeds rather than scandalous behavior.

Mark Harmon

The actor, best known for his roles on *St. Elsewhere* and *NCIS*, became a real-life hero in 1996 when two teenage boys crashed their Jeep near his Brentwood home. Harmon's wife, actress Pam Dawber, was the first on the scene, so when she saw the car in flames, she yelled for her husband to bring a sledgehammer. Harmon smashed a window, wrestled one of the boys from his seat belt, and then pulled him to safety. The boy was on fire, so the actor rolled him on the ground to extinguish the flames. A fire department spokesman praised Harmon for his heroics, stating, "These boys certainly owe their lives to the quick and selfless action of Mr. Harmon."

Harrison Ford

This movie star doesn't confine his heroics to the big screen when he's playing Han Solo or Indiana Jones. Ford has twice turned real-life hero to rescue stranded hikers in his Bell 407 helicopter. In July 2000, the accomplished pilot picked up the distress call from two female hikers on Table Mountain in Idaho. One was overcome with altitude sickness after a five-hour climb, so Ford flew in to airlift her to the hospital. The woman didn't recognize her famous rescuer until after she'd vomited in his hat.

A year later, Ford's flying skills were called upon again in the rescue of a 13-year-old Boy Scout who went missing in Yellowstone National Park. After scouring the area for two hours, Ford spotted the boy and swooped down to rescue him. He even shared a joke with the boy, who had managed to survive overnight wearing only a T-shirt and shorts. "Boy, you sure must have earned a merit badge for this one," said the actor.

Cuba Gooding Jr.

On the night of Memorial Day 2007, Cuba Gooding Jr. went to pick up dinner for his family from Roscoe's House of Chicken & Waffles in Hollywood. When the Oscar-winning actor saw a young man collapse, bleeding from a gunshot wound, he ran to help. He called into the restaurant for towels and managed to stem the bleeding. The *Jerry Maguire* (1996) star hailed a passing police car and cradled the injured man until an ambulance arrived at the scene.

Gerard Butler

Before he became famous as the heroic lead in *300*, the 2007 movie adaptation of Frank Miller's graphic novel, Gerard Butler was honored for his real-life heroism. The Scottish actor received a Certificate of Bravery from the Royal Humane Society of Scotland in 1997 after he risked his life to pull a drowning boy from the River Tay, the longest river in Scotland. Butler was enjoying a picnic nearby when he saw the child drowning and immediately dived in to rescue him.

Tom Cruise

Tom Cruise has a history of coming to the aid of folks in trouble, though the tabloid press seems to focus more on his couch-jumping and religious beliefs than his good deeds. In 2006, Cruise and his wife, Katie Holmes, assisted a young couple who had been in a car accident. Ten years earlier, Cruise rescued a young woman who had been hit by a car. He called an ambulance for her and then paid her emergency room bill. However charitable these acts were, they pale in comparison to an incident in London in 1998. While out walking, Cruise came across a woman being mugged. The woman was sitting in her Porsche when a man opened the car door and began grabbing the jewelry from her hands and arms. The woman screamed, and Cruise ran to her aid, chasing off the mugger in mid-theft. Reportedly, he prevented the loss of at least some of the jewelry the woman was wearing—worth between $120,000 and $150,000.

Todd Bridges

After his role as Willis Jackson on the popular sitcom *Diff'rent Strokes* came to an end in 1986, actor Todd Bridges tended to make headlines for all the wrong reasons. He endured a much-publicized battle with cocaine addiction and, in 1990, even stood trial for the attempted murder of a drug dealer. In 2001, however, Bridges made headlines for rescuing a paraplegic woman from drowning in Lake Balboa in Los Angeles. The 50-year-old woman was fishing while buckled into her motorized wheelchair. When the chair accidentally rolled into the lake and fell on its side, her head was trapped underwater. Bridges and his brother James ran to the woman's aid and managed to pull her to safety.

2017 Best Picture Oscar Flub

It was a moment that Hollywood—and moviegoers worldwide—won't soon forget.

With its hip, heartfelt story of love, jazz, acting, and dreams, 2016's *La La Land* was a critical and commercial darling. The star-studded musical landed a record-tying 14 Academy Award nominations and cemented writer-director Damien Chazelle as a gifted young talent.

So on the evening of the February 2017 Academy Awards ceremony, prognosticators anticipated it would score the evening's top honor.

It won, and then it didn't.

This Is Not a Joke

As the biggest award of the event was set to be announced, *La La Land* had already won six Oscars. Nominees for this Best Picture shoe-in readied to take the stage and accept the final award.

Hollywood legends Warren Beatty and Faye Dunaway took the stage, envelope in hand, to present the evening's ultimate honor. When Beatty opened the envelope, he paused and exchanged glances with his copresenter. He then handed her the envelope, and she announced the winner: *La La Land.*

When Dunaway announced *La La Land*, the theatre went wild with applause and cheers. Then filmmakers, cast and crew took the stage, and producer Jordan Horowitz spoke first with an Oscar in hand. But when fellow producer Marc Platt spoke next, it was evident something was amiss. Horowitz and Fred Berger, another producer, exchanged confused looks. A PricewaterhouseCoopers accountant ran on stage, and everyone quickly realized something was wrong.

La La Land producer Jordan Horowitz grabbed the microphone and acknowledged a mistake.

"*Moonlight*, you guys won Best Picture," he said. "This is not a joke."

Moonlight's filmmakers and cast appeared shocked and, like most everyone in the theatre, deeply confused. The show's host, Jimmy Kimmel, in an attempt to make light of the situation, quipped that he "blamed Steve Harvey for this." Harvey infamously stated the wrong winner at the 2015 Miss Universe pageant.

It turned out that an accountant backstage gave the *Bonnie and Clyde* duo the wrong envelope.

He Wasn't Trying to Be Funny

Beatty later sought to explain the now-infamous flub, noting that the envelope said "Emma Stone, *La La Land*."

"That's why I took such a long look at Faye and at you," he said. "I wasn't trying to be funny."

Following the flub, PricewaterhouseCoopers issued a statement, saying the accounting firm "deeply regret(s) that this occurred."

"At the end of the day, we made a human error," Tim Ryan, the U.S. chairman and senior partner of PwC, told *USA Today*. "We made a mistake."

Later that spring, the Academy announced it would add an additional accountant in the control room at all future ceremonies, and it also would bar accountants from having electronic devices backstage. And in a fitting move, Beatty and Dunaway returned in 2018 to once more to present the coveted award. That time, there were no surprises.

A Reckoning: Harvey Weinstein, #MeToo, and Time's Up

In Hollywood, everyone knew Harvey Weinstein's name.

Admired—and feared—by much of the film industry, the movie producer's career took off in the late 1970s and early 1980s when Weinstein and his brother Bob created a film production company called Miramax.

By the late 1980s and early 1990s, Miramax produced a number of hits, including *The Thin Blue Line* (1988), *Sex, Lies, and Videotape* (1989), *Tie Me Up! Tie Me Down!* (1990), and *Pulp Fiction* (1994). The company won its first Academy Award for Best Picture in 1997 for *The English Patient*. Weinstein himself took home an Oscar for *Shakespeare in Love* in 1999.

As Weinstein's clout among the industry's best and brightest grew, the movie mogul developed a reputation as a notorious executive who called for his films to be fundamentally restructured or reedited prior to release. He earned and proudly wore the moniker "Harvey Scissorhands"; for example, fellow producer Scott Rudin infamously fought Weinstein over the music and final cut of *The Hours* (2002).

Weinstein and his brother left Miramax to form their own production company, The Weinstein Company, in 2005. He became increasingly active in politics and outspoken on issues like gun control and health care. And his colleagues continued to praise him: an analysis found that, between 1966 and 2016, Weinstein tied with God as the second-most thanked person during Academy Award acceptance speeches.

By the end of 2017, however, Weinstein's reputation would wind up in tatters.

A Reckoning

Exposes by the *New York Times* and the *New Yorker*, each published days apart in early October 2017, painted a startling picture of the alleged harassment by the powerful producer.

The stories found that Weinstein harassed, assaulted, or raped more than a dozen women throughout his life and career. A number of prominent actresses, including Ashley Judd and Rose McGowan, described how Weinstein would appear in hotel rooms in nothing but a bathrobe and ask for a massage. A published audiotape from a 2015 New York Police Department sting found Weinstein pressuring model Ambra Battilana Gutierrez to come into his hotel room. In the tape, Weinstein admitted to groping Gutierrez.

Weinstein issued an apology and acknowledged "a lot of pain" but disputed the allegations. He said he was working with a therapist and was preparing to sue the *New York Times*.

But Weinstein's leave of absence was short-lived: three days after the first story broke about his misconduct, his company's board announced his ouster.

The accusations against Weinstein piled up, and within months, more than 80 women came forward to accuse Weinstein of a host of inappropriate behavior. Police in Los Angeles, New York, and the United Kingdom separately confirmed investigations into allegations involving Weinstein. New York state prosecutors filed a lawsuit against the Weinstein Company in February 2018.

The Academy of Motion Picture Arts and Sciences voted overwhelmingly to expel Weinstein. Institutions across the United States and the United Kingdom took similar actions to revoke honors or memberships in Weinstein's name.

Weinstein's legacy was eroding before his eyes, and the entertainment industry, alongside workplace culture across the nation, was undergoing rapid change.

#MeToo and Time's Up

Despite Weinstein's laundry list of allegations, the movie producer's behavior prompted a pair of wide-reaching campaigns.

In 2006, activist Tarana Burke created the phrase "Me Too" in an attempt to bring awareness to sexual assault victims. After the explosive allegations, Burke's 12-year-old phrase was coopted by actress Alyssa Milano when she encouraged people to reply to a tweet about sexual harassment or assault with the words "me too." Immediately, Milano's call lit social media abuzz, and thousands of women—young, old, and from different backgrounds—shared their own stories.

"In many regards Me Too is about survivors talking to survivors," Burke told the *Boston Globe*. " … It was about survivors exchanging empathy with each other."

And on January 1, 2018, a group of 300 women in the film, television, and theater industries launched a complementary initiative called Time's Up, a manifesto and coalition aimed at providing a wealth of resources for victims of assault, harassment, and inequality in the workplace. A legal fund developed to assist victims amassed $21 million in two months.

CHAPTER 9

FALLS FROM GRACE

Aaron Burr: Hero or Villain?

Mention the name Aaron Burr and the thing most people remember is his famous duel with Alexander Hamilton. That may have been the high point of his life, because by the time Burr died in 1836, he was considered one of the most mistrusted public figures of his era.

How to Make Friends

Burr seemed to have a knack for making enemies out of important people. George Washington disliked him so much from their time together during the Revolutionary War that, as president, he had Burr banned from the National Archives, didn't appoint him as minister to France, and refused to make him a brigadier general.

After the war, Burr became a lawyer in New York, frequently opposing his future dueling partner Alexander Hamilton. But it wasn't until Burr beat Hamilton's father-in-law in the race for a Senate seat that the problems between them really started.

In 1800, Burr ran for president against Thomas Jefferson. Back then, the candidate with the most votes got to be president; whoever came in second became vice president—even if they were from different parties. When the election ended in a tie in the Electoral College, it was thrown to the House of Representatives to decide. After 35 straight tie votes, Jefferson was elected president, and Burr became vice president.

Like Washington, Jefferson didn't hold Burr in high regard. So in 1804, Burr decided to run for governor of New York. When he lost, he blamed the slandering of the press in general and the almost constant criticism from Hamilton in particular.

Hamilton later shot off at the mouth at a dinner party, and Burr decided he'd had enough. After giving Hamilton a chance to take his comments back (Hamilton refused), Burr challenged him to the famous duel.

I Challenge You to a Duel

On July 11, 1804, Burr and Hamilton met at Weehawken, New Jersey. Some say that Hamilton fired first, discharging his pistol into the air; others say that he just missed. Burr, on the other hand, didn't miss, shooting Hamilton. He died the next day.

After the duel, Burr fled to his daughter's home in South Carolina until things cooled down. He was indicted for murder in both New York and New Jersey, but nothing ever came of it, and he eventually returned to Washington to finish his term as vice president. But his political career was over.

King Burr?

After his term as vice president, Burr decided to head west to what was then considered Ohio and the new lands of the Louisiana Purchase. It seemed that Burr had things on his mind other than the scenery, however. According to some (mostly his rivals), Burr intended to create a new empire with himself as king. As the story goes, he planned to conquer a portion of Texas still held by Mexico and convince some of the existing western states to join his new confederacy. Called the Burr Conspiracy, it got the attention of President Jefferson, who issued arrest orders for treason. Eventually, Burr was captured and in 1807 was brought to trial.

But Burr caught a break. The judge was Chief Justice John Marshall. Marshall and Jefferson didn't get along, and rather than give his enemy an easy victory, Marshall demanded that the prosecution produce two witnesses that specifically heard Burr commit treason. The prosecution failed to come up with anybody, and Burr was set free.

Burr then left the United States to live in Europe. Returning to New York in 1812, he quietly practiced law until his death in 1836.

Victoria Woodhull: An American Trailblazer

When Victoria Woodhull ran for president in 1872, some called her a witch, and others said she was a prostitute. In fact, the very idea of a woman casting a vote for president was considered scandalous— which may explain why Woodhull spent election night in jail.

Known for her passionate speeches and fearless attitude, Victoria Woodhull became a trailblazer for women's rights. But some say she was about 100 years before her time. Woodhull advocated revolutionary ideas, including gender equality and women's right to vote. "Women are the equals of men before the law and are equal in all their rights," she said. America, however, wasn't ready to accept her radical ideas.

Ahead of Her Time

Woodhull was born in 1838 in Homer, Ohio, the seventh child of Annie and Buck Claflin. Her deeply spiritual mother often took little Victoria along to revival camps where people would speak in tongues. Her mother also dabbled in clairvoyance, and Victoria and her younger sister Tennessee believed they had a gift for it as well. With so many chores to do at home (washing, ironing, chipping wood, and cooking), Victoria only attended school sporadically and was primarily self-educated.

Soon after the family left Homer, a 28-year-old doctor named Canning Woodhull asked the 15-year-old Victoria for her hand in marriage. But the marriage was no paradise for Victoria—she soon realized her husband was an alcoholic. She experienced more heartbreak when her son, Byron, was born with a disability. While she remained married to Canning, Victoria spent the next few years touring as a clairvoyant with her sister Tennessee. At that time, it was difficult for a woman to pursue divorce, but Victoria finally succeeded in divorcing her husband in 1864. Two years later she married Colonel James Blood, a Civil War veteran who believed in free love.

In 1866, Victoria and James moved to New York City. Spiritualism was then in vogue, and Victoria and Tennessee established a salon where they acted as clairvoyants and discussed social and political hypocrisies with their clientele. Among their first customers was Cornelius Vanderbilt, the wealthiest man in America.

A close relationship sprang up between Vanderbilt and the two attractive and intelligent young women. He advised them on business matters and gave them stock tips. When the stock market crashed in September 1869, Woodhull made a bundle buying instead of selling during the ensuing panic. That winter, she and Tennessee opened their own brokerage business. They were the first female stockbrokers in American history, and they did so well that, two years after arriving in New York, Woodhull told a newspaper she had made $700,000.

Presidential Ambitions

Woodhull had more far-reaching ambitions, however. On April 2, 1870, she announced that she was running for president. In conjunction with her presidential bid, Woodhull and her sister started a newspaper, *Woodhull & Claflin's Weekly*, which highlighted women's issues, including voting and labor rights. It was another breakthrough for the two, as they were the first women to ever publish a weekly newspaper.

That was followed by another milestone: On January 11, 1871, Woodhull became the first woman ever to speak before a congressional committee. As she spoke before the House Judiciary Committee, she asked that Congress change its stance on whether women could vote. Woodhull's reasoning was elegant in its simplicity. She was not advocating a new constitutional amendment granting women the right to vote. Instead, she reasoned, women already had that right. The Fourteenth Amendment says that "All persons born or naturalized in the United States . . . are citizens of the Unites States." Since voting is part of the definition of being a citizen, Woodhull argued, women, in fact, already possessed the right to vote. Woodhull, a persuasive speaker, actually swayed some congressmen to her point of view, but the committee chairman remained hostile to the idea of women's rights and made sure the issue never came to a floor vote.

Woodhull had better luck with the suffragists. In May 1872, before 668 delegates from 22 states, Woodhull was chosen as the presidential candidate of the Equal Rights Party; she was the first woman ever chosen by a political party to run for president. But her presidential bid soon foundered. Woodhull was on record as an advocate of free love, which opponents argued was an attack on the institution of marriage (for Woodhull it had more to do with the right to have a relationship with anyone she wanted). Rather than debate her publicly, her opponents made personal attacks.

That year, Woodhull caused uproar when her newspaper ran an exposé about the infidelities of Reverend Henry Ward Beecher. Woodhull and her sister were thrown in jail and accused of publishing libel and promoting obscenity. They would spend election night of 1872 behind bars as Ulysses Grant defeated Horace Greeley for the presidency.

Woodhull was eventually cleared of the charges against her (the claims against Beecher were proven true), but hefty legal bills and a downturn in the stock market left her embittered and impoverished. She moved to England in 1877, shortly after divorcing Colonel Blood. By the turn of the century she had become wealthy once more, this time by marriage to a British banker. Fascinated by technology, she joined the Ladies Automobile Club, where her passion for automobiles led Woodhull to one last milestone: In her sixties, Woodhull and her daughter Zula became the first women to drive through the English countryside.

Frances Farmer: Tortured Soul

When Frances Farmer's life spiraled out of control, the results proved devastating. Institutionalized for many years, the troubled actress miraculously fought her way back to the top. Unfortunately, her demons accompanied her every step of the way. She made very few films, but her story is remembered as a cautionary tale about the dark side of the Hollywood star system.

Hitting the Big Time

When moviegoers watched *Come and Get It* (1936), a film starring the effervescent flaxen-haired beauty Frances Farmer (1913—1970), they couldn't have guessed that in a few short years, the star would decline into a mentally tormented, alcohol-addicted figure. Certainly Farmer herself was unaware of the cruel fate that awaited her. Up to that point, the actress's ascent to stardom had gone according to plan. After studying at the University of Washington as a journalism and drama major, Farmer left her Seattle home and headed off to Hollywood. There she secured a seven-year contract with Paramount Pictures and was groomed for major stardom. While under Paramount's employ, Farmer was loaned out to the Samuel Goldwyn Company for the making of *Come and Get It*, a drama that proved the perfect vehicle to highlight Farmer's prodigious talents. Critics raved about Farmer's dual mother/daughter performance in the film. And director Cecil B. DeMille referred to the actress as the "screen's outstanding find of 1936." With this early victory acting as impetus, the 23-year-old Farmer thought she had the world on a string. Unfortunately, her good fortune would not last.

Downwardly Mobile

For the stage-trained Farmer, 1937 would bring further success. Fulfilling a dream that she'd had since first getting the acting bug, Farmer moved to New York City to work on the stage, joining the famed Group Theatre. She was cast in the production of *Golden Boy* and received praise for her portrayal of the emotionally charged Lorna Moon. She stayed with the production into its off-Broadway run.

But in 1939, things started to unravel for Farmer. Erratic behavior and an ever-increasing drinking habit began to take its toll on her. By the early 1940s, she had returned to Hollywood, but directors and producers took note of Farmer's sudden unreliability and responded in kind. By 1941, Farmer was no longer treated as a major player and was relegated to B-movies—the unimportant second features on a double bill. Then, in 1942, the bottom completely fell out. Confronted with a severely unstable actress who regularly fueled her mental demons with alcohol, the studio pulled the plug on her contract. Farmer's downward spiral was firmly on track.

The Snake Pit

In January 1943, Farmer was reportedly involved in a physical altercation with a studio hairdresser. After being arrested for her role in the assault, Farmer was placed in the custody of psychiatrist Thomas H. Leonard. The doctor determined that the uncooperative actress was "suffering from manic-depressive psychosis," a diagnosis that has since been contested. Farmer was then transferred to Rockhaven Sanitarium in La Crescenta, California, thus beginning an on/off ordeal of forced institutionalization that lasted for several years. In her autobiography *Will There Really Be a Morning?*, which was largely written by a longtime friend, Farmer recalled the horrors that she was subjected to as a patient in various sanitariums. Tales of shock treatments that did far more harm than good, hydrotherapy (submerging the patient in icy cold water for hours at a time), her use as an unwitting pawn to test unproven drugs, and even gang rape at the hands of hospital orderlies abound in her first-person account of those tortured years, but perhaps nothing is more heartbreaking than Farmer's realization that her own mother signed her commitment papers. It is believed that the actress was hospitalized against her will three separate times during the 1940s, spending a total of five years in mental institutions. Finally, in 1950, Farmer was released for good.

A Career Almost Resurrected

While Farmer's life easily could have continued its downward spiral, it didn't. In fact, it rebounded to a degree that seems improbable given her severe mental history, problems with addictions, and the tortures that she had endured. Starting small, Farmer first took a job working in a Seattle hotel laundry to help support her parents. After a failed marriage in 1954, she moved to Eureka, California, and found work at a photo studio. In 1957, a lucky break came when a talent scout rediscovered the actress and helped revive her career. Appearances on *The Ed Sullivan Show* and *This Is Your Life* led to a series of television dramas. Farmer's biggest break came in 1958, when she became hostess of *Frances Farmer Presents*, an afternoon movie and interview show on an NBC affiliate in Indianapolis. The show held the number one position for six straight years, but in a nod to her first mental downfall, Farmer's demons ultimately resurfaced. After Farmer fell back into the throes of alcoholism, the station pulled the plug on her show in September 1964.

A Bottle in Front of Me

While various sources have suggested that Farmer received a frontal lobotomy during her stay in a mental hospital, evidence does not support the claim. The 1978 book *Shadowland*, a purportedly factual account of her life that author William Arnold now calls "fictionalized," was largely responsible for popularizing the myth. Subsequent accounts of Farmer's treatments released by Western State Hospital have mostly laid this to rest. Certainly her successful stint as a television interviewer belies the limited capabilities of a person who has undergone a lobotomy. What cannot be debunked, however, was Farmer's dependency on alcohol. For most of her post-institution life, the actress fought a battle with the bottle, and the bottle usually won. Farmer's final years were spent operating a number of small businesses. The spell that the actress had once held over Hollywood had all but vanished and had been replaced by the lingering, silent hell of anonymity. In 1970, Frances Farmer developed esophageal cancer and quietly died at age 56. Her demons would torture her no more.

Wisconsin's Federal Scaremonger

Wisconsin has produced many notable U.S. senators, but the state also claims one very infamous senator, Joseph Raymond McCarthy, best known for his sensational communist witch-hunt.

A Promising Youth

Born to a farming family in rural Grand Chute on November 15, 1908, McCarthy was a bright but restless youngster. He dropped out of school after graduating from eighth grade and started his own chicken farm. Unfortunately, his birds fell victim to disease, and at the age of 20, McCarthy went back to school.

Somehow, he crammed an entire high school education into nine months, while also managing a grocery store in Manawa. He earned such stellar grades that Marquette University accepted him as a law student. At Marquette, he was known as "Smiling Joe" for his good humor and became a champion middleweight boxer, often felling larger opponents with his high-energy fighting style. McCarthy was so good that he even considered making a career in the ring, but a local boxing instructor talked him into getting his degree instead.

Throwing his energy into school, McCarthy dove into campus debate clubs where he proved he could be as much of a pit bull with his words as he was with boxing. After graduating in 1935, he became a lawyer in the small towns of Waupaca and Shawano and, by age 30, was elected judge in Wisconsin's Tenth Judicial Circuit.

Serving His Country

McCarthy put his legal practice on hold to join the Marines in 1942 and serve in World War II. He was an intelligence officer in the South Pacific and saw action as part of a bombing raid crew, which earned him a second nickname, "Tailgunner Joe."

McCarthy would later falsely say he carried 10 pounds of shrapnel in his leg, but in truth, he returned to Wisconsin unscathed and determined to regain his circuit judgeship. In 1946, he dared to run for the Republican candidacy for the U.S. Senate against the popular

21-year incumbent, Robert M. LaFollette Jr. McCarthy barely squeaked through to win the nomination and became the youngest U.S. senator at that time at age 38.

The Beginning of the End

The 1950 Senate election may have spurred McCarthy's monumental decline. Perhaps grasping for a campaign issue, McCarthy made the shocking claim that he had a list of 205 government officials who were communists. The government's House Un-American Activities Committee had already paved the way for such suspicion with its investigations of the Hollywood entertainment industry starting in 1947. The Senate opened hearings on McCarthy's allegations in March 1950, but McCarthy never proved his case. In 1952, the Senate turned the tables and began investigating McCarthy.

Although the committee found him guilty of unethical actions, his loyal base still reelected him in 1952. Ironically, McCarthy was made Chairman of the Committee on Government Operations and Investigations. "Tailgunner Joe" kept looking for communists, even going so far as to accuse the U.S. Army and the Eisenhower presidential administration. However, hearings broadcast via the new medium of television in 1954 helped discredit McCarthy. By December of that year, the Senate condemned McCarthy for abuse of power. He finished the two and a half years of his term, largely powerless and unpopular. At the same time, McCarthy began to drink heavily and suffered various physical ailments.

McCarthy succumbed to hepatitis on May 2, 1957. A gray granite headstone that simply reads "United States Senator" marks his grave in Appleton's St. Mary's Cemetery. He left behind a wife, Jean, an adopted daughter, Tierney, and a new word that's still in use: "McCarthyism." Thanks to this term, Joseph McCarthy's name will forever be associated with the act of aggressively hunting for certain people based on unsubstantiated charges.

Chappaquiddick

Following his election to the Senate in 1962, Edward M. "Ted" Kennedy had been known as a liberal who champions causes such as education and health care, but he had less success in his personal life.

On July 18, 1969, Kennedy attended a party on Chappaquiddick Island in Massachusetts. He left the party with 29-year-old Mary Jo Kopechne, who had campaigned for Ted's late brother, Robert. Soon after the two left the party, Kennedy's car veered off a bridge, and Kopechne drowned.

An experienced swimmer, Kennedy said he tried to rescue her but the tide was too strong. He swam to shore, went back to the party, and returned with two other men. Their rescue efforts also failed, but Kennedy waited until the next day to report the accident, calling his lawyer and Kopechne's parents first, claiming the crash had dazed him.

There was speculation that he tried to cover up that he was driving under the influence, but nothing was ever proven. Kennedy pleaded guilty to leaving the scene of an accident, received a two-month suspended jail sentence, and lost his driver's license for a year. The scandal may have contributed to his failed presidential bid in 1980, but it didn't hurt his reputation in the Senate. In April 2006, *Time* magazine named him one of "America's 10 Best Senators." Kennedy died in 2009 after a battle with brain cancer.

Bettie Page: From Girl Next Door to Impoverished Recluse

Dark and sometimes moody, mysterious and captivating, Bettie Page had a sunny smile that would melt butter. Whatever happened to this pinup who disappeared at the height of her notoriety?

Bettie Page, the sexy queen of pinups, easily transitioned from sweet to sultry to dark. The 2005 movie *The Notorious Bettie Page*, starring indie darling Gretchen Mol, only begins to skim the surface of her complex life. Page disappeared from the limelight at her peak, leaving many fans, fanzines, fan clubs, and products behind.

The Girl's Got Range

From 1950 to 1957, Bettie Page ruled everything from simple girl next door swimsuit spreads to taboo bondage films. The films eventually earned Page a subpoena from the U.S. government.

In his book, *The Real Bettie Page*, Richard Foster calls her "a swinging fifties chick who looks like the girl next door, yet tells you she knows the score. She winks, tosses back her famous gleaming black bangs, and flashes you her killer come-hither smile. Her curves entice, entrance, and devastate. She's a leggy, torpedo-chested weapon aimed at your heart . . . She's bikinis and lace. She's cotton candy and a ride on the Tilt-a-Whirl at Coney Island."

But Foster's love for the Dark Angel, as Bettie Page is sometimes called, led him to the awful truth—that after her queen-of-curves years, Page's life spiraled downward until she ended up in a mental institution after being convicted of attempted murder.

Humble Beginnings

Betty Mae Page, born in Tennessee in 1923, was the second of Edna and Roy Page's six children. Roy, a mechanic, couldn't find work during the Great Depression. Add Roy's supposedly insatiable sexual appetite—he sexually abused Bettie and impregnated a 15-year-old neighbor—and Edna's cold shoulder toward her children, and the result is a perfectly dysfunctional family pie.

Page was a good student and active in school—but she wasn't involved with boys. She was a typical goodie-goodie, raised as a faithful Christian by her devout, God-fearing mother, who didn't allow her to date. She escaped her oppressive upbringing by envisioning herself as a movie star. A few years after graduating from college, Page decided to follow her dream and moved to New York.

Between boyfriends, secretarial jobs, and small modeling gigs, Page met Jerry Tibbs on the beach at Coney Island in October 1950. Tibbs, a police officer from Harlem with a passion for photography, immediately asked Page if she'd ever thought about modeling. She agreed to let him shoot her. Tibbs showed Page tricks of the trade, doing her makeup and giving her tissues to stuff her bra. Eventually, he realized that her hairstyle—a simple part down the middle—was taking away from her beauty on camera. With a quick snip, the Bettie Page bangs arrived.

In Front of the Camera

Tibbs introduced Page to photographer Cass Carr, and her modeling career began. In 1952, Page met Irving Klaw, the man who would turn the Queen of Curves into the Dark Angel. Klaw ran a successful mail-order business and photo shop in New York, selling stills and headshots from famous movies. But his bread and butter was earned from bondage photos. Klaw shot photographs of girls being spanked, tied up, and wearing six-inch heels with black lingerie. Today, you'll see more suggestive displays in a Victoria's Secret ad, but this was the 1950s, and Page's carefree photos inspired sexually repressed Americans all around the country.

Klaw, along with his business partner and sister, Paula, took Page in like family. She enjoyed modeling, but she never gave up on her dream of being an actress. She spent her prosperous $75-per-day modeling payments on acting classes.

By 1955, Page was at her peak, gracing the pages of the January issue of *Playboy* in her most famous pose—wearing only a Santa hat and a naughty smile. But by 1957, Page was burned out on show business. She moved to Florida, rekindled a relationship with an old flame, and got married in 1958.

A Slow Slide

By New Year's Eve of that same year, however, the relationship fizzled. Frustrated, financially unstable, and brokenhearted, Page spent the night crying along the roads of Key West. She felt hopeless—and that's when she spotted a church. Page turned her life over to God, quit modeling, and spun into religious fervor. She spent the next few years in various Bible camps and schools; she wanted to be a missionary. But Page was a bit too fanatical, even for Baptist ministers. Her classmates and instructors began to see that her zeal was becoming frightening and dark; they speculated that Page, now pushing 40, wasn't well.

During the next few years, Page committed several violent acts. She pulled a gun on a missionary at a Bible camp; later, she attacked and stabbed an elderly woman and her husband, from whom she rented a trailer in California. Page was diagnosed with paranoid schizophrenia and sentenced to a psychiatric hospital.

However, because of good behavior, she was released early. Through a roommate service, she moved into the home of Leonie Haddad. After a few months of living together, Page heard Haddad on the phone with the agency asking for a new roommate and she snapped, stabbing Haddad 12 times.

Page went on trial for attempted murder in 1983 and spent seven years in a mental institution before being released on good behavior. Older, heavier, and with no money—even with all of those Bettie Page products swarming the globe—she became a recluse.

With her likeness on everything from posters to dioramas, Bettie Page is as popular now as she was in the 1950s. For women, Page represents the ultimate example of body confidence. She was comfortable posing in a leopard-print bathing suit as well as posing nude in a park. Through every wink and grin, she seems to be secretly speaking to young women about the power of curves—an important message today in a time when many female celebrities are diminishing before the public's very eyes.

Resigning in Disgrace

During the Great Depression, Wilbur Mills served as a county judge in Arkansas and initiated government-funded programs to pay medical and prescription drug bills for the poor. Mills was elected to the House of Representatives in 1939 and served until 1977, with 18 of those years as head of the Ways and Means Committee.

In the 1960s, Mills played an integral role in the creation of the Medicare program, and he made an unsuccessful bid for president in the 1972 primary. Unfortunately for Mills, he's best known for one of Washington's juiciest scandals.

On October 7, 1974, police stopped Mills's car in West Potomac Park near the Jefferson Memorial. Mills was drunk and in the back seat of the car with an Argentine stripper named Fanne Foxe. When the police approached, Foxe fled the car. Mills checked into an alcohol treatment center and was reelected to Congress in November 1974. But just one month later, Mills was seen drunk onstage with Fanne Foxe. Following the incident, Mills was forced to resign as chairman of the Ways and Means Committee and did not run for reelection in 1976.

Mills died in 1992, and despite the scandal, several schools and highways in Arkansas are named after him.

Robert Bauman's Double Life

Some politicians don't find their political calling until later in life, but Robert Bauman set his sights on the vocation when he was still a teenager, and he quickly worked his way up the political ladder. By the time he was in his mid-30s, he was a U.S. congressman, where the next few years would prove he had a knack for parliamentary procedure. In his own words, he said, "At the tender age of 43 I had reached a pinnacle of success few would have ever predicted for me and certainly I would have never predicted for myself." The world, as they say, was his. But a terrible decision, and the stress of hiding a secret life, would cost him his once-promising career.

The Rise of a Politician

Bauman graduated from the Capitol Page School at the Library of Congress when he was 18; he then earned a bachelor of science degree in international affairs from Georgetown University. In 1964, he received a juris doctor from Georgetown University Law Center and was admitted to the Maryland Bar. That same year, he attended his first Republican National Convention as a delegate; six years later, he was elected to the Maryland State Senate.

After congressman William O. Mills tragically died by suicide in 1973, Bauman was elected to the U.S. House of Representatives. He gained a reputation as a champion of a "family values" and an outspoken critic of declining morality, and he helped to form the Young Americans for Freedom youth activism group and the American Conservative Union. He married Carol Dawson, one of the cofounders of the Young Americans for Freedom group, and the couple had four children. The church-going family man was respected within his party as one of its rising stars, certain to be a fixture on Capitol Hill for years to come.

The Downfall

But Bauman's carefully composed life came crashing down on September 3, 1980. That day, in the middle of campaigning for reelection, Bauman arrived at his congressional office to find FBI agents waiting for him. The congressman was charged with solicitation for prostitution from a 16-year-old male prostitute. The charge was a misdemeanor and only resulted in a six-month suspended sentence for Bauman; but the political and personal fallout that followed was a much harsher punishment.

At first, Bauman blamed alcoholism for his transgression, checking himself into a rehab program and apologizing to his constituents. He continued his bid for reelection after the scandal, but he was easily defeated by Democrat Roy Dyson, who had been considered the underdog in the race. Although he would temporarily run again in 1982 before dropping out of the race, ultimately, Bauman's political career came to an abrupt end.

A Hidden Life Outed

The scandal cost Bauman his marriage and home and sent him into financial crisis. Years later, in an autobiography that he wrote, admittedly, for money, the disgraced politician would finally admit that he'd struggled with homosexuality since he was young, but he felt the need to hide that part of his life due to his Catholic upbringing. In his book *The Gentleman from Maryland: The Conscience of a Gay Conservative*, Bauman laments the torment he felt as a gay man leading a double life, and he suggests that perhaps subconsciously he wanted someone to discover his secret. He wrote, "Exposure of my secret life forced me to eventual acceptance of my sexual nature and slowly I am coming to terms with myself."

Today, Bauman serves as legal counsel for the Sovereign Society, a group that specializes in offshore banking and investing. He says he remains committed to conservative values but tends to avoid the circus of politics.

Gary Hart's Political Nosedive

During the 1984 race for the presidency, a little-known senator from Colorado named Gary Hart surprised the country. Hart had thrown his name in the ring for the Democratic nomination, alongside much more popular names like Vice President Walter Mondale, ex-astronaut and Senator John Glenn, and civil rights activist Jesse Jackson. After beginning his campaign with barely 1 percent of support in polls, Hart fought his way through primary season, gaining voter after voter, until the nomination finally came down to Hart and

Mondale. While Mondale would go on to secure the nomination, Hart had made a name for himself, and he was well-positioned to be a strong candidate in the 1988 race. But, as with so many political figures who served before and after Hart, his presidential aspirations were brought down by scandal.

I'm Not Involved in Any Relationship

Hart's political fall from grace was a surprisingly quick descent. On April 13, 1987, he officially announced his candidacy for president, and within a few days, rumors were already making the rounds. A *Washington Post* reporter was the first to get the ball rolling, asking Hart what he thought about his rivals categorizing him as a "womanizer." Hart shrugged off the label, saying his competitors would not "get to the top by tearing someone else down."

But the very next week, the *Miami Herald* broke a story that alleged that an anonymous source claimed Hart—who has been married to Lee Ludwig since 1958—was having an affair with a young woman. *Herald* reporters got a tip that the woman—Donna Rice—would soon be visiting Hart at his home, and they followed her as she flew from Miami to Washington, D.C. They then waited outside Hart's townhome, where they eventually saw him with a woman. But when they confronted the politician and asked about the relationship, he denied there was any "relationship" and suggested that someone had set him up.

Just Friends?

Regardless, the *Herald* ran with a story about Hart meeting up with a woman at his home, but once again, Hart and his campaign denied the accusation. A few days later, the media publicly identified Donna Rice, and she gave a press conference where she insisted her relationship with Hart was limited to her work as a campaign aide. But the story had already taken on a life of its own, with news outlets across the country speculating on the presidential candidate's fidelity. But voters seemed undeterred: polls showed that nearly two thirds of the country felt the media was treating Hart unfairly, and more than half thought a candidate's marital issues had nothing to do with the ability to run the country.

But even with the support of many voters, Hart couldn't prevent the *Washington Post* from threatening to release details about another alleged affair. In order to protect his wife and daughter from tabloid scrutiny, Hart dropped out of the race on May 8. On June 2, the *National Enquirer* published the now-famous photograph of Rice sitting on Hart's lap on a yacht in the Bahamas. Even after this compelling evidence, the pair continued to insist they were "just friends."

Moving On

In December of 1987, Hart made a dramatic reappearance, throwing himself back into the presidential race and proclaiming, "Let's let the people decide!" But after a poor showing in the New Hampshire primary, he once again withdrew. While Hart would never run for president again, he returned to politics in 2009 to vice chair President Obama's Homeland Security Advisory Council, and he later served as the U.S. Special Envoy to Northern Ireland. Through better and worse, Hart and his wife Lee have remained married for 60 years. As for Rice, the publicity of the scandal resulted in offers for books, movies, and even a *Playboy* interview, all of which she turned down. In 1994, she settled down and married businessman Jack Hughes, and she has led a quiet life since then, far from the scandal that made her famous.

Kobe Bryant: Adultery or Assault?

The 90th Academy Awards, held on March 4, 2018, called special attention to the women who'd recently come forward with stories of harassment and assault within the entertainment industry. The serious allegations leveled at producer Harvey Weinstein—as well as many others in the industry—led to the popular #MeToo and Time's Up movements, signaling that victims were no longer content with being silent, and demanding accountability.

But there was an unusual Oscar winner that night: former Los Angeles Lakers basketball player Kobe Bryant. Bryant won the Oscar for Best Animated Short for a film he wrote and narrated called *Dear Basketball*, which chronicles his lifelong love of the game. It may have been somewhat out of the ordinary for a sports star—instead of an actor or producer—to win an Oscar, but that wasn't the only reason many gave pause to Bryant's win, especially during a year when listening to women was the prevailing theme.

A Chance Meeting

Fifteen years earlier, Bryant was already enjoying a stellar career, having helped the Lakers earn three NBA Championships and having been featured in five All-Star games. He would eventually go on to win five NBA Championships and play in 18 All-Star games, but his life was about to take a disturbing turn. Bryant was scheduled to have surgery with Colorado knee specialist Dr. Richard Steadman on July 2, 2003, so he checked into The Lodge and Spa at Cordillera in Edwards, Colorado, on June 30.

It was at the hotel that Bryant—who has been married to Vanessa Laine since 2001—met a 19-year-old employee and invited her to his room the night before his surgery. Three days later, an arrest warrant was issued for the basketball star, after the employee accused him of rape, and on July 18, Bryant was formally charged with sexual assault.

Just Adultery? Or Also Assault?

As with many harassment and assault cases, the Bryant incident became a matter of one person's version of events versus the other. Bryant admitted that he'd had sex with the woman, but he insisted it was consensual. The woman, on the other hand, gave chilling testimony claiming Bryant had "strangled" her and that she was "held against my will in that room." Bryant's attorney attempted to call the accuser's credibility into question, saying she was taking antipsychotic drugs for schizophrenia at the time and had a history of depression. A bellman that worked at the resort testified that the woman seemed distraught when she was leaving the hotel on the night in question, and he said she "told me that Kobe Bryant had forced sex with her."

But all the back and forth was rendered moot on September 1, 2004, when the charges against Bryant were dropped. His accuser refused to testify, with many speculating that she feared for her life after receiving hate mail and death threats. A civil lawsuit was filed against Bryant, resulting in an undisclosed settlement, but as part of an agreement to dismiss the sexual assault charge, Bryant issued a statement of apology. In it, he expressed his remorse to his accuser, saying, "I want to apologize to her for my behavior that night and for the consequences she has suffered in the past year." But he stopped short of admitting to assault, stating, "Although I truly believe this encounter between us was consensual, I recognize now that she did not and does not view this incident the same way I did."

The incident tarnished Bryant's image with his fans, and sales of his once-popular jersey fell. He also lost endorsement contracts with McDonald's and Nutella, but within a few years, his popularity and endorsements would come bouncing back. And fifteen years later, he would be holding an Oscar, ironically during a year when women's voices and accusations were taken more seriously than ever.

John Edwards's Serious Error

In the world of the rich and famous—whether they are actors, sports stars, or politicians—affairs are so commonplace we barely bat an eye. It's certainly not unheard of for a famous name to publicly offer vehement denials and then later, fallen from grace, to come forward with apologies for their indiscretions. But the story of John Edwards adds even more drama: a wife fighting cancer, a baby with questionable paternity, and an expensive cover-up.

Presidential Aspirations

John Edwards began his career as a lawyer, making a name for himself in his home state of North Carolina, where he was eventually considered the top plaintiff's lawyer in the state. He was elected to the U.S. Senate in 1998, having had no political experience before winning the seat. By 2003, he had decided to run for president, later dropping out of the race as John Kerry took the lead. But Kerry chose him as his vice-presidential running mate, and Edwards was right back in the fray. Although Kerry/Edwards conceded to Bush/Cheney, Edwards was ready to throw his hat back in the ring a few years later, when he announced he would be running for president in 2008.

To gear up for what would be a long fight, the Edwards campaign hired a filmmaker named Rielle Hunter to produce a series of webisodes about life on the campaign trail. Edwards had met Hunter at a bar in New York when he was in town attending a business meeting. And soon after their professional relationship began, the *New York Post* hinted that there could be more to their pairing than met the eye: a gossip item in the paper claimed that a married political candidate had a girlfriend in New York, who he promised to marry "when his current wife is out of the picture." Although no names were mentioned, the story led some to believe that it was referring to Edwards and Hunter.

Tabloid Fodder

On October 10, 2007, the *National Enquirer* published a story that did, in fact, name Edwards. The *Enquirer* claimed that Edwards was having an affair with a campaign worker. On the same day, the *Huffington Post* published an article about Hunter, giving her name and listing some of the films she'd worked on. Finally, the next day, *New York* magazine published a story that linked Edwards and Hunter.

Edwards and Hunter both denied the allegations, with Edwards insisting he only had eyes for his wife, Elizabeth, who had been fighting breast cancer since 2004 and was "an extraordinary human being." And Hunter claimed that the story was a lie and "completely unfounded and ridiculous." The *Enquirer* fought back, saying their story was "100 percent accurate," and on December 19, 2007, they published another story, this time with a twist: the article included a photo of a visibly pregnant Hunter, with an anonymous source claiming that Edwards was the father of the child.

Lies and Admissions

A month later, Edwards suspended his race for the presidency, with many speculating that the affair rumors hurt his campaign and may have ruined his chances for a vice presidential bid. On February 27, 2008, Hunter's daughter, Frances Quinn, was born, but no father was listed on the birth certificate, fueling more suspicion. As late as July 23, Edwards was still denying the affair, but on August 8, he finally issued a statement admitting he "made a serious error in judgment" and that he had already told his wife about the affair and asked for forgiveness. But he continued to claim that Hunter's child was not his.

But more allegations were starting to arise: A member of Edwards's campaign team, Andrew Young, stated that Edwards asked him to "get a doctor to fake the DNA results" of a paternity test. Young even publicly claimed that he was the child's father, but later recanted that claim. What's more, a grand jury began investigating whether any of Edwards's campaign funds had been used to cover up the affair. As more facts came to light, it was discovered that Young had solicited funds from wealthy socialite Rachel Lambert Mellon (often known as Bunny Mellon). Mellon had paid $725,000 to Edwards's personal accounts, which had been used to support Hunter. On January 21, 2010, Edwards finally admitted that he was the father of Frances Quinn. And on June 3, 2011, he was indicted by a North Carolina grand jury on six felony charges, including conspiracy, issuing false statements, and violating campaign contribution laws. The trial ended with one not guilty verdict and five deadlocks, and a mistrial was declared.

Moving On

Sadly, Elizabeth Edwards succumbed to cancer on December 7, 2010. It was discovered that the affair between her husband and Hunter had been ongoing much longer than anyone realized, including during the time she was undergoing treatment for the disease. She had stated that she tried to forgive Edwards for his indiscretions, but it became more difficult as he continued to lie about the situation. Elizabeth intended to divorce her husband after a mandatory one-year separation.

After the scandal settled down, Edwards decided to return to his original career: law. He founded the law firm Edwards Kirby Attorneys at Law in Raleigh, North Carolina, and is now considered one of the leading personal injury lawyers in the state.

Rod Blagojevich: Another Corrupt Illinois Politician

It's not difficult to find corrupt politicians in any corner of the world. Perhaps it's a hunger for power and a desperation for votes that drives some people to unethical and illegal behavior. And in America, one state has developed a notorious reputation for producing more than its share of crooked political figures; in fact, Illinois's famous political corruption scandals have been around as long as the state itself. But while some names—like Governor Len Small, who defrauded the state a million dollars, or state official Orville Hodge, who embezzled more than $6 million in state funds—may not sound familiar, no doubt the name Rod Blagojevich rings a bell.

A Quick Rise to the Top

Blagojevich was born in Chicago, and he spent much of his childhood and teenage years working odd jobs to help support his family. After high school, he earned a bachelor of arts in history from Northwestern University, and he then went to the Pepperdine University School of Law. In 1990, he married Patricia Mell, who is the daughter of influential former Chicago alderman Richard Mell. With the help of his father-in-law, Blagojevich was elected to the Illinois House of Representatives in 1992. Four years later, he became a U.S. congressman, representing Illinois's 5th Congressional District. And in 2002, with his powerful father-in-law once again providing campaign assistance, Blagojevich was elected governor of Illinois. He was reelected four years later, seemingly at the top of his political game.

Mistakes and Media

And then, in 2008, Blagojevich's political career began to collapse. A complaint from the U.S. Department of Justice alleged the governor was engaging in "pay to play" schemes—using his position of power to demand favors in exchange for gubernatorial appointments or legislation. In particular, the Justice Department was concerned with the seat recently vacated by Barack Obama, as he resigned to begin his presidency. According to the complaint, Blagojevich was offering up Obama's empty seat to "the highest bidder." An FBI wiretap recorded the governor expressing his desire to get something in return for the senate seat, calling it "golden" and saying he would not fill the position for "nothing." Federal agents arrested Blagojevich at his home on December 9. Authorities charged him with conspiracy to commit mail and wire fraud and solicitation of bribery.

Within a month, the Illinois House and Senate voted to impeach the governor, and lieutenant governor Pat Quinn succeeded him. With his trial not set until June 3, 2010, Blagojevich hired a publicist named Glenn Selig, who founded the crisis management public relations firm "The Publicity Agency." Selig prompted the disgraced governor to go on a media tour to proclaim his innocence, and Blagojevich was soon popping up everywhere: He had appearances on *Today*, *Good Morning America*, and *The View*, as well as multiple programs on news channels like CNN and MSNBC. He stopped by *Late Show with David Letterman*, where he insisted that his impeachment was politically motivated revenge for his refusal to raise taxes. He even managed to publish an autobiography entitled *The Governor: The Truth Behind the Political Scandal That Continues to Rock the Nation.*

Conviction

At the trial in 2010, Blagojevich was indicted on 24 federal charges. Strangely, his defense team never called a single witness, believing that the prosecution could not prove their case. This may have resulted in some confusion for the jury, who were unable to agree on 23 of the 24 charges: Blagojevich was convicted on only one charge, but a mistrial was declared for the other charges. Not content with the outcome, the prosecution called for a retrial. While three of the charges were eventually dropped, on June 27, 2011, Blagojevich was found guilty of 17 charges pertaining to extortion and bribery, and he was sentenced to 14 years in prison.

Sadly, this man whose connections and career could've taken him right to the top of the U.S. political system now sits in a Colorado prison, where he won't be eligible for release until 2024.

A Socialite Topples a Four-Star General

Affairs and politics often go hand in hand. Political candidates or appointees have seen their popularity wane in the face of scandal. But it's not often that a seemingly harmless Tampa socialite—a socialite, who was once described as a "bimbo" by the former mayor of the city—brings down a four-star general.

The Socialite and the General

Jill Kelley and her husband, Scott, made a name for themselves on the Tampa social scene, throwing lavish parties and hobnobbing with some of the city's most important families. They even befriended the daughters of New York Yankees owner George Steinbrenner, as well as the mayor of Tampa and the governor of Florida. They also entertained high-ranking members of the military from nearby MacDill Air Force Base. So, in November 2008, when General David Petraeus was transferred to the base from Fort Leavenworth, Kansas, the Kelleys welcomed him and his wife, Holly, to the neighborhood by hosting one of their popular parties.

The two families quickly became friends, and the Kelleys continued to expand their military social circle, befriending General John R.

Allen and his wife, Kathy, as well. In fact, the Kelleys were so well known for their generosity toward the military that in March 2011, they were awarded medals during a ceremony in Washington, D.C., for "distinguished service to the military." Petraeus himself handed out the honor.

Mysterious Emails and a Shocking Admission

But not everyone was enamored by Jill Kelley. She was known to be quite a flirt with married men, and she often sent casual, chatty emails to the military men she befriended. General Allen's wife even complained to a family friend about Kelley's correspondence with her husband. And then one day around May 2012, Jill Kelley began to receive strange messages from someone who called themselves "kelleypatrol," which threateningly demanded she stay away from members of the military, including David Petraeus.

Kelley contacted a friend in the FBI, Frederick W. Humphries II, telling him she was afraid that she was being cyberstalked. The FBI, able to pinpoint the time, place, and IP addresses of the emails, named the source of the messages as Paula Broadwell. Broadwell was a U.S. Intelligence Officer and writer who coauthored Petraeus's biography titled *All In: The Education of General Petraeus*. But when the FBI brought Broadwell in for questioning, she admitted to being more than just the general's biographer: the two had been having an affair since 2011. It's unknown whether Broadwell became jealous of Kelley's contact with Petraeus, or whether Petraeus himself was bothered by it and Broadwell was attempting to protect him; but either way, Broadwell took it upon herself to anonymously email Kelley, inadvertently setting off a chain reaction.

Resignation

The "cyberstalking" investigation now took a new turn, as the FBI asked for Broadwell's computer and requested that Petraeus—who was now the director of the CIA—turn over all of his emails. They discovered classified documents on Broadwell's computer, which led to more questions about her relationship with the four-star general. Although the general was never found to be the source of the classified information, the affair prompted him to resign from the CIA on November 9, 2012, and Broadwell was stripped of her clearances to access classified information.

Had Jill Kelley not been so close to so many military members, Broadwell would have had no reason to send her "kelleypatrol" emails, and it's possible the Petraeus affair would not have come to light. Former Tampa Mayor Sandra Freedman is distressed that Kelley was so easily able to socialize with such high-ranking officials: "That a bimbo like Jill Kelley should be given any kind of recognition or access to the military—it's outrageous." Petraeus, once such a good friend of the socialite, probably now agrees.

Folly in the Big Apple

Many of the nation's juiciest scandals have sprung from the Big Apple. Here is a notorious quartet.

New York City is no stranger to scandal. In fact, over the centuries it probably ranks second only to Chicago in terms of politicians who get caught in compromising positions, the public revelation of high society's dirty little secrets, and assorted other embarrassments. Here are some highlights from among New York's worst scandals.

Eliot Spitzer's Sexual Shenanigans

Spitzer was the governor of New York and a promising up-and-comer in the Democratic Party until 2008, when he was fingered in a federal investigation that publicly revealed his penchant for high-priced call girls. Eliot!

The revelation had a devastating effect on Spitzer's political career, which had been built on his reputation as a squeaky-clean foe of organized crime and political corruption. The fact that the governor had been cheating on his wife was bad enough, political analysts noted, but more damning was the obvious fact that he was a bald-faced hypocrite.

Caught red-handed, Spitzer may have felt he had no choice but to resign as governor. After more than a year of lying low, he reentered the public eye as a political commentator. Observers' opinions are mixed as to whether he might one day seek political office again.

Miss America's Political Downfall

In 1945, Bess Myerson broke barriers as the first Jewish Miss America. Forty-two years later, the Bronx-born beauty was forced to resign from her job as New York City's commissioner of cultural affairs under a dark cloud of scandal. Among the allegations: that Myerson had used her political clout and winning personality to sway the judge overseeing the divorce of her paramour, Andy Capasso, a business executive 21 years her junior. Capasso, a wealthy sewer contractor, was later convicted of tax evasion and sentenced to four years in a federal prison.

According to an investigative report leaked to the *Village Voice*, Myerson, who was appointed by Mayor Ed Koch in 1983, manipulated Judge Hortense Gabel by placing that jurist's emotionally disturbed daughter, Sukhreet, on the city payroll as her assistant. Once Gabel had ruled in Capasso's favor, the newspaper reported, Myerson fired Sukhreet, initiated a cover-up, and lied about the entire affair. It was a sad end to the career of a woman who had given the city so much.

The Queen of Mean Takes a Fall

Everyone loves it when the obnoxiously rich fall from grace, and few wealthy New Yorkers have fallen as hard as hotel magnate Leona Helmsley. The wife of billionaire Harry Helmsley, who owned the lease on the Empire State Building, among other holdings, Leona Helmsley was convicted of tax evasion and sentenced to prison in 1989 following a widely publicized trial. Among the revelations: that she often terrorized her employees and routinely tried to stiff those who did work for her, including the contractors who renovated the couple's Connecticut mansion.

Perhaps most damning of all, however, was the testimony of a housekeeper who told the jury she had heard Helmsley comment, "We don't pay taxes. Only the little people pay taxes." Helmsley denied making such a statement but was never able to live it down. She died in 2007.

The Humiliation of the *New York Times*

Since its founding in 1851, the *New York Times* has enjoyed a reputation as the newspaper of record. But that reputation received a vicious black eye in 2003 when it was revealed that one of its star reporters, Jayson Blair, was guilty of plagiarism and of making up many of the stories he filed.

Blair was a promising young journalist when he joined the *Times* as an intern in 1998. However, within two years, his editors repeatedly took him to task for making too many errors in his reporting. Nonetheless, Blair was promoted to the national desk in 2002. A year later, Blair's conduct as a reporter had became so egregious that the *Times* was forced to conduct its own investigation which found numerous instances of plagiarism, falsification of information, and outright lying.

As a result, Blair was let go, and the *Times* published a 7,239-word mea culpa detailing Blair's errors and the newspaper's response.

CHAPTER 10

MYSTERIOUS DEATHS . . . OR MURDERS

◇◇

The Rise and Fall of Fatty Arbuckle

The bigger they are, the harder they fall. And when it comes to early Hollywood scandals, no star was bigger or fell harder than Roscoe "Fatty" Arbuckle.

The scurrilous affair that engulfed Roscoe "Fatty" Arbuckle (1887—1933) in 1921 remains one of the biggest Hollywood scandals of all time because of its repercussions on the film industry. (It was instrumental in the creation of organized film censorship in Hollywood.) The Fatty Arbuckle scandal rocked the world when it broke, and though few people today know the details, in 2007, *Time* magazine ranked it fourth on its list of the top 25 crimes of the past 100 years.

As one of Hollywood's first headline-grabbing scandals, it contained all the elements that make a scandal juicy: drunkenness, debauchery, and death. But what made the tawdry tale big was Arbuckle, who himself was big in size (nearly 300 pounds), big in popularity, and, as Tinseltown's highest paid comedian, one of the biggest stars in the Hollywood galaxy at the time.

The Rise

Arbuckle began his career as a child, performing in minstrel shows and sing-alongs. The young entertainer already carried a noticeable girth, but his remarkable singing voice, acrobatic agility, and knack for comedy made him a rising star on the vaudeville circuit.

In 1913, Arbuckle got his big break in film when Mack Sennett hired him on at Keystone Film Company. Arbuckle initially rollicked as one of Sennett's Keystone Cops, but he was soon developing his unique comic persona as the lovable fat man and honing his own slapstick specialties based on the seeming contradiction between his size and graceful agility. By 1914, Arbuckle was teamed with comedienne Mabel Normand for the extremely successful "Fatty and Mabel" shorts, in which the pair offered humorous interpretations of romantic rituals. Arbuckle's charming persona ensured that he always got the girl. He became so adept at working out the duo's physical gags for the camera that he soon took over direction of the films.

In 1917, Arbuckle formed Comique Film Corporation with Hollywood mogul Joseph Schenck, who offered Arbuckle creative control and an astounding paycheck. At Comique, Arbuckle launched the screen career of the great Buster Keaton, who played the rotund actor's sidekick in classic silent comedies such as *Coney Island* (1917), *Good Night, Nurse!* (1918), and *The Garage* (1920).

In 1919, Arbuckle reached unprecedented heights when Paramount Pictures handed him a monstrous three-year, $3 million contract to make several feature-length films. But Hollywood's first million-dollar man would have to work like a dog to meet production schedules. So on Labor Day weekend in 1921, a worn out Arbuckle headed to San Francisco for some rest and relaxation.

The Scandal

For the large-living, heavy-drinking Arbuckle, R&R meant a weekend-long bash at the St. Francis Hotel. On September 5, several people joined Arbuckle for a party, including a 26-year-old actress named

Virginia Rappe and her friend Maude Delmont. Much has been exaggerated about the sexual exploits of Rappe, but her bad reputation was largely the product of the sensationalized press of the day. However, Delmont was a convicted extortionist known for her penchant for blackmail.

Around three o'clock in the morning, Arbuckle left the party for his suite. Shortly thereafter, screams emanated from his room. According to press accounts of the day, several guests rushed in to find Rappe's clothing torn. She hysterically shouted at Arbuckle to stay away from her, supposedly uttering, "Roscoe did this to me." Though very dramatic, Rappe's accusation was most likely untrue and was probably invented to sell newspapers.

The story goes that the shaken Rappe was placed in a cold bath to calm her down and was later put to bed when a doctor diagnosed her as intoxicated. The next day, the hotel doctor gave her morphine and catheterized her when Delmont mentioned that Rappe hadn't urinated in some time.

Delmont later called a doctor friend to examine Rappe and said Arbuckle raped the young actress. The doctor found no evidence of rape but treated Rappe to help her urinate. Four days later Delmont took Rappe to the hospital, where she died of peritonitis caused by a ruptured bladder. Delmont called the police, and on September 11, Arbuckle was arrested for murder.

The Fall

Arbuckle told police—and would contend all along—that he entered his room and found Rappe lying on the bathroom floor. He said he picked her up, placed her on the bed, and rubbed ice on her stomach when she complained of abdominal pain.

Delmont told police that Arbuckle used the ice as a sexual stimulant, and years later, rumors circulated that Arbuckle had raped Rappe with a soda or champagne bottle. Yet, there was no mention of this in the press during the arrest and trial. Instead, police alleged that Arbuckle's immense weight caused Rappe's bladder to rupture as he raped her. But contemporary research speculates that Rappe was probably struck hard in the abdomen, not raped. Whatever the cause, the public— enraged by the extremely sensationalized reports in the newspapers— wanted Arbuckle hanged.

Over the next seven months, Arbuckle was tried three times for the death of Virginia Rappe. The first two ended with hung juries. In the final trial, the jury deliberated for six minutes before declaring Arbuckle not guilty and offering a written apology for the injustice placed upon him.

Arbuckle was exonerated, but the damage was done. In April 1922, the Hays Office, the motion picture industry's censorship organization, which was established in the wake of the scandal, banned Arbuckle's movies and barred him from filmmaking. Although the blacklisting was lifted in December 1922, it would be several years before Arbuckle resumed his Hollywood career. A few years after his acquittal, Arbuckle began directing under the name William Goodrich, and in the early 1930s, RKO hired him to direct a series of comic shorts. In 1933, Vitaphone—part of Warner Bros.—hired Arbuckle to appear in front of the camera again in a series of six sync-sound shorts shot in Brooklyn.

But his revitalized career was short-lived. On June 29, 1933, one day after finishing the sixth film and signing a long-term contract with Warner Bros., Arbuckle died of a heart attack at age 46. Eight decades later, Arbuckle is sadly remembered more for a crime that he *didn't* commit than as the comedic genius he was.

William Desmond Taylor: A Macabre Puzzle

The murder of actor/director William Desmond Taylor was like something out of an Agatha Christie novel, complete with a handsome, debonair victim and multiple suspects, each with a motive. But unlike Christie's novels, in which the murderer was always unmasked, Taylor's death remains unsolved nearly 90 years later.

On the evening of February 1, 1922, an unknown assailant shot Taylor in the back; a servant, Henry Peavey, discovered his body the next morning. News of Taylor's demise spread quickly, and several individuals, including officials from Paramount Studios, where Taylor was employed, raced to the dead man's home to clear it of anything incriminating, such as illegal liquor, evidence of drug use, illicit correspondence, and signs of sexual indiscretion. However, no one called the police until later in the morning.

Numerous Suspects

Soon an eclectic array of potential suspects came to light, including Taylor's criminally-inclined former butler, Edward F. Sands, who had gone missing before the murder; popular movie comedienne Mabel Normand, whom Taylor had entertained the evening of his death; actress Mary Miles Minter, who had a passionate crush on the handsome director who was 28 years her senior; and Charlotte Shelby, Minter's mother, who often wielded a gun to protect her daughter's tarnished honor.

Taylor's murder was the last thing Hollywood needed at the time, coming as it did on the heels of rape allegations against popular film comedian Fatty Arbuckle. Scandals brought undue attention on Hollywood, and the Arbuckle story had taken its toll. Officials at Paramount tried to keep a lid on the Taylor story, but the tabloid press did the exact opposite. A variety of personal foibles were made public in the weeks that followed, and both Normand and Minter saw their careers come to a screeching halt as a result. Taylor's own indiscretions were also revealed, such as the fact that he kept a special souvenir, usually lingerie, from every woman he bedded.

Little Evidence

Police interviewed many of Taylor's friends and colleagues, including all potential suspects. However, there was no evidence to incriminate anyone specifically, and no one was formally charged.

Investigators and amateur sleuths pursued the case for years. Sands was long a prime suspect, based on his criminal past and his estrangement from the victim. But it was later revealed that on the day of the murder, Sands had signed in for work at a lumberyard in Oakland, California—some 400 miles away—and thus could not have committed the crime. Coming in second was Shelby, whose temper and threats were legendary. Shelby's own acting career had fizzled out early, and all of her hopes for stardom were pinned on her daughter. She threatened many men who tried to woo Mary.

In the mid-1990s, another possible suspect surfaced—a long-forgotten silent-film actress named Margaret Gibson. According to Bruce Long, author of *William Desmond Taylor: A Dossier*, Gibson confessed to a friend on her deathbed in 1964 that years before she had killed a man named William Desmond Taylor. However, the woman to whom Gibson cleared her conscience didn't know who Taylor was and thought nothing more about it.

The Mystery Continues

Could Margaret Gibson (a.k.a. Pat Lewis) be Taylor's murderer? She had acted with Taylor in Hollywood in the early 1910s, and she may even have been one of his many sexual conquests. She also had a criminal past, including charges of blackmail, drug use, and prostitution, so it's entirely conceivable that she was a member of a group trying to extort money from the director, a popular theory among investigators. But according to an earlier book, *A Cast of Killers* by Sidney D. Kirkpatrick, veteran Hollywood director King Vidor had investigated the murder as material for a film script; through his research, Kirkpatrick pegged Shelby as the murderer. But out of respect for Minter, he never did anything about it.

Ultimately, however, we may never know for certain who killed William Desmond Taylor, or why. The case has long grown cold, and anyone with specific knowledge of the murder is likely dead. Unlike a Hollywood thriller, in which the killer is revealed at the end, Taylor's death is a macabre puzzle that likely will never be solved.

A 1924 Murder Mystery

Who's at the heart of the cloaked-in-secrets demise of Thomas Ince? Who, of the loads of lovelies and gallons of gents on the infamous Oneida yacht that night, was the killer? Curious minds demand to know.

The night is November 15, 1924. The setting is the Oneida yacht. The principal players are: Thomas H. Ince, Marion Davies, Charlie Chaplin, and William Randolph Hearst.

The Facts

By 1924, William Randolph Hearst had built a huge newspaper empire; he dabbled in filmmaking and politics; and he owned the Oneida. Thomas H. Ince was a prolific movie producer. Charlie Chaplin was a star comedian. Marion Davies was an actor. The web of connections went like this: Hearst and Davies were lovers; Davies and Chaplin were rumored to be lovers; Hearst and Ince were locked in tense business negotiations; and Ince was celebrating a birthday.

For Ince's birthday, Hearst planned a party on his yacht. It was lavish, with champagne all around. In the era of Prohibition, this was not just extravagant but illegal.

But Hearst had ulterior motives. He'd heard rumors that his mistress, Davies, was secretly seeing Chaplin, and so he invited Chaplin to the party. The Oneida set sail from San Pedro, California, headed to San Diego on Saturday, November 15.

An unfortunate but persistent fog settled once the coterie boarded the yacht. What is known definitively is that Ince arrived at the party late, due to business, and that he did not depart the yacht under his own power. Whether he was sick or dead depends on which version you believe, but it's a fact that Ince left the yacht on a stretcher on Sunday, November 16. What happened? Various scenarios have been put forward over the years:

- Possibility 1: Hearst shoots Ince. Hearst invites Chaplin to the party to observe his behavior around Davies and to verify their affair. After catching the two in a compromising position, he flies off the handle, runs to his stateroom, grabs his gun, and comes back shooting. In this scenario, Ince tries to break up the trouble but gets shot by mistake.

- Possibility 2: Hearst shoots Ince. It's the same end result as the first possibility, but in this scenario, Davies and Ince are alone in the galley after Ince comes in to look for something to settle the queasiness caused by his notorious ulcers. Seeing the two people together, Hearst assumes Chaplin—not Ince—is with Davies. He pulls his gun and shoots.

- Possibility 3: Chaplin shoots Ince. Chaplin, a week away from marrying a pregnant 16-year-old to avoid scandal and the law, is forlorn to the point where he considers suicide. While contemplating his gun, it accidentally goes off, and the bullet goes through the thin walls of the ship to hit Ince in the neighboring room.

- Possibility 4: An assassin shoots Ince. In this scenario, a hired assassin shoots Ince so Hearst can escape an unwanted business deal with the producer.

- Possibility 5: Ince dies of natural causes. Known for his shaky health, Ince succumbs to rabid indigestion and chronic heart problems. A development such as this would not surprise his friends and family.

Aftermath

Regardless of which of the various scenarios might actually be true, Ince was wheeled off Hearst's yacht. But what happened next?

That's not so clear, either. The facts of the aftermath of Ince's death are as hazy as the facts of the death itself. All reports agree that Ince did, in fact, die. There was no autopsy, and his body was cremated. After the cremation, Ince's wife, Nell, moved to Europe. But beyond those certainties, there are conflicting stories.

The individuals involved had various reasons for wanting to protect themselves from whatever might have happened on the yacht. If an unlawful death did indeed take place, the motivation speaks for itself. But even if nothing untoward happened, Hearst was breaking the Prohibition laws. The damage an investigation could have caused was reason enough to make Hearst cover up any attention that could have come his way from Ince's death. As a result, he tried to hide all mention of any foul play. Although Hearst didn't own the *Los Angeles Times*, he was plenty powerful. Rumor has it that an early edition of the paper after Ince's death carried the screaming headline, "Movie Producer Shot on Hearst Yacht." By later in the day, the headline had disappeared.

For his part, Chaplin denied being on the Oneida in the first place. In his version of the story, he didn't attend the party for Ince at all. He did, however, claim to visit Ince—along with Hearst and Davies—later in the week. He also stated that Ince died two weeks after that visit. Most reports show that Ince was definitely dead within 48 hours of the yacht party.

Davies agreed that Chaplin was never aboard the Oneida that night. In her version, Ince's wife called her the day after Ince left the yacht to inform her of Ince's death. Ince's doctor claimed that the producer didn't die until Tuesday, two days later.

So, what really happened? Most of the people on the yacht never commented on their experience. Louella Parsons certainly didn't. The famed gossip columnist was reportedly onboard the Oneida that night (although she denied it as well). She had experienced some success writing for a Hearst newspaper, but shortly after this event, Hearst gave her a lifetime contract and wide syndication, allowing her to become a Hollywood power broker. Coincidence? No one can say for certain.

The Mysterious Death of Thelma Todd

Old Hollywood has more than its share of secrets. Here's another one.

On December 16, 1935, at about 10:30 a.m., actor Thelma Todd was found dead behind the wheel of her Lincoln Phaeton convertible. Her maid, Mae Whitehead, had come to clean the luxurious apartment Todd lived in above her rollicking roadhouse, Thelma Todd's Sidewalk Café. The maid discovered Thelma in a nearby garage. Some sources claim the ignition of her car was still turned on and the garage door was opened a crack.

An obvious suicide? Not quite.

Humble Beginnings

Thelma Todd was born in Lawrence, Massachusetts, on July 29, 1905 or 1906, depending on the source. She was an academically gifted girl who went on to attend college, but her mother pushed her to use her physical assets as well as her intellectual gifts. She made a name for herself in local beauty pageants, winning the title "Miss Massachusetts" in 1925. Though she did not take the top prize in the "Miss America" pageant, she was discovered by a talent agent and soon began appearing in the short one- and two-reel comedy films of producer/ director Hal Roach.

Before Thelma knew it, she was starring with big names, including Gary Cooper and William Powell, and working at an exhausting pace on as many as 16 pictures a year. Her forte was comedy, however, and she found her biggest success as a sidekick to such legends as the Marx Brothers and Laurel and Hardy. Around Hollywood, she was known as "The Ice Cream Blonde" or "Hot Toddy" (a nickname she assigned to herself). But Thelma knew that fame was fleeting, and she decided to invest in a nightclub and restaurant with her sometimes boyfriend, director Roland West. The upscale gin joint became a favorite with Hollywood's hard-partying, fast set.

A Complicated Girl

To say that Thelma's love life was messy would be an understatement. Her marriage to playboy Pasquale "Pat" DiCicco (from 1932 to 1934) was a disaster, filled with domestic abuse. She turned to West after her divorce but was reportedly also seeing mobster Charles "Lucky" Luciano on the side. It was said that Luciano wanted a room at the Sidewalk Café for his gambling operation, and he was willing to go to great lengths to get it. The rumor was that even after he got Thelma hooked on amphetamines, she was still of sound enough mind to refuse. Supposedly, the couple got into a huge screaming match about the subject one night at another restaurant, The Brown Derby, and various threats were exchanged.

So, Who Did It?

All of the romantic drama and hard living came to a head on the evening of December 14, 1935. Thelma had been invited to a party involving a good friend of hers, Ida Lupino, and her chauffeur, Ernest Peters, drove her there. Unfortunately for Thelma, her ex-husband showed up with another woman and made a scene. After a nasty argument, DiCicco left with his date, and a drunken Thelma informed Lupino that there was a new man in her life, a rich businessman from San Francisco.

Peters dropped Thelma back at her apartment at about 3:30 a.m. on December 15. She apparently couldn't get into the building and instead retreated to the garage, perhaps to sleep there. She might have turned on the car for warmth, not paying attention to the carbon monoxide. Authorities determined the time of death had been between 5:00 and 8:00 a.m.

Making the circumstances even more mysterious is the fact that, although Thelma was determined to have died early on Sunday morning, December 15, her body was not found until Monday morning. There were uncorroborated reports that she had been seen during the day on Sunday in Beverly Hills. Is it possible that Thelma actually died 24 hours later than was reported?

The coroner's report listed carbon monoxide asphyxiation as the cause of death and ruled it a suicide, but Thelma's crazy life led many to dismiss that verdict. With so many intriguing suspects—the violent ex-husband, the jealous boyfriend, the ruthless gangster lover, and the mysterious out-of-town paramour—who could blame them? That initial report was reconsidered and overturned, with the ruling changed to accidental death, but some observers believe the incident was never investigated thoroughly.

Ohio's Greatest Unsolved Murder Mystery

From 1935 until 1938, a brutal madman roamed the Flats of Cleveland. The killer—known as the Mad Butcher of Kingsbury Run—is believed to have murdered 12 men and women. Despite a massive manhunt, the murderer was never apprehended.

In 1935, the Depression had hit Cleveland hard, leaving large numbers of people homeless. Shantytowns sprang up on the eastern side of the city in Kingsbury Run—a popular place for transients—near the Erie and Nickel Plate railroads.

It is unclear who was the Butcher's first victim. Research suggests it may have been an unidentified woman found floating in Lake Erie—in pieces—on September 5, 1934; she would be known as Jane Doe I but dubbed by some as the "Lady of the Lake." The first official victim was found in the Jackass Hill area of Kingsbury Run on September 23, 1935. The unidentified body, labeled John Doe, had been dead for almost a month. A mere 30 feet away from the body was another victim, Edward Andrassy. Unlike John Doe, Andrassy had only been dead for days, indicating that the spot was a dumping ground. Police began staking out the area.

After a few months passed without another body, police thought the worst was over. Then on January 26, 1936, the partial remains of a new victim, a woman, were found in downtown Cleveland. On February 7, more remains were found at a separate location, and the deceased was identified as Florence Genevieve Polillo. Despite similarities among the three murders, authorities had yet to connect them—serial killers were highly uncommon at the time.

Tattoo Man, Eliot Ness, and More Victims

On June 5, two young boys passing through Kingsbury Run discovered a severed head. The rest of the body was found near the Nickel Plate railroad police station. Despite six distinctive tattoos on the man's body (thus the nickname "Tattoo Man"), he was never identified and became John Doe II.

At this point, Cleveland's newly appointed director of public safety, Eliot Ness, was officially briefed on the case. While Ness and his men hunted down leads, the headless body of another unidentified male was found west of Cleveland on July 22, 1936. It appeared that the man, John Doe III, had been murdered several months earlier. On September 10, the headless body of a sixth victim, John Doe IV, was found in Kingsbury Run.

Ness officially started spearheading the investigation. Determined to bring the killer to justice, Ness's staff fanned out across the city, even going undercover in the Kingsbury Run area. As 1936 drew to a close, no suspects had been named, and no new victims were discovered. City residents believed that Ness's team had run the killer off. But future events would prove that the killer was back . . . with a relentless and unforgiving vengeance.

The Body Count Climbs

A woman's mutilated torso washed up on the beach at 156th Street on February 23, 1937. The rest would wash ashore two months later. (Strangely, the body washed up in the same location as the "Lady of the Lake" had three years earlier.)

On June 6, 1937, teenager Russell Lauyer found the decomposed body of a woman inside of a burlap sack under the Lorain-Carnegie Bridge in Cleveland. With the body was a newspaper from June of the previous year, suggesting a timeline for the murder. An investigation indicated the body might belong to one Rose Wallace; this was never confirmed, and the victim is sometimes referred to as Jane Doe II. Pieces of another man's body (the ninth victim) began washing ashore on July 6, just below Kingsbury Run. Cleveland newspapers were having a riot with the case that the "great" Eliot Ness couldn't solve. This fueled Ness, and he promised justice.

Burning of Kingsbury Run

The next nine months were quiet, and the public began to relax. When a woman's severed leg was found in the Cuyahoga River on April 8, 1938, however, people debated its connection to the Butcher. But the rest of Jane Doe III was soon found inside two burlap sacks floating in the river (sans head, of course).

On August 16, 1938, the last two confirmed victims of the Butcher were found together at the East 9th Street Lakeshore Dump. Jane Doe IV had apparently been dead for four to six months prior to discovery, while John Doe VI may have been dead for almost nine months.

Something snapped inside Eliot Ness. On the night of August 18, Ness and dozens of police officials raided the shantytowns in the Flats, ending up in Kingsbury Run. Along the way, they interrogated or arrested anyone they came across, and Ness ordered the shanties burned to the ground. There would be no more confirmed victims of the Mad Butcher of Kingsbury Run.

Who Was the Mad Butcher?

There were two prime suspects in the case, though no one was ever charged. The first was Dr. Francis Sweeney, a surgeon with the knowledge many believed necessary to mutilate the victims the way the killer did. (He was also a cousin of Congressman Martin L. Sweeney, a known political opponent of Ness.)

In August 1938, Ness, two other men, and the inventor of the polygraph machine, Dr. Royal Grossman, interrogated Dr. Sweeney. By all accounts, Sweeney failed the polygraph test (several times), and Ness believed he had his man, but he was released due to lack of evidence. Two days after the interrogation, on August 25, 1938, Sweeney checked himself into the Sandusky Veterans Hospital. He remained institutionalized at various facilities until his death in 1965. Because Sweeney voluntarily checked himself in, he could have left whenever he desired.

The other suspect was Frank Dolezal, who was arrested by private investigators on July 5, 1939 as a suspect in the murder of Florence Polillo, with whom he had lived with for a time. While in custody, Dolezal confessed to killing Polillo, although some believe the confession was forced. Either way, Dolezal died under mysterious circumstances while incarcerated at the Cuyahoga County Jail before he could be charged.

As for Eliot Ness, some believe his inability to bring the Butcher to trial weighed on him for the rest of his life. Ness went to his grave without getting a conviction. To this day, the case remains open.

The Black Dahlia Murder Mystery

One of the most baffling murder mysteries in U.S. history began innocently enough on the morning of January 15, 1947. Betty Bersinger was walking with her young daughter in the Leimert Park area of Los Angeles when she spotted something lying in a vacant lot that caused her blood to run cold. She ran to a nearby house and called the police. Officers Wayne Fitzgerald and Frank Perkins arrived on the scene shortly after eleven o'clock in the morning.

A Grisly Discovery

Lying only several feet from the road, in plain sight, was the naked body of a young woman. Her body had numerous cuts and abrasions, including a knife wound from ear to ear that resembled a ghoulish grin. Even more horrific was that her body had been completely severed at the midsection, and the two halves had been placed as if they were part of some morbid display. That's what disturbed officers the most: the killer appeared to have carefully posed the victim close to the street because he wanted people to find his grotesque handiwork.

Something else that troubled the officers was that even though the body had been brutally violated and desecrated, there was very little blood found at the scene. The only blood evidence recovered was a possible bloody footprint and an empty cement package with a spot of blood on it. In fact, the body was so clean that it appeared to have just been washed.

Shortly before removing the body, officers scoured the area for a possible murder weapon, but none was recovered. A coroner later determined that the cause of death was from hemorrhage and shock due to a concussion of the brain and lacerations of the face, probably from a very large knife.

Positive Identification

After a brief investigation, police were able to identify the deceased as Elizabeth Short, who was born in Hyde Park, Massachusetts, on July 29, 1924. At age 19, Short had moved to California to live with her father, but she moved out and spent the next few years moving back and forth between California, Florida, and Massachusetts. In July 1946, Short returned to California to see Lt. Gordon Fickling, a former boyfriend, who was stationed in Long Beach. For the last six months of her life, Short lived in an assortment of hotels, rooming houses, and private homes. She was last seen a week before her body was found, which made police very interested in finding out where and with whom she spent her final days.

The Black Dahlia Is Born

As police continued their investigation, reporters jumped all over the story and began referring to the unknown killer by names such as "sex-crazed maniac" and even "werewolf." Short herself was also given a nickname: the Black Dahlia. Reporters said it was a name friends had called her as a play on the movie *The Blue Dahlia*, which had recently been released. However, others contend Short was never called the Black Dahlia while she was alive; it was just something reporters made up for a better story. Either way, it wasn't long before newspapers around the globe were splashing front-page headlines about the horrific murder of the Black Dahlia.

The Killer Is Still Out There

As time wore on, hundreds of police officers were assigned to the Black Dahlia investigation. They combed the streets, interviewing people and following leads. Although police interviewed thousands of potential suspects—and dozens even confessed to the murder—to this day, no one has ever officially been charged with the crime. More than 60 years and several books and movies after the crime, the Elizabeth

Short murder case is still listed as "open." We are no closer to knowing who killed Short or why than when her body was first discovered.

There is one bright note to this story. In February 1947, perhaps as a result of the Black Dahlia case, California became the first state to pass a law requiring all convicted sex offenders to register themselves.

Lana Turner and the Death of a Gangster

On the evening of April 4, 1958, Beverly Hills police arrived at the home of actress Lana Turner to discover the dead body of her one-time boyfriend Johnny Stompanato, a violent gangster with underworld ties. He had been stabbed to death, but sensational reporting of the tabloid press muddied the exact circumstances of his demise.

Sweater Girl

Lana Turner's first credited film role came in 1937 with *They Won't Forget*, which earned her the moniker "Sweater Girl," thanks to the tight-fitting sweater her character wore. Turner went on to star in hits such as *Honky Tonk* (1941), *The Postman Always Rings Twice* (1946), and *Peyton Place* (1957).

Hanging with the Wrong Crowd

Off-screen, Turner was renowned for her many love affairs. During her lifetime, she amassed eight marriages to seven different husbands. It was shortly after the breakup of her fifth marriage to actor Lex Barker in 1957 that Turner met Johnny Stompanato. When she discovered that his name was not John Steele (as he had told her) and that he had ties to underworld figures such as Mickey Cohen, she realized the negative publicity that those ties could bring to her career, so she tried to end the relationship. But Stompanato incessantly pursued her, and the pair engaged in a number of violent incidents which came to a head on the night of April 4.

Turner's 14-year-old daughter, Cheryl Crane, rushed to her mother's defense after hearing Stompanato threaten to "cut" Turner. Fearing for her mother's life, the girl grabbed a kitchen knife and ran upstairs to Turner's bedroom. According to Crane's account, Turner opened the door and Cheryl saw Stompanato with his arms raised in the air in a fury. Cheryl then rushed past Turner and stabbed Stompanato, killing him. Turner called her mother, who brought their personal physician to the house, but it was too late. By the time the police were called, much time had passed and evidence had been moved around. According to the Beverly Hills police chief, who was the first officer to arrive, Turner immediately asked if she could take the rap for her daughter.

At the crime scene, the body appeared to have been moved and the fingerprints on the murder weapon were so smudged that they could not be identified. The case sparked a media sensation, especially among the tabloid press, which turned against Turner, essentially accusing her of killing Stompanato and asking her daughter to cover for her. Mickey Cohen, who paid for Stompanato's funeral, publicly called for the arrests of Turner and Crane. For years, ugly rumors surrounding the case persisted.

The Performance of a Lifetime

During the inquest, the press described Turner's testimony as "the performance of a lifetime." But police and authorities knew from the beginning that Turner did not do it. At the inquest, it took just 20 minutes for the jury to return a verdict of justifiable homicide, so the district attorney decided not to bring the case to trial. However, Turner was convicted of being an unfit mother, and Crane was remanded to her grandmother's care until she turned 18, further tainting Turner's image. There was an aura of "guilt" around Turner for years, though she was never seriously considered a suspect in the actual murder.

As fate would have it, Turner's film, *Peyton Place*, which features a courtroom scene about a murder committed by a teenager, was still in theaters at the time of the inquest. Ticket sales skyrocketed as a result of the sensational publicity, and Turner parlayed the success of the film into better screen roles, including her part in a remake of *Imitation of Life* (1959), which would become one of her most successful films. She appeared in romantic melodramas until the mid-1960s, when age began to affect her career. In the 1970s and 1980s, she made the transition to television, appearing on shows such as *The Survivors, The Love Boat,* and *Falcon Crest.*

Marilyn Monroe, an Untimely Death

Marilyn Monroe was—and still is—one of the most enchanting women ever to grace the silver screen. But, like so many of her fellow movie stars, Monroe's deeply troubled personal life often overshadowed her professional achievements. This was especially true when the world learned of the 36-year-old's tragic death on August 5, 1962.

Troubled Beginnings

Marilyn Monroe was born Norma Jean Baker on June 1, 1926. Her life was troubled almost from the start: Her mother was institutionalized with mental problems, and the man she was told was her father, Edward Mortensen, was killed in a motorcycle accident when she was three. As a result, Norma Jean spent most of her childhood in foster care.

Norma Jean married at 16 and found success as a model, which eventually led to a name change and a brief contract with 20th Century Fox. Her first credited role came in *Dangerous Years* (1947). It was a critical flop, and studio head Darryl F. Zanuck didn't know what to do with this breathy starlet, so her contract was not renewed. However, she later returned and made most of her films for Fox.

Monroe's chaotic personal life made constant news. She married baseball legend Joe DiMaggio in 1954, but their union was tumultuous, and they divorced nine months later. In 1956, she married playwright Arthur Miller, who was nearly 11 years her senior; the marriage lasted until 1961. Rumors swelled that Monroe was also involved with President John F. Kennedy and his brother, Robert.

A Hollywood Starlet's Tragic End

In her final months, Monroe was living in a house in the Brentwood section of Los Angeles. On the evening of August 4, she was visited by her psychiatrist, Dr. Ralph Greenson; she then made several phone calls from her bedroom, including one to actor Peter Lawford, a Kennedy family confidante.

Late that night, Monroe's housekeeper, Eunice Murray, noticed an odd light coming from under the actress's bedroom door. When Monroe didn't respond to her knocks, Murray went around to the side of the house and peered through the bedroom window. Monroe looked peculiar, Murray later told police, so she called Greenson, who broke into Monroe's bedroom and found her on the bed unconscious. Greenson then called Monroe's personal physician, Dr. Hyman Engelberg, who pronounced the actress dead. It was then that the police were notified.

Los Angeles Police Sgt. Jack Clemmons was the first on the scene. He said he found Monroe naked and facedown on her bed with an empty bottle of sleeping pills nearby. A variety of other pill bottles littered the nightstand.

Monroe's body was taken to Westwood Village Mortuary and then transferred to the county morgue; her house was sealed and placed under guard. Los Angeles Deputy Medical Examiner Dr. Thomas T. Noguchi performed Monroe's autopsy and concluded in his official report that the actress had died from an overdose of Nembutal (a sleeping pill) and chloral hydrate (a mild sedative) and ruled that it was a "probable suicide."

Suicide, Murder, or Accidental Overdose?

Over the years, Monroe's death has drawn the interest of conspiracy theorists because of numerous inconsistencies between Noguchi's autopsy report and the evidence at the scene, as well as in the stories of those who were at the scene. Some conspiracy theorists believe that Monroe was murdered and that her death was made to look like a suicide.

The most prevalent theory—unproved by anyone—is that the Kennedy family had her killed to avoid a scandal. However, given Monroe's habit of taking more medication than doctors prescribed because she thought she had a high tolerance for it, accidental overdose cannot be ruled out.

Today, Marilyn Monroe remains as popular as ever. Her image graces a wide variety of products worldwide, and the resulting royalties generate nearly a million dollars per year. Even in death, Hollywood's most famous blonde goddess continues to bask in the bright spotlight of fame.

Anything but Splendor: Natalie Wood

The official account of Natalie Wood's tragic death is riddled with holes. For this reason, conspiracy theorists continue to run hog-wild with conjecture. Here's a sampling of the questions, facts, and assertions surrounding the case.

A Life in Pictures

There are those who will forever recall Natalie Wood as the adorable child actress from *Miracle on 34th Street* (1947) and those who remember her as the sexy but wholesome grown-up star of movies such as *West Side Story* (1961), *Splendor in the Grass* (1961), and *Bob & Carol & Ted & Alice* (1969). Both groups generally agree that Wood had uncommon beauty and talent.

Wood appeared in her first film, *Happy Land* (1943), in a bit part alongside other people from her hometown of Santa Rosa, California, where the film was shot. She stood out to the director, who remembered her later when he needed to cast a child in another film. Wood was uncommonly mature and professional for a child actress, which helped her make a relatively smooth transition to ingénue roles.

Although Wood befriended James Dean and Sal Mineo—her troubled young costars from *Rebel Without a Cause* (1955)—and briefly dated Elvis Presley, she preferred to move in established Hollywood circles. By the time she was 20, she was married to Robert Wagner and was costarring with Frank Sinatra in *Kings Go Forth* (1958), which firmly ensconced her in the Hollywood establishment. The early 1960s represent the high point of Wood's career, and she specialized in playing high-spirited characters with determination and spunk. She added two more Oscar nominations to the one she received for *Rebel* and racked up five Golden Globe nominations for Best Actress. This period also proved to be personally turbulent for Wood, as she suffered through a failed marriage to Wagner and another to Richard Gregson. After taking time off to raise her children, she remarried Wagner and returned to her acting career.

Shocking News

And so, on November 29, 1981, the headline hit the newswires much like an out-of-control car hits a brick wall. Natalie Wood, the beautiful, vivacious 43-year-old star of stage and screen, had drowned after falling from her yacht the *Splendour*, which was anchored off California's Santa Catalina Island. Wood had been on the boat during a break from her latest film, *Brainstorm*, and was accompanied by Wagner and *Brainstorm* costar Christopher Walken. Skipper Dennis Davern was at the helm. Foul play was not suspected.

In My Esteemed Opinion

After a short investigation, Chief Medical Examiner Dr. Thomas Noguchi listed Wood's death as an accidental drowning. Tests revealed that she had consumed "seven or eight" glasses of wine, and the coroner contended that in her intoxicated state Wood had probably stumbled and fallen overboard while attempting to untie the yacht's rubber dinghy. He also stated that cuts and bruises on her body could have occurred when she fell from the boat.

Doubting Thomases

To this day, many question Wood's mysterious demise and believe that the accidental drowning theory sounds a bit too convenient. Pointed questions have led to many rumors: Does someone know more about Wood's final moments than they're letting on? Was her drowning really an accident, or did someone intentionally or accidentally *help* her overboard? Could this be why she sustained substantial bruising on her face and the back of her legs? Why was Wagner so reluctant to publicly discuss the incident? Were Christopher Walken and Wood an item as had been rumored? With this possibility in mind, could a booze-fueled fight have erupted between the two men? Could Wood have then tried to intervene, only to be knocked overboard for her efforts? And why did authorities declare Wood's death accidental so quickly? Would such a hasty ruling have been issued had the principals not been famous, wealthy, and influential?

Ripples

At the time of her death, Wood and Wagner were seven years into their second marriage to each other. Whether Wood was carrying on an affair with Walken, as was alleged, may be immaterial, even if it made for interesting tabloid fodder. But Wagner's perception of their relationship could certainly be a factor. If nothing else, it might better explain the argument that ensued between Wagner and Walken that fateful night.

Case Closed?

Further information about Wood's death is sparse because no eyewitnesses have come forward. However, a businesswoman whose boat was anchored nearby testified that she heard a woman shouting for help, and then a voice responding, "We'll be over to get you," so the woman went back to bed. Just after dawn, Wood's body was found floating a mile away from the *Splendour*, approximately 200 yards offshore. The dinghy was found nearby; its only cargo was a stack of lifejackets.

In 2008, after 27 years of silence, Robert Wagner recalled in his autobiography, *Pieces of My Heart: A Life*, that he and Walken had engaged in a heated argument during supper after Walken had suggested that Wood star in more films, effectively keeping her away from their children. Wagner and Walken then headed topside to cool down. Sometime around midnight, Wagner said he returned to his cabin and discovered that his wife was missing. He soon realized that the yacht's dinghy was gone as well. In his book, he surmised that Wood may have gone to secure the dinghy that had been noisily slapping against the boat. Then, tipsy from the wine, she probably fell into the ocean and drowned. Walken notified the authorities.

And what about Walken, who was supposedly flirting with the star before she disappeared? He has mostly stayed silent about the whole incident over the last few decades, offering only occasional terse comments. But he did speak out two years after Wood's drowning to say, "The people who are convinced that there was something more to it than what came out in the investigation will never be satisfied with the truth. Because the truth is, there is nothing more to it. It was an accident."

Was Natalie Wood's demise the result of a deadly mix of wine and saltwater as the coroner's report suggests? This certainly could be the case. But why would she leave her warm cabin to tend to a loose rubber dinghy in the dark of night? Could an errant rubber boat really make such a commotion?

Perhaps we'll never know what happened that fateful night, but an interview conducted shortly before Wood's death proved prophetic: "I'm frightened to death of the water," said Wood about a long-held fear. "I can swim a little bit, but I'm afraid of water that is dark."

Unsolved: JonBenét Ramsey

In the early hours of December 26, 1996, Patsy Ramsey reported that her 6-year-old daughter, JonBenét, had been abducted from her Boulder, Colorado, home. Police rushed to the Ramsey home where, hours later, John Ramsey found his little girl dead in the basement. She had been battered, sexually assaulted, and strangled.

Police found several tantalizing bits of evidence—a number of footprints, a rope that did not belong on the premises, marks on the body that suggested the use of a stun gun, and DNA samples on the girl's body. The ransom note was also suspicious. Police found that it was written with a pen and pad of paper belonging to the Ramseys. The amount demanded, $118,000, was a surprisingly small amount, considering that John Ramsey was worth more than $6 million. It is also interesting to note that Mr. Ramsey had just received a year-end bonus of $118,117.50.

A number of suspects were considered, but one by one they were cleared. Finally, the police zeroed in on the parents. For years, the Ramseys were put under intense pressure by authorities and the public alike to confess to the murder. However, a grand jury investigation ended with no indictments. In 2003, a judge ruled that an intruder had killed JonBenét. Then, in August 2006, John Mark Karr confessed, claiming that he was with the girl when she died. However, Karr's DNA did not match that found on JonBenét. He was not charged, and the case remains unsolved.

The Deaths of Tupac and The Notorious B.I.G.

Tupac Shakur—known as Tupac—and Christopher Wallace—known as The Notorious B.I.G.—were two of the biggest rappers in the 1990s and arguably in history. Onetime friends, the young rappers later become rivals. Sadly, both would end up dead following drive-by shootings just six months apart. And more than 20 years after the slayings, both murders remain unsolved.

Difficult Upbringings, Big Successes

Born in 1971, Tupac Shakur came from a family of Black Panthers and radical politics. He grew up in challenging homes and homeless shelters, but his creative chops landed him at the Baltimore School for the Arts, where he studied ballet, poetry, and acting. His family later moved from Baltimore to the San Francisco Bay Area; there, Shakur joined a rap group and signed a record deal. In 1991, Shakur released his debut solo album, *2Pacalypse Now*, which caused controversy with its biting social commentaries.

One year younger than his contemporary, Christopher Wallace grew up in Brooklyn. He was an accomplished student who, by age 15, was selling drugs. Wallace also began rapping as a teenager, at that time for fun. An editor at a rap scene national magazine got hold of one of Wallace's rap tapes, and the young rapper subsequently appeared in the magazine.

Shakur and Wallace would later meet in the early 1990s. When they met, Shakur was already an accomplished artist, while Wallace was working on his first album, *Ready to Die*, which would go on to sell millions of copies. The two struck up a friendship, and Wallace even asked Shakur to become his manager, an offer Shakur declined. But a feud ultimately developed between their dueling record labels, and this feud turned personal in 1994 when Shakur was shot five times during a robbery at a New York City recording studio. Shakur—who miraculously survived—believed Wallace was behind the shooting.

Unsolved Mysteries

On September 7, 1996, Shakur attended a Mike Tyson boxing match in Las Vegas. After leaving the event with Suge Knight, the then-CEO of Death Row Records, Shakur got into a brawl with Orlando Anderson, a Crips gang member, in the MGM Grand casino's lobby. Shortly after the fight, a white Cadillac pulled up beside Shakur's vehicle at a traffic light, and an occupant in the Cadillac fired into Shakur's vehicle, striking the rapper four times. Six days later, Shakur died at a Las Vegas hospital.

A 2002 investigation by *Los Angeles Times* suggested that the gang Southside Crips carried out Shakur's killing in retaliation for the brawl in the MGM Grand lobby hours before the attack on Shakur's vehicle. The story also said that Wallace supplied the weapon for Shakur's murder, and he agreed to pay the gang $1 million for Shakur's killing. Orlando Anderson—a suspect involved in MGM Grand brawl—later died in a drug-related shooting.

Meanwhile, Wallace was shot dead on March 9, 1997 in Los Angeles, after leaving a music industry party. A dark-colored Chevrolet Impala pulled up next to his vehicle and an occupant fired into Wallace's side of his vehicle. An unsealed autopsy later revealed that a single bullet that pierced several vital organs killed Wallace.

Though speculation swirled about the role of corrupt police officers in Wallace's killing, the FBI ended its inquiry in 2005 after prosecutors concluded that there was scant evidence to pursue a case. That year, a federal judge concluded that a Los Angeles police detective intentionally withheld evidence in a wrongful death lawsuit filed against the city by Wallace's family; the lawsuit, however, was dismissed in 2010. Kevin McClure, a former LAPD captain who oversaw the investigation into Wallace's murder, told the *Los Angeles Times* in 2017 that the shooter is likely dead.